Iain Sinclair

MANCHESTER
1824

Manchester University Press

Contemporary British Novelists

Series editor:
Daniel Lea

already published

Iain Sinclair

Brian Baker

Manchester University Press

Manchester and New York

distributed exclusively in the USA by Palgrave

Published by Manchester University Press
Oxford Road, Manchester M13 9NR, UK
and Room 400, 175 Fifth Avenue, New York, NY 10010, USA
www.manchesteruniversitypress.co.uk

Distributed exclusively in the USA by
Palgrave, 175 Fifth Avenue, New York,
NY 10010, USA

Distributed exclusively in Canada by
UBC Press, University of British Columbia, 2029 West Mall,
Vancouver, BC, Canada V6T 1Z2

British Library Cataloguing-in-Publication Data
A catalogue record for this book is available from the British Library

Library of Congress Cataloging-in-Publication Data applied for

ISBN   978 0 7190 6904 8 *hardback*
ISBN   978 0 7190 6905 5 *paperback*

First published 2007

16 15 14 13 12 11 10 09 08 07   10 9 8 7 6 5 4 3 2 1

Typeset
by Florence Production Ltd, Stoodleigh, Devon
Printed in Great Britain
by Antony Rowe Ltd, Chippenham, Wiltshire

For the Baker, Vigors and Staples families

Contents

Series editor's foreword

Contemporary British Novelists offers readers critical introductions to some of the most exciting and challenging writing of recent years. Through detailed analysis of their work, volumes in the series present lucid interpretations of authors who have sought to capture the sensibilities of the late twentieth and twenty-first centuries. Informed, but not dominated, by critical theory, *Contemporary British Novelists* explores the influence of diverse traditions, histories and cultures on prose fiction, and situates key figures within their relevant social, political, artistic and historical contexts.

The title of the series is deliberately provocative, recognising each of the three defining elements as contentious identifications of a cultural framework that must be continuously remade and renamed. The contemporary British novel defies easy categorisation and rather than offering bland guarantees as to the current trajectories of literary production, volumes in this series contest the very terms that are employed to unify them. How does one conceptualise, isolate and define the mutability of the contemporary? What legitimacy can be claimed for a singular Britishness given the multivocality implicit in the redefinition of national identities? Can the novel form adequately represent reading communities increasingly dependent upon digitalised communication? These polemical considerations are the theoretical backbone of the series, and attest to the difficulties of formulating a coherent analytical approach to the discontinuities and incoherencies of the present.

Contemporary British Novelists does not seek to appropriate its subjects for prescriptive formal or generic categories; rather it aims to explore the ways in which aesthetics are reproduced, refined and repositioned through recent prose writing. If the overarching architecture of the contemporary always eludes description, then the grandest ambition of this series must be to plot at least some of its dimensions.

Daniel Lea

Acknowledgements

Although the work contained in this book is my own, as are any errors or omissions, every project rests upon the support and help of others, and I would like to express my gratitude here. Firstly, I would like to thank my colleagues in the English department of the University of Chester for their support, where I was allocated study leave to enable progress on this book. I would also like to thank the staff at the libraries at the Universities of Liverpool and Chester for their help in sourcing documents. Friends and colleagues, and their relevant Departments, hosted conferences and seminar papers at which earlier versions of this material was delivered, at the following institutions: the University of Chester, Edge Hill College, Goldsmith's College, University of London, the University of Greenwich and Lancaster University.

Personal thanks must go to the following friends and colleagues for their help and encouragement: Arthur Bradley, Robert Bond, Jenny Bavidge, Paul Newland, Boris Vidovic, Keith Wilson (University of Ottawa), Daniel Lea, Eliot Atkins, Sebastian Groes, and Ed and Sarah for late London nights. Special thanks must go to Alan Wall, who read some of these chapters and made many excellent suggestions, and to Simon Lee, who set me on this road in the first place. I owe a considerable debt of gratitude to Matthew Frost and the editorial team at Manchester University Press for their benign forebearance. Finally, my love and thanks go to Deniz, who put up with all this for far too long.

Introduction: maps of the London Underground

Of course, we don't only find ourselves in situations,
we also make situations. (Raymond Williams)[1]

'Situations'

Iain Sinclair was born in Cardiff in 1943, and was raised in Maesteg, in Wales. He was, as the jacket blurb tells us, the 'son of a doctor', and his paternal forebears (father and grandfather were doctors) moved to South Wales from Scotland. He attended Cheltenham College, a public school, then Trinity College, Dublin, during the early 1960s. He then moved to London where he went to film school, before embarking on a succession of labouring jobs (including Truman's brewery in Whitechapel, and Tower Hamlets parks and gardens department), finally becoming a bookdealer, all of which would provide him with some of the materials for his two prose/poem sequences, *Lud Heat* (1975) and *Suicide Bridge* (1979), and his first novel, *White Chappell, Scarlet Tracings* (1987).

This is not to say that Sinclair occupies the position of some kind of provincial *naïf*, still less the patronised, alienated role of a 'native' or 'unschooled' poet such as the Romantic John Clare, who is, it is worthy of note, the subject of Sinclair's *Edge of the Orison* (2005). Nor is he a poet of 'the street', wearing his non-establishment attitudes on his sleeve. As we will see in this Introduction, and in the rest of this book, Sinclair does indeed value the figure of the visionary outsider, which may well be connected to his upbringing; however, this book will not pursue a biographical mode of analysis, though it will place Sinclair's work in context and with an eye to chronological development. Sinclair's connection to the 'outsider' is less a political than a literary one, though, as I will argue below, his career is indebted to the politics of the counter-culture of the 1960s. Sinclair's literary antecedents are modernist, and his immediate poetic influences, particularly the Cambridge neo-modernist J. H. Prynne, and the group of writers and artists with whom Sinclair may be said to be associated – among them Brian Catling, Doug Oliver, Chris Petit – could be characterised as experimental, avant-gardist, or non-mainstream in their orientation and interests.

Sinclair's major early works, *Lud Heat* (1975) and *Suicide Bridge* (1979), were self-published by his own Albion Village Press, which also produced books by Sinclair's friends and contemporaries. It was part of the 'British poetry revival' scene of the early 1970s, which found its locus in the bookshop Compendium Books. One should not see Sinclair's early works as being produced in a vacuum, then, although as the 1980s unwound, Sinclair's self-produced 'chapbooks' eventually were made in runs of no more than a dozen. His first novel, *White Chappell, Scarlet Tracings* (1987), published by the Rutland gallery owner Mike Goldmark in a very fine hardback edition, was subsequently republished by Paladin in paperback, and was sole runner-up for the *Guardian* Fiction Prize for 1987. His second novel, *Downriver* (1991), won the James Tait Black Memorial Prize. Sinclair has continued to publish fiction, though to less acclaim; his popular profile, however, was raised enormously by the success of his non-fiction, particularly *Lights Out for the Territory* (1997) and *London Orbital* (2002). He has continued, in slightly less 'fugitive' forms, his poetry publications, though these have tended to be with small-press imprints rather than large publishers; and he has worked with Chris Petit on a series of films that connect with his fiction and non-fiction. With his reviewing, journalism and occasional television appearances (usually on the subject of London), Sinclair is now a high-profile writer whose fiction is (at the time of writing) published by Penguin. One might argue, perhaps, that he has achieved a kind of 'cross-over' from the avant-garde to mainstream success.

The shape of Sinclair's personal trajectory is not, one suspects, an unusual one for someone of his background and generation. Coming to maturity at the beginning of the 1960s, Sinclair, I will argue in this book, exemplifies the utopian aspirations of the late-1960s counter-culture, disillusionment with its failure, and the subsequent realignment of critiques of contemporary conditions of life from an explicitly Marxian politics to an oppositional stance concerned with the configurations of urban space. Sinclair is also connected to the 'British poetry revival' of the late 1960s and early 1970s, a connection investigated further in Chapter 1. In figures such as Allen Fisher, the British poetry revival also exemplifies a different 'poetics of space', both with regard to poetic form (influenced by Charles Olson's 'field poetics') and in its interest in 'site-specific' ideas and images. Sinclair, I shall argue, invests this 're-enchantment' of space with a modernist/ avant-gardist poetic practice in order to forge a non-Marxian critical praxis, one which, ironically, echoes similar reworkings of the Marxist critical tradition in the 1970s and 1980s in adopting topographical or geographical approaches to late capitalism. I will consider these later in this Introduction.

This is not to say, however, that Sinclair's poetry, fiction, non-fiction prose or film work reflects a total withdrawal from political commitment. It is clear that in his description of his adolescent meeting with the Welsh poet Vernon Watkins – who is praised for 'the sense of that public role, and political engagement of the poet, prepared to meet strangers out of the blue who've just turned up on the doorstep and generously give his time' – the necessity of poetry's political connection with life, with the everyday life of 'meeting a stranger', is central to Sinclair's appreciation of the poet's responsi-bility and role.[2] The form that commitment takes, however, is certainly at issue in Sinclair's writing. In his book of 'conversations' with Kevin Jackson, *The Verbals* (2003), Sinclair confesses his presence at the Grosvenor Square demonstrations against the Vietnam War, but delimits his participation with the caveat that he attended 'more or less as an observer'.[3] When questioned, Sinclair returns to the position of the disinterested observer that he first adopts in his first published text (by his own Albion Village Press), *The Kodak Mantra Diaries* (1971), which attempts to record the 'Dialectics of Liberation' Congress held at the Roundhouse in London in July 1968. The Congress is described by Jonathon Green as the 'brainchild' of the anti-psychiatrists R. D. Laing and David Cooper, both important to *The Kodak Mantra Diaries* and, as I will argue, to Sinclair's own world-view. Sinclair reiterates the position of disinterested observer or 'documenter' when asked by Jackson about his intentions at the Congress. How to occupy a position of critique in the light of this is a question that I hope to address throughout this book. Emmit Grogan of the San Francisco group The Diggers (whose drug-addicted state is described by Sinclair as 'pretty grisly' in *The Verbals*) is at the centre of a penetrating critique in *The Kodak Mantra Diaries*:[4]

> it's all bullshit. TV will have endless programmes on Ginsberg, on [Stokely] Carmichael, even on Grogan. Turn them into faces. Into more brand names. They won't have programmes BY them. And they won't have programmes FOR them. And nobody is clear-sighted enough to see it. But it doesn't matter. It's all maya. It will all pass.[5]

Sinclair understands, in 1971, that Emmit Grogan, Stokely Carmichael and Allen Ginsberg, all participants at the Congress, are already reinscribed into a circulation of mediated images and consumption, signified by the term 'TV'. Ironically, as *The Kodak Mantra Diaries* itself narrates in part, Sinclair was himself making a television documentary about Ginsberg's participation for West German television, a project sold to the BBC but never shown. (It received its first UK 'public broadcast' at an academic conference on Sinclair held at the University of Greenwich in the summer of 2004.) Sinclair, I think, deliberately implicates himself in the 'bullshit', the Ginsbergian term 'maya' (which Ginsberg, later in *The Kodak Mantra Diaries*, describes as '*a total illusion*', a universe of 'quixotic & illusory' appearance).[6] Perhaps, Sinclair indicates, the 'dialectics of Liberation' was itself 'maya', a staged event which bore little relation to 'real' political struggles elsewhere; 'there were acres of bullshit around'.[7]

Ginsberg is at the centre of *The Kodak Mantra Diaries* and the film *Ah Sunflower*. Much of the second, longest 'Book' of *The Kodak Mantra Diaries* are transcriptions of interviews with Ginsberg, interviews that are repeated in visual terms in *Ah Sunflower*. In Book 2, Tape Fifteen, two paired poems, 'The End Now (HOW BURROUGHS SEES IT)' and 'The Way Out (GINSBERG'S HOPE)' identify what seems to be the tension between apocalyptic imagining and utopian/revolutionary desire at the heart of counter-cultural thinking. Both poems are 'unauthored': although in form and 'voice' they appear to be Ginsberg's poems, it is possible that they could be transcriptions of Ginsberg's monologues, 'cut up' into poetic form by Sinclair himself. The question of observation and participation is at issue here, clearly; also, the seeming lack of distinction between Ginsberg's voice and Sinclair's tends to suggest that Sinclair himself validates the arguments. In '*The End Now*', the vision is apocalyptic, ascribed to William Burroughs's world-view:

So Burroughs sees the United States now
on a point of balance
everything is falling apart & getting worse

WELL, IS THERE A WAY OUT?[8]

The stagnation that inevitably leads to violence (and the revolutionary energy that leads to reaction) dominates the poem. In the 'replying' poem, a capitalised programme of action is offered as a source of hope:

1) THE IMMEDIATE FORMATION OF COMMUNITIES
2) THE ACTION & WORKING TOGETHER THAT IS FOUND IN PLEASURABLE WORK
3) THE SLOW WOOING & SEDUCTION OF PEOPLE INVOLVED WITH MASS COMMUNICATIONS
SO THAT THE MEDIA ARE TURNED TO MORE HUMANE AFFECT[9]

This seems unashamedly utopian or perhaps Marxian, particularly in the direction towards communities and unalienated labour. It is also worth noting that there is a strong distrust in revolutionary energies, a distrust which also appears in the later *Suicide Bridge* (1979) where a political use of myth (even in the service of 'resistance') is characterised thus: 'it climbs out of the book into a vertical energy called: FASCISM'.[10] Robert Bond has suggested that Sinclair's apparent hesitation before these energies is a critical and ideological gesture: that Sinclair deploys a 'non-willed, visionary–contemplative mode which *enables* interruptive materialist revelation', a release of the pressures of everyday life which enables us to contemplate the world truly.[11] I will have more to say about the displacement of agency later. Here, though, it is perhaps enough to indicate that while Sinclair was excited about the Congress, there is a continuing aversion to the violent expression of those desires: 'we were debating violent action, but I wasn't going to do that' says Sinclair; 'It wasn't part of my remit. I thought it was wrong at the time – showbiz rather than anything else'.[12] While the poet must remain committed, then, certain actions are problematic; or perhaps, if Robert Bond is correct, the idea of action at all is problematic. While R. D. Laing's validation of the anti-agency position seems to be in tune with Ginsberg's Buddhism at this point, the problem remains that cessation of activity may in fact lead to quietism and the failure to advance the possibility of social change. What *is* important, curiously, is that Ginsberg and the Congress creates the material for Sinclair to mine over the next few years, rather than a programme to act on, producing both *The Kodak Mantra Diaries* and *Lud Heat*.

Sinclair seems perhaps rather more interested, and less neutral, in *The Kodak Mantra Diaries* than his later pronouncements, and even some sceptical comments in the 1971 text, would admit. Clearly, Sinclair is, in part, attracted to Ginsberg's rhetoric and 'vision', but perhaps even more so to that of R. D. Laing. Marianna DeKoven describes Laing's 'revolutionary' anti-psychiatry:

> Laing was part of an ongoing modern, particularly twentieth-century, synthetic project, generally rejected by postmodernity, of conjoining not just Marx and Freud – politics and psychoanalysis – but also philosophy, aesthetics, ethics, cultural history, in a unified, integrated theory and critique of all human culture and society, culminating in a totalised, utopian plan for a revolutionary change: the ultimate 'master narrative'.[13]

I believe the connection to Laing to be vital in understanding Sinclair's means of critiquing contemporary London. Simon Perrill, in a relatively early but incisive commentary on Sinclair, notes Laing's influence. Laing, writes Perrill, researched the phenomenon of schizophrenia, 'elucidating it as a condition for which the fundamental units of society, the family, the environment, lovers, were responsible'.[14] He had achieved 'guru-like status among the counter-culture':

> His works from this period, *The Politics of Experience*, *Bird of Paradise* saw him, in the eyes of many psychiatrists and psychotherapists, to have made the mistake of equating psychotic with psychedelic states of mind. He began to view schizophrenia as a redemptive, healing voyage away from social alienation and 'sanity'.[15]

Laing's redemptive, or even Romantic view of madness (schizophrenia), is revealed by the following quotation of Laing in *The Kodak Mantra Diaries*: 'it seems that *what is most realistic, most sensible, most obvious, most sane, appears to most people to be starry-eyed idealism, absolutely unrealistic, & completely crazy & mad*'.[16] 'Madness' is actually presented as a form of freedom. The connection between 'madness', alienation and political activism achieves a kind of currency in the counter-culture, the connection between them important because both indicate forms of thought and behaviour that mainstream, normative, 'sane' society excludes because it compromises the assumptions upon which that society is based. To be 'mad' is to be 'alienated' from the inauthentic, artificial consumerism of late capitalism; to become 'mad' is to reach a space of authenticity outside of contemporary society. Ginsberg later characterises what Laing means by 'psychosis' in *The Kodak Mantra Diaries* as '*a breakthrough of the old consciousness formation into an insight into the new*'.[17]

The influence of Laing never really disappears in Sinclair's work. He is referred to in *Downriver*, where the narrator 'remembers 1967 talking with R. D. Laing in a waste garden alongside the Round-house',[18] and the way in which Sinclair reintroduces him in *London Orbital* – as 'Ronnie, the charismatic Glaswegian antispychiatrist' whose work at Shenley, an asylum outside London, is described as 'ships of fools with crazed or inspired captains'– again makes clear the connection between madness and a revolutionary poetic practice: 'crazed' and 'inspired' are equated.[19] This influence also helps decode Sinclair's later interest in J. G. Ballard. Unacknowledged, Laing seems the model for the 'renegade scientists' of Ballard's fiction: Vaughan in *Crash* (1973), Wilder in *High-Rise* (1973), Wilder Penrose in *Super-Cannes* (2001). These scientists encourage the self-deceiving narrators to undergo a psychic journey (Ballard in *Crash*, Lang in *High-Rise*), very similar to a Laingian self-discovery.

Ballard's imprecations on suburbanites who must find out what lies 'on the other side of alienation' is directly analogous to a Laingian 'voyage to schizophrenia'. Ballard's fiction, which even up to *Millennium People* (2003) conforms to this narrative trajectory, does not offer modes of resistance to the deformations of 'boring' contemporary life; rather, total immersion in it is the way to 'healthy' repressed psychosis. As Laing himself stated (quoted by Roy Porter): 'Madness need not be all breakdown. It may also be break-through. It is potential liberation and renewal as well as enslavement and existential death'.[20] Sinclair's latter-day interest in Ballard (who appears in both text and film of *London Orbital* and in Sinclair's book on David Cronenberg's film of *Crash*) might otherwise seem curious, considering Ballard's focus in his fiction. Sinclair writes of him:

> Ballard's poetic is anti-populist, anti-city. It's a demented meltdown of Thatcher and Aleister Crowley: do what you will is all of the law, repression is death. No interference from the state, no nannying. Canary wharf triumphalism and the inalienable right to kill yourself on an orbital motorway as you fight your way to work. What is astonishing is the courage, the recklessness of Ballard's argument; the unashamed trust in his own psychopathology.[21]

Ballard's suburban, car-obsessed individuals seem a long way from Sinclair's urban pedestrians. As I will suggest in Chapter 6, Sinclair identifies the world of Ballard's fiction with the actual organisation of contemporary life: Ballard's 'predictive mythologies' came true. *London Orbital* can be read, in this way, as a means to 'exorcise', rather than validate, Ballard's vision. The presence of Laing, however, connects the two writers. While the connection between Laing and Ballard is never made explicit in either Ballard or Sinclair's work, the ongoing legacy of the equation between 'madness' and 'vision' can be traced in both.

Sinclair uses the Laingian word 'breakthrough' to describe his trajectory from the 'scepticism' of the *Kodak Mantra Diaries* period, the late 1960s, to that of *Lud Heat* and the early 1970s: 'That was the real breakthrough. It required this cataclysmic thing of the sixties, a sudden charge coming from every direction, a real battery [. . .] I pulled back, got into my own territory, created my own space, and took things on my own terms'.[22] Curiously, although Sinclair suggests that the counter-cultural moment 'petered out into general lethargy and malcontent in the seventies', it is this very period of 'decline' (or perhaps 'disillusion') which he represents as the critical time for his own writing.[23] If there is a breakthrough, then perhaps it is to a belated recuperation of the position of the Laingian outsider. Social alienation seems key to the kind of poetry, and therefore poetic practice, that Sinclair values. In the Introduction to *Conductors of Chaos* (1996), an anthology of poetry from key figures in the British poetry revival and their inheritors, Sinclair writes that: 'the work I value is that which seems most remote, alienated, fractured'.[24] In *Lights Out for the Territory* (1998), in another sense a 'breakthrough' work for Sinclair, he characterises the activities of such outsider artists/poets as 'shamanism', 'heroically perverse experiments' in redemption. Sinclair adds: 'They were associated in my mind with other avatars of unwisdom: scavengers, dole-queue antiquarians, bagpeople, out-patients, muggers, victims, millennial babblers'.[25] In the form of the 'shaman', Simon Perrill argues, Sinclair's Laingian inheritance allows him to forge 'a mythological vocabulary for the discussion of social alienation'.[26] This Romanticism of the 'mad' outsider is analogous to Sinclair's occulting or Gothicised mode of critique found throughout his fiction and non-fiction.

While Sinclair's valuation of the 'alienated' poet seems directly connected to his involvement with the ideas of the counter-culture in the late 1960s, this explicit depoliticisation of modes of resistance is a problem for Sinclair's critique of contemporary life. This is connected, I believe, to his adoption of a neo-modernist poetics, one which is vital to both *Lud Heat* and *Suicide Bridge*, and to the poets of the 'British Poetry Renaissance' (or 'Revival') that Sinclair identifies and anthologises in *Conductors of Chaos*. Marianne DeKoven, in her book *Utopia Limited*, suggests an important connection between modern(ist) poetics and the counter-culture:

> Implicit throughout sixties ideologies is the utopian Enlightenment assumption of the capability of an avant-garde (by the end of the decade, a revolutionary avant-garde) to locate itself sufficiently outside of – at a critical distance from – society to see its ills clearly and to imagine alternatives that will cure them all.[27]

A Laingian anti-psychiatry – which itself rests upon a notion of 'alienation' in its formulations of the 'mad outsider' that DeKoven points to as peculiarly of the 1960s – provides that 'critical distance', the space 'outside' of society. DeKoven argues that the 'sixties' is a cultural point where 'Enlightenment utopianism' (identified with a yearning for wholeness that supplements a modernist poetics of the fragment) becomes articulated through a 'politics of the self' to create 'the primacy of individual meaningfulness', a condition DeKoven identifies as 'postmodern'.[28] This tension between modernity and modernism, and the conditions of postmodernity, is historically and culturally central to the development of Sinclair's work and also enables us to decode the means by which Sinclair offers his critique of late twentieth-century London. I will argue later in this book that traces of a (counter-cultural) utopianism survive in Sinclair's work, but here I would like to suggest that Sinclair's reliance upon a modernist avant-gardism to structure his poetics (and thinking) means that he tends to rearticulate the Laingian 'mad outsider' (or poet) as a space 'outside' contemporary London's structures of domination. DeKoven characterises Laing's anti-psychiatry as offering the possibility of change 'only as a result of a collective set of acts of willed individual self-liberation . . . redefining politics as a question of subjectivity (consciousness) rather than structural social change'.[29] Sinclair's own self-confessed position – neo-modernist in poetic practice, yet with a scepticism towards political activity ('not a joiner') that aligns him with a postmodern 'politics of the self' – tends to effectively undermine a material critique of contemporary Britain.

The loss of political agency, perhaps analogous to Laing's 'cessation of desire', implied by the turn to a postmodern 'willed individual self-liberation' indicates a major problem for considering Sinclair's urban walking to be any more than a strictly textual practice. This turn away from 'politics' perhaps helps to explain Sinclair's own continual turn towards the discourses of the mystical, occult or Gothic in analysing formations of power and domination.

Sinclair argues that the counter-cultural scene was 'bogus', but, he adds, 'it [was] real, it [was] crazy, and everything seem[ed] to be opening, splitting in new ways'.[30] 'Split' is a word that recurs in the Sinclair œuvre, particularly in *White Chappell, Scarlet Tracings*. I would like to stress here the probable Laingian derivation of this word. In Laing's 1965 text *The Divided Self*, Laing begins Chapter 1:

> The term schizoid refers to an individual he totality of whose experience is split in two main ways: in the first place, there is a rent in his relation to the world and, in the second, there is a disruption of his relation to himself. Such a person is not able to experience himself 'together with' others or 'at home in' the world, but, on the contrary, he experiences himself in despairing aloneness and isolation; moreover, he does not experience himself as a complete person but rather as 'split' in various ways, perhaps as a mind more or less tenuously linked to a body, as two or more selves, and so on.[31]

This dissociation is 'schizoid' rather than schizophrenic; further down the page, Laing avers that he uses 'the terms *schizoid* and *schizophrenic* for the sane and psychotic positions respectively'.[32] If 'schizoid' equates with 'sanity', then the sane person is already split, dissociated, 'mad'. This division between rational subject and 'mad' poet or preacher is repeated in the insistence on the status of the sceptical 'documenter' in *The Kodak Mantra Diaries* (inside yet outside the counter-culture), and also in recurrent images of splitting and bifurcation in *White Chappell, Scarlet Tracings*. If the psyche, body and culture are 'split' in Sinclair's work, so is the space of London.

The spatial turn

In his turning from documenting the counter-culture (and its failure by 1971, the year *The Kodak Mantra Diaries* was published), to the 'lines of force' emanating through the fabric of London in *Lud Heat* (1975), Sinclair also demonstrates a change of focus which corresponds to what has been called the 'spatial turn' in critical and social theory since the days of the counter-culture, the late 1960s. Brian Jarvis, in *Postmodern Cartographies* (1998), writes:

> Amongst critics on the left the turn to geography has been universally applauded as a radical and emancipatory challenge to the hegemony of historicism and of capitalist spatiality. It can also be read, however, as symptomatic of the crisis in faith in the grand narratives of classical Marxist prophecy. It may be far from coincidental that the upsurge in interest in spatial politics follows rapidly on the heels of a series of devastating disappointments for the left on the historical stage: the failure of 1968 in France, the rise to politicocultural hegemony of the New Right since the 1970s and the collapse of various communist regimes.[33]

While one might take exception to the characterisation of Marxism as 'prophecy' (perhaps substituting 'teleology' or 'historical determinism'), the period 1968 to 1972, the period of the counter-culture and its perceived failure, is clearly crucial in the realignment of politics on the Left. Fredric Jameson identifies a 'dual break' to periodise the 'end of the 60s', one occurring culturally in 1967, the other more decisively and economically in 1972–4. In his essay 'Periodizing the Sixties', he suggests:

> [I]t seems appropriate to mark the definitive end of the '60s' in the general area of 1972–74 [. . .] For 1973–4 is the moment of the onset of a worldwide economic crisis, whose dynamic is still with us today, and put a decisive full stop to the economic expansion and prosperity characteristic of the postwar period generally and of the 60s in particular.[34]

In relation to Sinclair's work, the 'rupture' takes place between the 'Dialectics of Liberation' Congress and the publication of *Lud Heat* in 1975, what I have suggested (in DeKoven's terms) as a trajectory from a collective politics (the counter-culture) to a Laingian 'politics of the self'. What this rupture inaugurates, according to Jameson, is what he will later analyse as the conditions of 'late capitalism': postmodernity. In 'Periodizing the Sixties', Jameson proposes several (now highly familiar) characteristics of postmodernism or postmodernity: the 'death of the subject'; the '*culture of the simulacrum*' or 'society of the spectacle'; an 'aesthetic of *textuality*' or what is often described as 'schizophrenic time'; and the 'waning of [the opposition between high modernism and mass culture], and some new conflation of the forms of high and mass culture'.[35] The 'spatial turn' can be characterised, perhaps, as a response to the 'postmodern' failure of the 'Master Narratives', a turn away from totalising metanarrative to the contingent, the fragmentary, and the spatial. The 'spatialising' of left critique is perhaps most insistently apparent in the influence of Michel Foucault. Foucault, in his article 'Of Other Spaces' (1984), wrote:

> The great obsession of the nineteenth century was, as we know, history: with its themes of development and of suspension, of crisis and cycle [. . .] The present epoch will perhaps be above all the epoch of space. We are in the epoch of simultaneity: we are in the epoch of juxtaposition, the epoch of the near and far, of the side-by-side, of the dispersed.[36]

Foucault's insistence upon the culturally determinations affecting critique is an important one, and we will return to some of the terms by which he characterises the 'epoch of space' later. Victor Burgin, writing of Jameson's 1984 essay 'Postmodernism, or, the Cultural Logic of Late Capitalism', writes:

> The preoccupation of cultural theorists with questions of space had begun before Jameson's article, to the extent that his remarks about time seemed *at the time* to be 'behind their time' – a futile last shot fired in a battle, already lost, on behalf of Marxist historicism.[37]

If spatial critique is determined, in part, by what Jameson diagnoses in his 1991 book *Postmodernism* as a 'weakening of historicity' or even 'crisis in historicity', their turning towards spatial concepts becomes a symptom of postmodernity (and the exhaustion of Marxism) as much as a critique.[38] We can see this in the work of 'postmodern geographers'.

Edward Soja's work of the 1980s and particularly *Postmodern Geographies* (1989), part of the so-called 'L.A. School' of Marxist geography, was an important redefinition of the field of human geography and an attempt to recover spatial thinking in terms of a Marxist materialism. Mike Crang and Nigel Thrift, in their 'Introduction' to a work introducing the major theorists of the 'spatial turn', *Thinking Space* (2000), follow Soja in suggesting that 'spatiality has been a repressed element of much social thought'.[39] The bringing forth of this repressed element, argues Soja, replenishes the resources of 'Western Marxism' rather than indicating its exhaustion:

> This historico-geographical materialism is more than a tracing of empirical outcomes over space or the description of spatial constraints

and limitations on social action over time. It is a compelling call for a
radical reformulation of critical social theory as a whole, of Western
Marxism in particular, and of the many different ways we look at,
conceptualise, and interpret not only space itself but the whole range
of fundamental relationships between space, time, and social being at
every level of abstraction. As Lefebvre suggests [. . .] it is an invitation
to 'resume the dialectic' on a different interpretative terrain.[40]

Not only will geography be transformed by Marxism, claimed Soja;
Marxism itself will be changed and replenished with its 'encounter'
with geography. A 'postmodern geography', then, is not one that
simply explores the spatial configurations of contemporary capital
and their (de)forming relations to power, subjectivity and the social;
rather, the 'passage to postmodernism' results in a 'disassembl[ing]
and rearrang[ing]' effect, a radicalisation of the possibilities of social
critique from the geographical perspective.

Soja, like Jameson, identifies Los Angeles as the city where 'it
all comes together': the key city for investigating 'postmodern
geographies'. If Paris is the city which 'haunts' theories of the modern
urban space, then Los Angeles is the paradigmatic postmodern city.
Soja's method consciously avoids totalisation, which can 'never
capture all the meanings and significations of the urban'; instead,
'the perspectives explored are purposeful, eclectic, fragmentary,
incomplete, and frequently contradictory, but so too is Los Angeles'.[41]
Soja's critique is, then self-avowedly complicitous with contemporary
conditions, the 'fragmentary' nature of the analysis analogous to
the dislocation experienced by the inhabitants of 'postmodern' Los
Angeles. Fredric Jameson's conception of postmodern hyperspace
also stands in metonymic relation to the 'incapacity of our minds
. . . to map great global multinational and decentred communicational
network in which we find ourselves caught as individual subjects'.[42]
The traces of the 'crisis in historicity' are strong in both Soja's and
Jameson's thinking here. The latter's critique of 'postmodern
hyperspace' is fully elucidated in *Postmodernism*:

> This latest mutation is space – postmodern hyperspace – has finally
> succeeded in transcending the capacities of the individual human body
> to locate itself, to organize its immediate surroundings perceptually,
> and cognitively to map its position in a mappable external world.[43]

Although 'postmodern hyperspace' signifies a certain condition of
spatial relations and spatial representation, it is also a 'real' (as in

lived or experienced) space. Jameson identifies an emblematic postmodern hyperspace' in the Bonaventure Hotel in Los Angeles. The Bonaventure, writes Jameson,

> Aspires to being a total space, a complete world, a kind of miniature city; to this new total space, meanwhile, corresponds a new collective practice, a new mode in which individuals move and congregate, something like the practice of a new and historically original kind of hypercrowd.[44]

The glass skin of the building 'repels the city outside', achieving a 'peculiar and placeless dissociation of the Bonaventure from its neighborhood'.[45] Therefore, not only does postmodern hyperspace, made glass and concrete in the form of the Bonaventure, produce new conditions of spatial relationships within it, it also acts as a kind of disruption to the urban space in which it is (dis)located.

Jameson's description of a material 'postmodern hyperspace' are echoed in Sinclair's response to the 'Siebel' building he discovers in *London Orbital*:

> Siebel, I recognised at once, was the future. *Post*-surveillance. A discretion so absolute, that criminality and vandalism were impossible concepts [. . .] Siebel could be an illusion. A photo-realist hoarding. We walk towards the central tower, the bottle-glass Panopticon. And then we're inside – with no memory of having passed through an automatic door. The building has no inside.[46]

The Siebel building is an example of Jameson's formulation of 'hyperspace', the boundary between outside and inside impossible to locate. The Siebel building symbolises a self-effacement which borders on virtuality; Sinclair notes that he cannot identify what product the Siebel corporation makes. The positionality of the building in space represents the ideological construction of contemporary corporate organisation, the presentation of absence the most effective of ideological gestures. Throughout *London Orbital*, Sinclair diagnoses the privatisation of space and the erasure of the markers of history and community that had heretofore provided a system of orientation for urban life. The 'spatial turn' in critical theory is echoed in Sinclair's own 'spatial turn', one particularly evident in his books of 'excursions' like *Lights Out for the Territory* and *London Orbital*. Elsewhere in Sinclair's work, the representation of spatial relations and forces is critiqued through a variety of different themes: the 'lines of force' and occult alignments of the Hawksmoor churches in *Lud Heat*; the traces of violent history of Spitalfields in *White Chapell, Scarlet Tracings*; Thatcher's London in *Downriver*; 'psychogeography' and walking in *Lights Out*; and the spatial exclusion of London's others in the asylums of *London Orbital*. I will deal with each of these in subsequent chapters. Sinclair's recurrent emphasis on space and spatial relations indicates that the form of critique is, like Jameson, Foucault and other theorists of space, dependent upon the 'rupture' in the early 1970s that Jameson and David Harvey locate as the beginning of 'postmodern' conditions.

Mike Davis, another of the 'L.A. School' of Marxist geographers, identifies similar forces at work in late 1980s Los Angeles: the principle behind the reconfiguration of Los Angeles's urban centre, he argues, is the 'destruction of urban public space'.[47] Instead of the delocation found in Jameson's Bonaventure hotel, Davis insists upon the enclosure and policing that characterise the contemporary American city:

> The American city, as many critics have recognized, is systematically being turned inside out – or, rather, outside in. The valorized spaces of the new megastructures and super-malls are concentrated in the center, street frontage is denuded, public activity is sorted into strictly functional components, and circulation is internalised in corridors under the gaze of private police.[48]

Note how the Siebel building, like Davis's mall, was an 'inside out' or 'outside in' space. Sinclair's recurrent emphasis upon surveillance as a means of control in contemporary spaces (cameras, security guards) indicates a similar critique of the privatisation of public space. It is little wonder, then, that a British 'super-mall', the Bluewater complex at Dartford in Kent is also the 'destination' of a visit and the object of satirical critique in *London Orbital*, where it is described as a 'Ballardian resort'.[49] Bluewater mixes Davis's panoptic space – 'Security (discreet but firm)' – with the postmodern dislocation of Jameson's Bonaventure: 'you meet trembling humans who have lost their cars'.[50] For Sinclair, Bluewater becomes the space where the consumerist dynamic of contemporary capitalism reaches its British apogee, but the experience of visiting the mall, where 'only the fake is authentic', induces trauma, 'incubates rage' and the desire to flee.[51] Consumerism itself is occulted, becoming a superstitious act that protects the consumer from the overwhelmingly negative experience of Bluewater's space: 'buy and live'.[52]

Sinclair's description of the Siebel building as 'Panopticon', as in Davis's work on 'Fortress L.A.', also signifies the importance of Foucauldian conceptions of the centrality of power and policing to the organisation of space to both analyses. Although the policing and privatisation of space is central to Sinclair's writing from the early 1990s (and especially in *Lights Out for the Territory* (1998), it is not until *London Orbital* that Sinclair directly refers to Foucault, and there in connection with the asylum. Chris Philo implicitly indicates a significant connection between Foucault's spatial critique and the Laingian anti-psychiatry which seems to have had such an impact upon Sinclair's world-view. Philo suggests that:

> One way of characterising Foucault's projects [. . .] is to suggest that his sensitivity to spatial relations amounts to the introduction of a *geometric turn* into histories of 'social otherness', and it is also possible to find various commentaries portraying his studies as primarily concerned with excavating the geometries of power that have structured the historical experiences of the mad, the sad, and the bad.[53]

Philo also argues that 'a simple geometry of "inclusion" and "exclusion", of "inside" and "outside", is therefore projected onto the history of Western madness' in *Madness and Civilization*, a binary structure which distorts rather than reveals history.[54] 'Postmodern geographies' attempt to complicate the binary structure of inside and outside, inclusion and exclusion, but it remains a structuring principle of Foucault's spaces of power and exclusion, Laingian anti-psychiatry (the 'mad' or schizophrenic excluded by the 'sane'), theories of 'alienation', and, it should be noted, Sinclair's conception of the poet/artist as 'shaman'. These discourses intersect in Sinclair's work in the recurrent references to David Rodinsky, the mysterious and emblematic outsider of *Rodinsky's Room* (1999) and *Dark Lanthorns* (1999). Rodinsky, whose room was discovered 'abandoned' much later, is discovered to have been removed from his home in Princelet Street, Whitechapel, to an 'asylum' in Epsom, where he died. It can also be found in Sinclair's meditation on the Romantic poet John Clare, *Edge of the Orison* (2005). For Sinclair, the post-war movement of families or communities from London to suburb is symbolically enacted in this forced relocation.

The M25 'ring' that Sinclair investigates in *London Orbital* is central to a post-war history that Sinclair attempts to recover, a history of the dispersal of urban communities into the suburbs and dormitory towns where history has been erased. This impetus towards dispersal and dislocation is not, according to other theorists of space, coincidental to contemporary capital's organisation of space. Andy Merrifield, writing about Henri Lefebvre's *The Production of Space* (1991) in the edited collection *Thinking Space*, argues that 'Lefebvre sees fragmentation and conceptual dislocation as serving distinctively ideological purposes. Separation ensures consent, perpetuates misunderstanding, and worse: it reproduces the status quo'.[55] Edward Soja also suggests that Lefebvre revealed an 'increasingly embracing, instrumental and socially mystified spatiality' at the heart of capitalism, a spatiality hidden beneath 'illusion and ideology'.[56]

In *London Orbital*, Sinclair undertakes a walk up the Lea Valley, 'tame country' that extrudes from the north-east of the city into London's hinterlands. This chapter of *London Orbital* is as close as Sinclair comes to campaigning journalism. Rather than an 'Edwardian sense of excursion, pleasure, time out', Sinclair discovers a different history, that of the 'military/industrial complex'.[57] The area was once dominated by a now-demilitarised munitions factory (or 'brownfield site') at Enfield, which itself has been redeveloped into 'Enfield Island Village': ' "Village" is the giveaway. Village is the sweetener that converts a toxic dump into a slumber colony. You can live ten minutes away from Liverpool Street Station and be in a village. With CCTV, secure parking and uniformed guards'.[58] The 'first Island Village', asserts Sinclair soon after, is the City of London: 'sealed off, protected, with its own security'.[59] In the course of his walks around the M25, Sinclair encounters an archipelago of such enclosed estates and gated communities, such as 'Repton Park', on the outskirts of Watford: 'by day, the Crest Homes estate is deserted (no sign of children); you feel the eyes tracking you, the soft hum of surveillance cameras'.[60] Here we find another connection to J. G. Ballard, whose *Running Wild* (1988), *Super-Cannes* (2000) and *Millennium People* (2003) all posit the kind of enclosed, 'gated' communities that Sinclair encounters and satirises in *London Orbital*. Where, for Ballard, the gated community is the privileged site where liberating, Laingian 'voyages to schizophrenia' can be enacted, for Sinclair they indicate an evacuation of 'real life', an erasure of history and its replacement with an entirely artificial and atomistic simulacrum of community, and the fake 'history' of the heritage industry. The gated communities and fabricated 'villages' of the M25 ring and Lea Valley are symptomatic of the means by which contemporary capital organises urban (and suburban) space.

The practice of space

Sinclair's practice of investigating the spatial configurations of contemporary life is, famously, walking. The walking subject has been theorised in the twentieth century in several ways, but here I wish to concentrate on, first, the *flâneur*, the 'stroller' of Baudelaire's writing which was critiqued by Walter Benjamin; and secondly, the practice of 'tactical' walking in the city as theorised by Michel de Certeau. The *flâneur* has been a figure to conjure with in contemporary critical and urban theory; it is not without its problems, as I shall show, not least for this study that Sinclair has explicitly repudiated the idea in relation to his own work.

The *flâneur* is an urban stroller, and is historically bound up with Paris in the nineteenth century, and particularly the work of Charles Baudelaire. Famously, Benjamin, in 'On Some Motifs of Baudelaire', identifies Baudelaire's phrase 'a *kaleidoscope* with a consciousness' to characterise the *flâneur*, the man of modernity who experiences the 'shocks and collisions' of the streets, symbolic of the sensory energies of modernity.[61] Though the *flâneur* moves in the crowd, he is not of it, and in his essay Benjamin is careful to critique Baudelaire's identification of the *flâneur* with the 'man of the crowd': 'It is hard to accept this view', wrote Benjamin. 'The man of the crowd is no *flâneur*. In him, composure has given way to manic behaviour. Hence he exemplifies, rather, what had become of the *flâneur* once he was deprived of the milieu to which he belonged.'[62] The 'man of the crowd', identified with the spectral figure of Edgar Allan Poe's short story, is, curiously, a dislocated *flâneur*, without the ease and 'idleness' that Benjamin associates with the activities of the *flâneur* in *The Arcades Project* (1999). The crowd or 'masses' in Baudelaire, suggests Benjamin, 'do not stand for classes or any sort of collective; rather they are nothing but the amorphous crowd of passers-by, the people in the street'.[63] Benjamin suggests that the crowd is simply, for the *flâneur*, a further articulation of urban space: 'within the labyrinth of the city, the masses are the newest and most inscrutable labyrinth'.[64]

This distinction of the *flâneur* from the mass or 'crowd' signifies that the *flâneur* is a particular type of urban bourgeois sensibility. Where the masses 'efface all traces of the individual',[65] the *flâneur* is an assertion of the sovereignty of the individual subject within the urban mass. (Again, we find the tension between totality and separation identified earlier.) This subjectivity is, however, caught up in the processes of production and reproduction. Keith Tester argues that 'the *flâneur* is a passive spectator who is duped by the spectacle of the public as the consumer who is duped by the glittering promises of consumption'.[66] Benjamin calls the *flâneur* the 'spy for the capitalists, on assignment in the realm of consumers', which, while identifying the *flâneur* with consumption, indicates a different mode of consumption: the *flâneur* is the 'observer of the marketplace'.[67] For the *flâneur*, observation *is* consumption, the consumption of spectacles, and the streets the place of consumption. Tester suggests that '*flânerie* is invariably identified as an activity located in the realm of the empire of the gaze and the spectacle';[68] activity is perhaps the wrong word here, for critique of the *flâneur* often emphasises, as Tester himself does, quoted above, the *passivity* of *flânerie*. Strolling, drifting through the streets, becomes simply a rarefied form of the consumption-directed subject-position enforced by commodity capitalism.

Early in *Lights Out for the Territory*, Sinclair writes:

> Walking is the best way to explore and exploit the city; the changes, shifts, breaks in the cloud helmet, movement of light on water. Drifting purposefully is the recommended mode, tramping asphalted earth in alert reverie, allowing the fiction of an underlying pattern to assert itself. To the no-bullshit materialist this sounds suspiciously like *fin-de-siècle* decadence, a poetic of entropy – but the born-again *flâneur* is a stubborn creature, less interested in texture and fabric, eavesdropping on philosophical conversation pieces, than in noticing *everything*.[69]

Sinclair, in the above quotation, seems to mark out the 'born-again *flâneur*' as different from the '*fin-de-siècle* decadent'. Sinclair's attempt to distance his walking practice is signified by '[d]rifting purposefully': Sinclair's conception, avowedly *purposeful*, with an aim if not a destination, avoids allegations of passivity and consumption. This distancing is emphasised further in *Lights Out for the Territory*:

> The concept of 'strolling', aimless urban wandering, the *flâneur*, had been superseded. We had moved into the age of the stalker [. . .] This was walking with a thesis. With a prey.[70]

As we noted above, the turn towards 'willed self-liberation' in Sinclair's work (from the political engagement of *The Kodak Mantra Diaries* to the occult formulations of *Lud Heat*) perhaps implicates Sinclair's urban stroller in *flânerie* more than Sinclair is able to acknowledge: there is in Sinclair's writing a distinction between the walking subject and the 'mass' or crowd, largely effected through the *absence* of others on London's streets. Sinclair and his companions seemingly walk empty pavements, decoding the urban fabric but not part of the mass urban transits that make up much of the traffic of the city. The *flâneur*, the bourgeois individualist connoisseur of the streets, rather ironically approximates Kevin Jackson's description of Sinclair on his walks: Sinclair is a 'scholar and a gentleman . . . [a] wit and raconteur'.[71]

Helping distance 'stalking' from *flânerie*, and politicising the act of walking in Sinclair's texts is 'psychogeography', a word coined by the situationists, but used rather differently by Sinclair. Chris Jenks describes it thus:

> A psycho-geography, then, derives from the subsequent 'mapping' of an unrouted route which, like primitive cartography, reveals not so much randomness and chance as spatial intentionality. It uncovers compulsive currents within the city along with unprescribed boundaries of exclusion and unconstructed gateways of opportunity. The city begins, without fantasy or exaggeration, to take on the characteristics of a map of the mind.[72]

Sinclair, in *The Verbals*, rather deprecates his use of the term, suggesting that 'psychogeography could be adapted to forge a franchise'.[73] He redefines his own practice as a '*psychotic* geography', 'the belief that something which happens in a place permanently affects that place'.[74] This formulation, and the reiteration of the phrase 'stalking the city', again indicates the continuing influence of Laingian conceptions of 'madness' as counter-cultural resistance, the 'mad' or alienated outsider able to discern the true or underlying patterns or histories of the city. Sinclair's psychogeography is a depth-model, revealing the 'hidden' strata of the city. In this, psychogeography connects both with Sinclair's interest in the 'archives' of London (for which, see Chapter 4 in this volume) and also his past role as bookseller and antiquarian. Sinclair avers that he appropriated psychogeography not from the situationists but from Stewart Home, cultural provocateur and pulp novelist. Home is involved in the London Psychogeographical Association and related groups. In *Mind Invaders*, a collection of pamphlets edited by Home, psychogeography is described as 'one antithetical pole amongst many which realises the conflict between our idealised role as citizens and our subjectivity arising from the material conditions of our life'; it 'investigates the intersection of time and space'; and perhaps most importantly, 'Psychogeography is not a substitute for class struggle, but a tool of class struggle'.[75] Rather than the 'soggy' occult formulations of ley-lines, Sinclair seems to propose a political conception of the deformative effects of the urban environment, attempting to trace the inscription of power in policed and excluded spaces. For Sinclair, psychogeography is 'more than a metaphor',[76] and assumes the status of a practice of space, because it both resists the contemporary configurations of urban space, and reveals the history of that space which is deliberately erased or overlaid by late capitalism. His excoriation of the Millennium Dome in *London Orbital* and *Sorry Meniscus* (1999) is partly driven by the erasure of spatial and communal histories, and his desire to reclaim the 'pre-forgotten' or 're-forgotten'. This is perhaps another reason why Sinclair resists categorisation as a *flâneur*, as *flânerie* depoliticises walking as a spatial practice. What Sinclair attempts to do is not to consume the spectacle of urban space, but to produce it through a reinscription of its histories.

'Stalking the city', as a metaphor of pedestrian practice, is not without its sinister undertones. It has also been suggested that it constructs a distinctly masculine subjectivity, directly analogous to that of the *flâneur*. Judith Walkowitz, in *City of Dreadful Delight* (1992), critiques the *flâneur*, suggesting that 'the fact and fantasy of male bourgeois exploration had long been an informing feature of nineteenth-century bourgeois male subjectivity'.[77] The *flâneur* offers the not only a fantasy of unseen agency, privileged knowledge and voyeuristic power, but also a fantasy of possible violence and sexual domination. Deborah Parsons also emphasises the gendered subject position of the *flâneur*, stating that 'Benjamin never admits the possibility of a *flâneuse* (and in fact defines it in such a way as to preclude this possibility)';[78] instead, she suggests, the female subject-position identified with *flânerie* is the 'passante' (or streetwalker): the prostitute. Parsons goes on to argue that 'the prostitute and the *passante* are figures in opposition to, rather than reflection of, the *flâneur*, and are objects of his gaze in the city'.[79] Where the male subject consumes, the female 'object' becomes a commodity to be consumed.

The fantasy involved is of experiencing the city 'as a whole', the diversity of London's districts and locations made coherent through the unifying gaze of the male subject. It is also a fantasy of sovereign desire, the male desiring subject freed from social, economic and spatial constraints. Both Parsons and Rob Shields emphasise the gaze of the *flâneur*, but where Parsons suggests that 'the act of walking, as a body *within* the city, seems incompatible with the need to be a totalizing, panoramic and authoritative viewpoint, of being an eye *observing* it',[80] Shields emphasises the 'self-implication' that is necessary for *flânerie*:

> An interpretative attempt to grasp the totality of social relations through a *verstehen*-like experiencing of the 'aura' of the scene of commodity consumption in the arcades requires the *flâneur* to become part of the process of commodity exchange as a 'participant observer'.[81]

To grasp the totality of social relations is therefore to acknowledge or 'see' the *flâneur's* own part in the system of commodity exchange.

The implication of the 'participant observer' in the process of commodity exchange, in attempting to grasp the 'totality of social relations', relates to our consideration of Sinclair's role as 'documenter' of the 'Dialectics of Liberation' Congress we explored earlier. We noted how Sinclair emphasised his own 'scepticism' about the possibility of radical change or 'liberation', both in *The Kodak Mantra Diaries* and in his later recollections in *The Verbals*. Perhaps the narrative Sinclair proposes of his own relationship to the 'spiritual' or 'mystic' elements of counter-cultural thinking can be connected to his repudiation of the *flâneur* (he even calls dabbling in those areas being a 'flaneur of the mystic' in *The Verbals*, suggesting a dilettante consumerism).[82] When Sinclair declares that he 'went right in' to mystical or non-materialist beliefs in the early 1970s, he attempts to decouple his activities from the leisured, privileged 'strolling' consumption of the *flâneur*, yet perhaps in his gestures towards belief *and* scepticism Sinclair would like to have it both ways. The figure of the 'born-again *flâneur*' indicates Sinclair's paradoxical critical position, half inside, implicated in the processes of production and consumption (walker, writer, bookseller) and half-outside, critical of them (poet, shaman, 'mad walker').

Sinclair offers a different walking subject in *London Orbital*. There, he considers the *flâneur* to be 'overworked' (2002a: 120), itself an interesting word in relation to the 'man of leisure'. Instead, he posits the *fugueur*, 'the right description for our walk, our once-a-month episodes of transient mental illness. Madness as a voyage'.[83] Here, the walker is passed through the medium of R. D. Laing's redemptive schizophrenia. Notably, the *fugueur* walks outside the city, and is symbolised by John Clare's 'journey out of Essex' cited towards the end of *London Orbital* and published in 2005 as *Edge of the Orison*. The connection between walking and hypnagogic or narcotic states is also found in Virginian Woolf's 'Street Haunting: A London Adventure', one of the texts cited by critics as positing a particularly female walking subject. In 'Street Haunting', the pedestrian subject encounters the crowds on the streets, who are

> wrapt, in this short passage from work to home, in some narcotic dream [. . .] Dreaming, gesticulating, often muttering a few words, they sweep over the Strand and across Waterloo Bridge, whence they will be slung in long rattling trains, to some prim little villa in Bares or Surbiton where the sight of the clock in the hall [. . .] puncture[s] the dream.[84]

In the flow of crowds over Waterloo Bridge, there is more than an echo here of T. S. Eliot's *The Waste Land*. The characterisation of the 'crowd', either dead (metaphorically or literally) or narcotised, signifies a critique of the effects of contemporary urban life. However, the contrast between somnambulism and the very definitely perceptive and alive subjectivity of the narrator in 'Street Haunting' repeats the distinction between 'crowd' or mass and bourgeois subject that we found in the figure of the *flâneur*.

For Woolf's walking subject, very much like the *flâneur* (the '*kaleidoscope* with a consciousness'), the experience of walking in the city is primarily a visual one. Once the walker leaves the domestic space of the home (the 'soul' leaving its shell) it becomes a 'central oyster of perceptiveness, an enormous eye'.[85] Like Sinclair's 'born-again *flâneur*' it notices everything. Perception here, though, induces reverie; freed of its shell, the walking subject can be projected into the consciousnesses of those she encounters. In this way, the subjects of the city become a totality through the perception or gaze of the 'street haunter', a totality that is brought into being by the *dissolution* of the subject; it is only when she returns home that 'the old possessions, the old prejudices, fold us round; and the self . . . sheltered and enclosed'.[86] Curiously, then, 'Street Haunting' both differentiates the walking subject from the narcotised crowd, and (temporarily) immerses and dissolves the subject into the consciousnesses of London's denizens. The subject becomes a 'ghost', material yet immaterial, haunting the streets of the city.

The figure of 'haunting' has been a recurrent one in thinking about urban formations and spatial practice. Julian Wolfreys, in *Deconstruction: Derrida* (1998), proposes a 'hauntological' reading of Sinclair's *Lights Out for the Territory*, a reading itself prompted by Jacques Derrida's *Specters of Marx* (1998). (Perhaps unsurprisingly, Wolfreys also refers to Woolf's 'spectral essay'.) Wolfreys suggests that 'the psychogeography which Sinclair traces raises spectres which are always there, revenants of the city, endlessly recalled through walking, memory and writing'.[87] He proposes a 'hauntological' reading partly through Sinclair's own recourse to the language of ghosts, spectres and haunting to represent the layered or 'palimpsest' constructions of urban space, and effectively traces the recurrence of this language in *Lights Out for the Territory*. While the figure of 'haunting' is certainly evident throughout Sinclair's work, in the language of the texts and in the conceptual framework Sinclair employs to represent the intertextual fabrics of London writing (see Chapter 2 on *White Chappell, Scarlet Tracings* for more on this idea), Wolfreys' own occulted critical discourse is open to critique as simply a reflection of the terms of Sinclair's own. Wolfreys anticipates this at the end of the chapter on Sinclair, when he admits: 'it might be suggested on the part of those wishing to criticise a hauntological or spectropoetical analysis [that much of what I address] is merely a question of intertextuality given a ghostly guise'.[88] However, we can bring Derrida's analysis of Marx to bear on Sinclair's conception of the role of the urban walking subject.

In *Specters of Marx*, Derrida conducts a reading of Marx's *The Communist Manifesto* in order to propose an aporia at the heart of Marx's materialist discourse. On the first page of Marx's text, Derrida identifies three usages of the noun 'spectre' or ghost, most famously in the phrase 'A spectre is haunting Europe, the specter of communism'.[89] (Both Mike Crang and Nigel Thrift, and the London Psychological Association deploy variants of this phrase in the texts I have already cited, indicating their Marxian lineage.) Derrida develops his argument to suggest that Marx proposes Communism as a spectre that haunts capital from the future: 'Marx, for his part, announces and calls for a presence to come. He seems to predict and prescribe: What for the moment figures as only a spectre in the ideological representation of old Europe must become, in the future, a present reality, that is, a living reality'.[90] The *Manifesto* is then a text which calls up a spectral manifestation, a Communist future which 'haunts' Europe's present. Once material Communism exists, Marxian materialism proposes to banish the non-material basis of belief of religion, the 'opiate of the masses', 'ghosts which are bound to the categories of bourgeois economy'.[91] Slavoj Žižek proposes the same tension between materialism and religion in Marx's writings in his essay 'The Spectre of Ideology'. He argues that 'the point of Marx is that the commodity universe provides the necessary fetishistic supplement to the "official" spirituality: it may well be that the "official" ideology of our society is Christian spirituality, but its actual foundation is none the less the idolatry of the Golden calf, money'.[92] It is not that religion or spirituality ideologically 'masks' the structuring presence of capitalist economy, in Derrida's argument: it is that the discourse of materialist critique itself rests upon the terms of the non-material (even in the concept of ideology itself).

The 'real presence of the specter [is] thus the end of the spectral' according to Derrida:

> One must also underscore the instant immediacy with which, as Marx would like us to believe or to make us believe, mysticism, magic and the ghost would disappear: they *will vanish* (indicative), they will dissipate in truth, according to him, as if by magic, as they had come, at the very second in which one will (would) see the end of market production.[93]

This banishment cannot be complete, as indicated by Derrida's deployment of the term 'as if by magic': Marx's materialism remains 'haunted' by non-materialism, is haunted by belief. Derrida extends his analysis of Marx's discourse to propose an inescapable connection between the figures of a critique of ideology and those of religion itself: 'If the objective relation between things (which we have called a *commerce between commodities*) is indeed a phantasmagoric form of the social relation between men, *then* we must have recourse to the *only analogy possible*, that of religion'.[94] The material, then, contains and proposes a 'spectral' other or supplement; material critique is thereby 'haunted' by the terms of non-materiality.

This has clear importance for our reading of the activity of the walking subjects in these texts. In *Echographies of Television* (2002), Derrida's collaboration with Bernard Stiegler, the 'specter' is described by Derrida as 'both visible and invisible, phenomenal and nonphenomenal: a trace that marks the present with its absence in advance', a phrase which returns to the idea of Communism 'haunting' the present from the future.[95] The destabilising and disruptive figure of the 'specter' does indeed seem useful for thinking Woolf's walking subject in 'Street Haunting', which both differentiates itself from, and subsumes itself within, the others of London. However, it is actually Derrida's remarking of the visual formation of the 'ghost' or 'spectre' that has greatest bearing upon our consideration of the urban walker, the spectacle, and the gaze. Derrida proposes a 'visor effect' (prompted by a reading of the ghost of Hamlet's father) in relation to the spectre:

> The ghost looks at or watches us, the ghost concerns us. The specter is not simply some we see coming back, it is someone by whom we feel ourselves watched, observed, surveyed [. . .] [The] fact that there is a visor symbolizes the situation in which I can't see who is looking at me, I can't meet the gaze of the other, whereas I am in his sight [. . .] The specter enjoys the right of absolute inspection. He is the right of inspection itself.[96]

Woolf's 'street haunter' is certainly spectral, in this formulation, 'inspecting' the other pedestrians without seeming reciprocity. Not all urban walkers assume the same explicit spectrality: the flâneur, by contrast, is bound up both with materialism (consumption) and with looking and visibility. Rob Shields argues that 'the flâneur is out to see and be seen, and thus requires a crowd to be able to watch others and take in the bustle of the city in the security of his anonymous status as part of the metropolitan throng. The crowd is also an audience': visibility is central to flânerie.[97] Sinclair's walking subject, the 'stalker', seems to hesitate between materiality (the 'born-again flâneur' associated with the 'no-bullshit materialist', the investigations of the concrete lived spaces of London) and non-materiality ('lines of force', triangulations, Sinclair's direct assertion in The Verbals that he is not a materialist). Psychogeography itself, a way of uncovering and recovering the lost or occulted strata of the city, is perhaps a means of negotiating the material and the non-material, the physical experience of London through walking and the mystical. If a 'ghost of the future' haunts London's streets, it Jameson's 'postmodern hyperspace' that we encountered above: the Siebel building, gated communities, Ballardian suburbs, all of which partake of a willing erasure of history and memory. Sinclair's own, rather occult formulation of a 'psychic geography' (which he relates to a kind of séance) somewhat masks the centrality of this conception for

Sinclair's political 'practice of space': recovering, and giving voice to, lost, erased or forgotten histories or memories. This tension between the material and the non-material is illuminated by Derrida's argument in *Specters of Marx*. Sinclair's critique of the material conditions of London's urban fabric must inevitably turn to the language of the non-material or mystical, for that discourse is inevitably bound up with the terms of materialism.

In Michel de Certeau's *The Practice of Everyday Life* (1984), the 'ghost' is used to signify the trace of memory in space: 'there is no place that is not haunted by many different spirits hidden there in silence, spirits one can "invoke" or not. Haunted places are the only one people can live in'.[98] We can read this alongside Certeau's emphasis upon the enunciative act he ascribes to walking: 'the act of walking is to the urban system what the speech act is to language or to the statements uttered'.[99] This enunciative function of walking, the production of stories about the places people live, is indissolubly connected to memory, history, the traces of the past: 'the dispersion of stories points to the dispersion of the memorable as well'.[100] In 'Walking in the City', de Certeau contrasted the 'panoramic' view from above with the 'practices' of city life as it is lived by its inhabitants. Looking from the 103rd floor of the World Trade Center, then serving as a 'prow' for Manhattan, the viewer was able to take in the whole of New York in his or her gaze. This view from above, however, like the map, while organising the city through the look of a 'totalising eye', 'construct[s] the fiction that creates readers, makes the complexity of the city readable and immobilizes its opaque mobility in a transparent text'.[101] This legibility is a fiction, 'a "theoretical" (that is, visual) simulacrum' which obscures the true nature of the city space as it is lived.[102] Opposed to this, de Certeau offers the idea of 'practices' of life, conducted every day, which undermine and oppose a totalising view of the city.

> The ordinary practitioners of the city live 'down below', below the thresholds at which visibility begins. They walk – an elementary form of this experience of the city; they are walkers, *Wandersmänner*, whose bodies follow the thicks and thins of an urban 'text' they write without being able to read it.[103]

De Certeau's emphasis is on the 'practices that are foreign to the "geometrical" or "geographical" space of visual, panoptic, or theoretical constructions'.[104] The 'geometrical space' is material, lived physical space made into a diagram, an abstraction: a map. The map becomes an organised illusion of the totality of the city, a totality incomprehensible in the everyday lives of its citizens. It is, as I shall explore further in Chapter 5, a diagrammatic reduction of complexity to enable legibility. The walker, through his or her everyday practices of life, resists the organising power of both the gaze and the map. His or her city is produced every day, inscribed with his or her journeys, journeys that create the city but 'elud[e] legibility'. Sinclair's narratives, narratives of walking in both fiction and non-fiction, similarly enunciate the 'ghosts' of lived space.

While de Certeau's formulation of the 'practices' of walking, the 'tactics' which in a micro-political way disrupt the determining fabric of the space of power and the strategy, seem to offer a way of theorising Sinclair's own walking practice as a political act, its very contingency and lack of totalising gaze restricts its use as a material agent of social change. Micro-political practices indicate resistance to domination available in the space of everyday life, but does not offer a way in which the material conditions of 'gridded' or panoptic space can be changed or overthrown. Urban walking may offer a practice of everyday life which allows a resisting reading of urban spaces (and its strata of memory and history), but perhaps indicates in Sinclair the failure of a totalising politics that I have diagnosed in positing his turn from the communal energies of the counter-culture to the 'politics of the self' informing the practice of the urban walker.

The idea of inscribing a walk upon the material fabric of the city is articulated on the first page of *Lights Out for the Territory*:

> I had developed this curious conceit while working on my novel *Radon Daughters*: that the physical movements of the characters across the territory might spell out the letters of a secret alphabet [. . .] trace the line on the map. These botched runes, burnt into the script in the heat of creation, offer an alternative reading – a subterranean, preconscious text capable of divination and prophecy.[105]

Sinclair usually deploys the metaphor of vertical space to suggest the culturally hidden or 'invisible', the histories that have been erased. Sinclair's city is a sign-system of accretions, a palimpsest. Reading (or writing/ enunciating) the signs imprinted upon the city reveals the hidden or 'subterranean', that which, in de Certeau's terms, is 'below the threshold' of visibility. Walking in the city, then, makes the invisible legible, whereby the overwritten histories of London's spaces are recovered. In *Lights Out for the Territory*, Sinclair's 'stalking' both decodes and calls into being the signs of the 'real' city, the 'fiction of an underlying pattern': the city is text, a system of signs: the material city becoming the (non-material) map. The first excursion in *Lights Out* begins by describing the layering of 'tags' sprayed by graffiti artists on the walls of east London. The city is itself inscribed by language, but its linguistic materiality and *legibility* is invoked by the presence of the stalking subject. In all of these cases, the subject who witnesses or sees is not simply a transcriber of the 'truth' of city life, they are also readers, and their presence creates the readings, just as the *flâneur* becomes the 'participant observer', and Sinclair the 'documenter' becomes Sinclair the 'non-materialist' who 'dives in'. As in de Certeau's formulation, 'the fiction . . . creates readers'.[106] They are active agents in, and participant creators of, the social and topographic space they describe, and this extends to the languages and discourses they use to articulate the city. Where Woolf's 'street haunter' assumed a spectrality that is a 'right of inspection', and whose gaze proposed a distinction between the 'haunter' and the urban mass, Sinclair's walking subject is engaged in a 'practice of space', helping to produce a tactical rewriting of the power-inscribed configurations of urban space, but this materialism is itself caught up in a discourse of the non-material, of 'haunting' and the 'ghosts' of memory.

Notes

1   Raymond Williams, *Resources of Hope*, Robin Gable (ed.) (London and New York: Verso, 1989), p. 73.
2   Iain Sinclair, with Kevin Jackson, *The Verbals* (Tonbridge: Worple Press, 2003), p. 53.
3   Sinclair, with Jackson, *The Verbals*, p. 56.
4   Sinclair, with Jackson, *The Verbals*, p. 58.
5   Iain Sinclair, *Kodak Mantra Diaries* (London: Albion Village Press, 1971), unpaginated, Book 1, Ch. 15.
6   Iain Sinclair, *Kodak Mantra Diaries*, unpaginated, Book 2, Ch. 2, Tape Three.
7   Sinclair, with Jackson, *The Verbals*, p. 58.
8   Sinclair, *Kodak Mantra Diaries*, unpaginated, Book 2, Ch. 9, Tape Fifteen.
9   Sinclair, *Kodak Mantra Diaries*, unpaginated, Book 2, Ch. 9, Tape Fifteen.
10 Iain Sinclair, *Lud Heat and Suicide Bridge* (London: Granta, 1995), p. 149.
11 Robert Bond, e-mail, 17 November 2004b.
12 Sinclair, with Jackson, *The Verbals*, p. 57.

13 Marianne DeKoven, *Utopia Limited: The Sixties and the Emergence of the Postmodern* (Durham: Duke University Press, 2004), p. 202.

14 Simon Perril, 'A Cartography of Absence: The Work of Iain Sinclair', *Comparative Criticism: An Annual Journal*, 19 (1997), 309–39 (334).

15 Perril, 'A Cartography of Absence', 334.

16 Sinclair, *Kodak Mantra Diaries*, unpaginated, Book 2, Ch. 3, Tape Five.

17 Sinclair, *Kodak Mantra Diaries*, unpaginated, Book 2, Ch. 4, Tape Seven.

18 Iain Sinclair, *Downriver* (1991) (London: Vintage, 1995), p. 302.

19 Iain Sinclair, *London Orbital* (London: Granta, 2002a), p. 127.

20 Roy Porter, *Madness: A Brief History* (Oxford: Oxford University Press, 2002), p. 210.

21 Iain Sinclair, *Crash* (London: BFI, 1999), p. 110.

22 Sinclair, with Jackson, *The Verbals*, pp. 59–60.

23 Sinclair, with Jackson, *The Verbals*, p. 57.

24 Iain Sinclair, 'Introduction', in I. Sinclair (ed.), *Conductors of Chaos: A Poetry Anthology* (London: Picador, 1996), p. xvii.

25 Iain Sinclair, *Lights Out for the Territory: 9 Excursions in the Secret History of London* (London: Granta, 1998), p. 240.

26 Perril, 'A Cartography of Absence', 334.

27 DeKoven, *Utopia Limited*, p. 134.

28 DeKoven, *Utopia Limited*, p. 137.

29 DeKoven, *Utopia Limited*, p. 201.

30 Sinclair, with Jackson, *The Verbals*, p. 54.

31 R. D. Laing, *The Divided Self* (Harmondsworth: Penguin, 1965), p. 17.

32 Laing, *The Divided Self*, p. 17.

33 Brian Jarvis, *Postmodern Cartographies: The Geographical Imagination in Contemporary American Culture* (London: Pluto, 1998), p. 45.

34 Fredric Jameson, 'Periodizing the Sixties', in Patricia Waugh (ed.), *Postmodernism: A Reader* (London: Edward Arnold, 1992), pp. 125–52 (p. 149).

35 Jameson, 'Periodizing the Sixties', p. 140.

36 Michel Foucault, 'Of Other Spaces', *Diacritics* 16, spring (1986), 22–7 (22).

37 Victor Burgin, *In/Different Spaces: Place and Memory in Visual Culture* (London, Berkeley and Los Angeles: University of California Press, 1996), p. 195.

38 Fredric Jameson, *Postmodernism, or, the Cultural Logic of Late Capitalism* (London: Verso, 1991), pp. 6 and 25.

39 Mike Crang, and Nigel Thrift (eds), 'Introduction', in M. Crang and N. Thrift (eds), *Thinking Space* (London: Routledge, 2000), pp. 1–30, p. 10.

40 Edward W. Soja, *Postmodern Geographies: The Reassertion of Space in Social Theory* (London: Verso, 1989), p. 44.

41 Soja, *Postmodern Geographies*, p. 247.

42 Jameson, *Postmodernism*, p. 44.

43 Jameson, *Postmodernism*, p. 44.
44 Jameson, *Postmodernism*, p. 40.
45 Jameson, *Postmodernism*, p. 42.
46 Sinclair, *London Orbital*, pp. 215 and 217.
47 Mike Davis, *City of Quartz: Excavating the Future in Los Angeles* (1990) (London: Pimlico, 1998), p. 226.
48 Davis, *City of Quartz*, p. 226.
49 Sinclair, *London Orbital*, p. 338.
50 Sinclair, *London Orbital*, p. 339.
51 Sinclair, *London Orbital*, p. 390.
52 Sinclair, *London Orbital*, p. 390.
53 Chris Philo, 'Foucault's Geography', in Crang and Thrift (eds), *Thinking Space*, pp. 205–38 (p. 222).
54 Philo, 'Foucault's Geography', p. 224.
55 Andy Merrifield, 'Henri Lefebvre: A Socialist in Space', in Crang and Thrift (eds), *Thinking Space*, pp. 167–82 (p. 171).
56 Soja, *Postmodern Geographies*, p. 50.
57 Sinclair, *London Orbital*, p. 35.
58 Sinclair, *London Orbital*, p. 58.
59 Sinclair, *London Orbital*, p. 58.
60 Sinclair, *London Orbital*, p. 138.
61 Walter Benjamin, 'On Some Motifs of Baudelaire', in Hannah Arendt (ed.), trans. Harry Zohn, *Illuminations* (London: Fontana, 1992), pp. 152–96 (p. 171).
62 Benjamin, 'On Some Motifs of Baudelaire', p. 168.
63 Benjamin, 'On Some Motifs of Baudelaire', pp. 161–2.
64 Walter Benjamin, *The Arcades Project*, trans. Howard Eiland and Kevin McLaughlin (Cambridge, MA and London: Belknap Press, 1999), Konvolute M16, 3; p. 446.
65 Benjamin, *The Arcades Project*, Konvolute M16, 3; p. 446.
66 Keith Tester, 'Introduction', in *The Flâneur* (London: Routledge, 1994), pp. 1–21 (p. 14).
67 Benjamin, *The Arcades Project*, Konvolute M5, 6; p. 427.
68 Tester, 'Introduction', p. 18.
69 Sinclair, *Lights Out for the Territory*, p. 4.
70 Sinclair, *Lights Out for the Territory*, p. 75.
71 Sinclair, with Jackson, *The Verbals*, p. 8.
72 Chris Jenks, 'Watching Your Step: The History and Practice of the *flâneur*', in C. Jenks (ed.), *Visual Culture* (London and New York: Routledge, 1995), pp. 142–60 (p. 154).
73 Sinclair, with Jackson, *The Verbals*, p. 75.
74 Sinclair, with Jackson, *The Verbals*, p. 76.
75 London Psychogeographical Association, 'Why Psychogeography?', in S. Home (ed.), *Mind Invaders: A Reader in Psychic Warfare, Cultural*

     Sabotage and Semiotic Terrorism (London: Serpent's Tail, 1997), pp. 136–9 (pp. 137 and 138).
76 Sinclair, with Jackson, *The Verbals*, p. 76.
77 Judith Walkowitz, *City of Dreadful Delight: Narratives of Sexual Danger in Late-Victorian London* (London: Virago, 1992), p. 16.
78 Deborah L. Parsons, *Streetwalking the Metropolis: Women, the City and Modernity* (Oxford: Oxford University Press, 2000), p. 23.
79 Parsons, *Streetwalking the Metropolis*, p. 37.
80 Parsons, *Streetwalking the Metropolis*, p. 36.
81 Rob Shields, 'Fancy Footwork: Walter Benjamin's Notes on *flânerie*', in Tester (ed.), *The Flâneur*, pp. 61–80 (p. 75).
82 Sinclair, with Jackson, *The Verbals*, p. 59.
83 Sinclair, *London Orbital*, p. 120.
84 Virginia Woolf, 'Street Haunting: A London Adventure', *Collected Essays* Vol. 4 (London: Hogarth Press, 1967), pp. 155–66 (p. 163).
85 Woolf, 'Street Haunting', p. 156.
86 Woolf, 'Street Haunting', p. 166.
87 Julian Wolfreys, *Deconstruction: Derrida* (New York: St. Martin's Press and Basingstoke: Macmillan, 1998), p. 140.
88 Wolfreys, *Deconstruction: Derrida*, p. 158.
89 Jacques Derrida, 'from *Specters of Marx*', in Julian Wolfreys (ed.), *The Derrida Reader: Writing Performances* (Edinburgh: Edinburgh University Press, 1998), pp. 140–68 (p. 143).
90 Derrida, 'from *Specters of Marx*', p. 145.
91 Derrida, 'from *Specters of Marx*', p. 153.
92 Slavoj Žižek, 'The Spectre of Ideology', in Elizabeth Wright and Edmond Wright (eds), *The Žižek Reader* (Oxford: Blackwell, 1999), pp. 53–86 (p. 73).
93 Derrida, 'from *Specters of Marx*', p. 153.
94 Derrida, 'from *Specters of Marx*', p. 154.
95 Jacques Derrida and Bernard Stiegler, *Echographies of Television* (Cambridge: Polity, 2002), p. 117.
96 Derrida, 'from *Specters of Marx*', pp. 120 and 121.
97 Shields, 'Fancy Footwork', p. 65.
98 Michel de Certeau, *The Practice of Everyday Life* (Berkeley, CA and London: University of California Press, 1984), p. 108.
99 de Certeau, *The Practice of Everyday Life*, p. 96.
100 de Certeau, *The Practice of Everyday Life*, p. 108.
101 de Certeau, *The Practice of Everyday Life*, p. 100.
102 de Certeau, *The Practice of Everyday Life*, p. 128.
103 de Certeau, *The Practice of Everyday Life*, p. 128.
104 de Certeau, *The Practice of Everyday Life*, p. 128.
105 Sinclair, *Lights Out for the Territory*, p. 1.
106 de Certeau, *The Practice of Everyday Life*, p. 128.

1

Space and time, myth and place

Iain Sinclair's major works of poetry, *Lud Heat: A Book of Dead Hamlets* (1975) and *Suicide Bridge: A Book of the Furies, A Mythology of South and East* (1979) (both subsequently collected in a 1995 Granta edition I will use here), represent Sinclair's engagement with what was described and promoted by Eric Mottram (professor at King's College, London) as a 'British poetry revival' (or alternately 'renaissance') from the mid-1960s to the end of the 1970s. The 'poetry revival' was organised around three bookshops in London, which consecutively provided the focal point for an upsurge in small-press poetry publication, of which Sinclair's own Albion Village Press (which published *The Kodak Mantra Diaries*, *Lud Heat* and *Suicide Bridge*) was one. These three bookshops were Better Books (run by the poets Lee Harwood and Bob Cobbing), Indica (managed by Barry Miles, later to become one of the chroniclers of the 1960s and the beat poets), and finally Compendium. Peter Barry also notes Turret bookshop in Kensington and Oriel in Cardiff as other key sites. There was, says Sinclair, a 'community [. . .] people who didn't know each other would meet at readings and give readings together [. . .] people were doing extraordinary things'.[1]

The origin point of this 'underground' poetry scene is identified by Jonathon Green in *All Dressed Up* (1999) in the poetry reading at the Royal Albert Hall in 1965, documented by Peter Whitehead in his film and book *Wholly Communion*. (Peter Whitehead is connected with Sinclair through the film *The Falconer* that we will consider in Chapter 5.) Green suggests that it was the 'timely arrival' of Allen Ginsberg – often a catalytic figure in counter-cultural events in the later 1960s, as we saw in the Introduction – and his stay at Better Books which provided the impetus for the poetry reading.

Ginsberg and the Better Books circle, and later Alex Trocchi, according
to Green, organised the event around major international figures
such as Lawrence Ferlinghetti and Gregory Corso from the beat
generation, Pablo Neruda, Pablo Fernandez from Cuba and Andrei
Voznesensky, all of whom were in London or within easy travel at
that point. 'The central readings', argues Green from a viewing of
Whitehead's film, 'came from Ginsberg, from Ferlinghetti, from
[Christopher] Logue – the old pros'.[2] Michael Horovitz, the British
beat who also read that night, somewhat disparages the *Wholly
Communion* film, stating that 'an event which was at least three-
dimensional is reduced to a (literally) framed photo-reduction'.[3]
Horovitz gives a rather more ecstatic version in the 'Afterwords' to
his key edited collection, *Children of Albion* (1969):

> What did happen – for whoever suspended disbelief – is that poem
> after poem resonated mind-expanding ripples of empathy – uncut and
> precious stones in a translucent pool. The buds of a spreading poetry
> internationale the Esperanto of the subconscious sown by dada & the
> surrealists & the beats bore fruit.[4]

The utopian and transcendental terms in which Horovitz describes
the evening – which he later promotes as 'the greatest stimulus for
poetry this century' – connects the poetry reading to counter-cultural
hopes for 'enlightenment' and revolutionary change, and also looks
forward to psychedelia.[5] The connections Horovitz forges, not only
to a modernist avant-garde (Dada and surrealism) but to Ginsberg,
and through him, to Blake – 'the initial moving spirit of our co-
operative was the transmission, through Ginsberg, or the heritage
of Blake'– is vital to an understanding of the cultural and poetry
milieu in which Sinclair produced *Lud Heat* and *Suicide Bridge*.[6] It
is no coincidence that Sinclair's own small press was named the
Albion Village Press, and I will trace the importance of Blake,
particularly to *Suicide Bridge*, later in the chapter. The inheritance
of Blake provides a connection to a particularly English tradition of
counter-hegemonic poetry which couches its resistance to, and critique
of, prevailing conditions in mythological and transcendent, rather
than 'realist' and materialist, terms.

The resistance to 'realism' also indicates the traces of 'neo-
modernism' within British poetry which were used to define the
poetic practice of the British poetry revival poets in opposition to the
anti-intellectual, parochial and 'realist' imperatives of the Movement

poets (exemplified by Philip Larkin). In form and poetic practice, many poets of the 'revival', including Sinclair, look to modernism for their inspiration. Peter Barry, in *Contemporary British Poetry and the City* (2000) identifies a confluence between left-wing politics and a commitment to 'various forms of neo-modernist, avant-garde practice in poetry', a conjunction which, as I suggested in the Introduction, is not without its problems for Sinclair in terms of sustaining a critique of contemporary London.[7] However, it is not to what Neil Corcoran identifies as the 'Pound/Eliot' version of British modernism to which Sinclair connects, but the 'Pound/Williams/ Olson' triumvirate which is central to the development of American poetry in the twentieth century.[8] (William Carlos Williams was himself a major influence on Ginsberg.) Sinclair and others are indebted to the Black Mountain poet Charles Olson, who, admits Sinclair in *The Verbals*, made a 'very big impact' on him; 'I would say that he became the major figure for me', Sinclair confesses.[9]

In 'Projective Verse', a 1950 manifesto of poetics, Olson undertakes a tripartite prescription of what he calls 'COMPOSITION BY FIELD': first, 'kinetics'. The poem is a 'high energy-construct' and an 'energy-discharge', whereupon the poem communicates from poet to reader not through the 'metronome' of verse form, but through the 'track [. . .] the poem under hand declares, for itself'.[10] The poet, then, in putting herself in the 'FIELD' of composition, while seeming to be the originator/maker of poetic meaning, is in fact only the conduit: the poem, rather than the poet, achieves autonomy. The poem itself is an energy field. In 'Intimate Associations: Myth and Place', what I take to be the defining prose piece of *Suicide Bridge* and key to Sinclair's poetic practice, Sinclair characterises 'Man' as a 'raised tube, opened at crown of head & base of feet – so that it flows through him, conscious or unconscious, the power, the surge, the tachyonic voltage'.[11] This energy discharge is between *myth* and *place*, but similarly to Olson, displaces the meaningful act and renders the human (poet) as a means of transmission rather than an originator of meaning. Understanding poesis as energy-transmission also ensures the centrality of activity ('kinesis') rather than either a static model of the poem as a metrical form, or the poem as a linguistic or symbolic enunciation. Paradoxically, the poet shapes what is already present.

Here we can also trace the importance of J. H. Prynne (himself influenced by Black Mountain poetics). Describing Prynne's poetics,

Geoffrey Ward writes: 'poetic language is there in order to reveal what was already pursuing an unseen life'.[12] In this sentence, Ward also provides a concise summary of Sinclair's practice, an interest in what Sinclair himself calls the 'what-is-going-on, unseen'.[13] In *The Verbals*, Sinclair confesses to be 'knocked out' by Prynne's 1969 collection *The White Stones*, and it seems Prynne supplanted Ginsberg as a touchstone for Sinclair's thinking: 'what he said lasted much longer for me than what Ginsberg had said. Extraordinary vistas were opened up by a long, long afternoon's conversation'.[14] Prynne was, and still is, an academic as well as a neo-modernist poet, at Gonville and Caius College, Cambridge, and he is surrounded by a 'Cambridge school' of like-minded poets and critics (such as Rod Mengham and Drew Milne). Prynne's poetry is, according to Neil Corcoran, 'notoriously difficult'; Corcoran also identifies an Olsonian 'open field' poetic at work in Prynne's poetry, 'relying on a combination of long and short lines in an arrangement of some pictorial delicacy'.[15] Part of Sinclair's inheritance from Prynne is a tension between the material and the non-material, the impulse towards the transcendent or mystical in the critique of contemporary conditions. Corcoran suggests that Prynne's poem 'The Numbers' (from his first collection, *Kitchen Poems* of 1968) attempt to locate a ' "place" of opposition to unthinking social valuations [. . .]; the poem may effect a kind of dilation, an opening up into light of the customary world'.[16] This is perhaps analogous to what Robert Bond has diagnosed as the gesture towards a 'non-willed, visionary–contemplative mode' in Sinclair's work. It also suggests a mode of 'estrangement' (or Brechtian *Verfremsdungseffekt*), an alienation from naturalised representations of life which enables us to see their formation more clearly, a suggestion I will return to later in this book.

It needs to be emphasised, however, in making this connection, that Prynne and Sinclair are effecting a (neo-)modernist poetics in place of a Marxian or materialist critique, even if the intentions are similar. The 'difficulty' of Prynne's work, its very neo-modernist poetics, of course precludes the possibility of translating this place of opposition into collective (or popular) social action. Corcoran, analysing Prynne's 1969 poem 'Moon Poem', suggests that Prynne's seeming

> disbelief in the revolution of 1968 is no disbelief in the possibility of social change, but the recommendation of a gradualism, of the patient extension of 'a community of wish'. The poem saves itself from the

charge of privileged quietism by confessing its own place of origin as
a version of pastoral rather than a confrontation with *realpolitick*. [*sic*][17]

'Moon Poem' indeed make gestures towards gradualism and calm
(a 'modesty about conduct in/the most ethical sense') – 'Since I must
hold to the gradual in/this, as no revolution but a slow change/like
the image of snow' – but further on in the poem Prynne alters the
terms of this 'space' of contemplation to something more active, and
more positive: 'we go in this way/on and on and the unceasing image
of hope/is our place in the world'.[18] Prynne repeats the figure 'diffuses'
and 'diffusion' to suggest the connection between the 'wide personal
vacancy' and the 'wishes that are now too far beyond/us': in this
figure, the desire for change, although expressed in a seemingly
passive way, transcends the historical and contingent and becomes
a mystical (or quasi-religious) resource.[19]

In 'Questions for the Time Being', also from *The White Stones*,
Prynne opposes the 'diffusion' of community to alienated existence:
'living in hope is so silly when our desires/are so separate', and we
find a suspicion of the counter-cultural moment very much like
Sinclair's: 'Really it's/laughable & folks talk of discontent or waiting/to
see what they can make of it'.[20] At the end of the poem, however,
Prynne adopts a much more urgent, even astringent, tone:

> The up-
> shot is simple & as follows: 1. No one has any right
> to mere idle discontent, even in conditions of most
> extreme privation, since such a state of arrested
> insight is actively counter-productive; [. . .]
>   4. Luminous
> take-off shows through in language forced into any
> compact with the historic shift, but in a given con-
> dition such as now not even elegance will come
> of the temporary nothing in which life goes on.[21]

The 'historic shift', which we can perhaps read as counter-cultural
ferment, Prynne describes in terms of the transcendent, 'luminous
take-off'; this is again opposed to the 'temporary nothing' of contemporary conditions. If desire for change is inscribed as a desire for
transcendence of contemporary conditions, however, how does
this translate into material action? One suspects it must remain
constrained within the terms of the mystical. The same opposition
between the material and non-material (transcendent, mystical, occult)

is found throughout Sinclair's writing, and particularly in the image of the 'muck-rake' Sinclair uses as the title of the first (and only) 'book' of *Lud Heat*. The derivation of this image, from an episode in Book 2 of John Bunyan's *The Pilgrim's Progress*, is given as an epigraph to *Lud Heat*. In it, Christiana is taken by the Interpreter into a room,

> where there was a man that could look no way but downwards, with a muck-rake in his hand. There stood also one over his head with a celestial crown in his hand, and proffered to give him that crown for his muck-rake; but the man did neither look up, nor regard, but raked to himself the straws, the small sticks, and dust of the floor.[22]

Within Bunyan's text, this symbolic figure is glossed by the Interpreter as showing 'that earthly things when they are with power upon men's minds quite carry their hearts away from God'.[23] The man with the muck-rake is clearly an avatar of Sinclair himself. Peter Barry reads this image as indicating the 'sombrely pessimistic topography of Sinclair's London vision', that Sinclair is trapped within a close-reading materialism that occludes 'broad new horizons of ideas'.[24] This characterisation is to miss the continual gestures towards the non-material in Sinclair's writings, from the occulted 'lines of force' in *Lud Heat* to the 'ghosts' haunting late Victorian texts. Rather, the figure of the muck-rake exposes the unresolved tension in Sinclair's texts between materialist critique and the non-material 'vision' of the alienated poet-outsider who is able to forge a place 'outside' society through an avant-gardist poetic practice, and thereby 'see' contemporary conditions both more clearly and in totality.

Sinclair's appropriation of Bunyan, to the extent that several paragraphs are inserted verbatim into *Lud Heat*, indicates the influence of Olson's second prescription: 'FORM IS NEVER MORE THAN AN EXTENSION OF CONTENT'.[25] The poem is an 'open field': its form is not delimited by traditional metrical arrangements, and anything can be imported into it (so long as 'right form' is an 'extension of content')[26]. If Sinclair wanted to 'include everything', then 'open field' poetics allow him to do so. Form follows content. The shape of both *Lud Heat* and *Suicide Bridge* conforms to Olson's poetics, and therefore themselves can be considered 'fields' rather than poems. Of the sixteen sections of *Lud Heat*, six contain both poetry and prose; three prose only; seven poetry only. Throughout, Sinclair deploys Egyptian hieroglyphics as visual annotations; the section 'The Vortex of the Dead! The Generous!' contains a typographic poem in the shape of a downward-pointing arrow; and there are three hand-drawn diagrams by Brian Catling: 'Being a Map of the 8 Great Churches', 'Lunar South is Solar East' and 'The Oracle Bunker/The Step Obstacles'. Most tellingly, the second section of *Lud Heat* is called 'Closed Field, the Dogs of the Moon', punning on Olson's term. *Suicide Bridge* has many more pieces of prose and poetry (thirty in all), organised into four sections: 'Bone-Muscle', 'Dupes', 'Victims' and 'The Older Hidden Powers', though the first prose piece and first poem ('Intimate Associations' and 'A Cosmogony for Hand and Hyle') are actually situated before any section titles. This again signifies the openness of the structure: form is purposefully asymmetrical, arrhythmic, disruptive.

Olson's third prescription is that 'ONE PERCEPTION MUST IMMEDIATELY AND DIRECTLY LEAD ON TO ANOTHER PER-CEPTION', again insisting on kineticism: 'get on with it, keep moving' enjoins Olson, 'keep in, speed, the nerves, the speed, the perceptions, theirs, the acts, the split second acts, the whole business, keep it moving as fast as you can, citizen'.[27] Olson's language use here anticipates not only Sinclair's stripped, compressed poetry and prose, but also the kineticism of the beats and Burroughs's cut-ups, both of which also have marked similarities to the urgency and estranging, unusual linguistic collisions found in Sinclair's work. This kineticism can also be found in the work of Tom Raworth, a British poet also connected to the 'revival' scene, of whose 'cinematic' work Sinclair writes that 'shaped word clusters [frolic] between generous white margins. Speed-reading is the preferred option'.[28] What this process reflects is 'daily reality'; what is leads to is to the artist's intervention *into* reality: 'the projective act, which is the artist's act in the larger field of objects, leads to dimensions larger than the man'.[29] Let us consider this statement for a moment. It is, apparently, materialist: 'reality' is 'the field of objects', and the artist's 'act' assumes the same materiality as those objects. However, the material act *projects* into a sphere beyond the material: 'dimensions larger than the man'. Here, Olson's materialism intersects with transcendental, even mystical thought; similarly, his whole conception of the 'field' con-nects both with earlier science and speculations into 'dimensions' larger than our own. This trajectory from material to non-material has, as we saw in the Introduction, particular resonance for Sinclair's own work.

The 'field'

The concept of 'field', in science, is most associated with physics. More precisely, it was the work of Michael Faraday in the nineteenth century, into electro-magnetism, which introduced the term 'field'. Faraday was interested in electricity and magnetism, and his experiments proved that the two were connected phenomena. He did this by passing an electric current through a wire, and producing a magnetic effect; and by rotating a magnet around a wire, producing a faint electric current. Magnetism intrigued Faraday. Phenomena such as magnetism and gravity seemed to presuppose that objects were influenced at a distance, a quasi-magical idea that compromised the empirical tenets of classical mechanics. Faraday, in *Experimental Researches in Electricity*, argued that a magnetic field was produced from a structure of 'lines of magnetic force'; these magnetic lines of force 'have a physical existence independent, in a manner, of the body radiating, or of the body receiving the rays'.[30] Faraday, and, possibly, ourselves as schoolchildren, saw those rays marked out by iron filings surrounding a magnet. Inside the field were places of strong and weak force; a specially magnetised object would tend to move from areas of strong force to areas of weak force. Faraday was able to consider 'actions at a distance' by formulating a multi-dimensional space, or 'field', constituted by the 'lines of force' he saw in his experiments.

These 'lines of force' were, according to A. E. E. McKenzie, 'in tension, like threads of stretched elastic . . . tending to push each other sideways'.[31] Faraday's theory, in McKenzie's words, 'postulated the occurrence of magnetic action from point to point, between contiguous particles of the æther, and not at a distance. The lines represented a state of strain, or the transmission of some kind of stress, through the æther'.[32] Of course, 'æther' is a discredited concept in scientific terms, and Faraday himself was suspicious of its use. It is interesting to note, however, that even James Clerk Maxwell, who confirmed Faraday's experiments with mathematical proofs (Faraday was himself a weak mathematician), considered that an ætherial 'medium' was necessary to effect a transfer of energy (signified by lines of force, or light waves). Perhaps unexpectedly, we can see connections between Faraday and Maxwell's physics, and Olson's poetics: both are described in terms of a 'field'; both consider effect to be attendant on a transfer of energy; both ultimately move from a material description ('field of objects', 'lines of magnetic force') to a reliance upon the numinous ('another dimension', 'æther'). Perhaps most importantly, both have a strongly spatial conception of the energies they describe.

John Berger, in his essay 'The Moment of Cubism', also makes the connection between Faraday and modernism, but through painting rather than poetics. He writes:

> The concept of the field, first put forward by Faraday when wrestling with the problem – as defined in traditional terms – of 'action at a distance', entered now, unacknowledged, into all modes of planning and calculation and even into many modes of feeling. There was a startling extension through time and space of human power and knowledge. For the first time the world, as a totality, ceased to be an abstraction and became *realisable*.[33]

I will return to the terms of Berger's connection between modernist representations of space and time, and the concept of the field, in Chapter 5. It is important to note here that Sinclair's conscious or unconscious indebtedness to Faraday is probably mediated through his alignment with modernism. Sinclair quotes J. G. Frazer (author of *The Golden Bough*) in *Lud Heat*: 'Things which have once been in physical contact continue to act on each other at a distance after contact has been broken', a magical version of Faraday's magnetic fields.[34] 'Lines of force' is a phrase that recurs in Sinclair's writing, describing the configurations of power, control and cultural memory as they are inscribed upon the (symbolic) landscape, a phrase directly taken from Faraday. Like Olson and Faraday, Sinclair uses a spatial conception of energies to mark out his engagement with contemporary life. In fact, Sinclair's imagination of the cultural field is very much akin to Faraday's understanding of the magnetic field. As M. Norton Wise writes in the *Companion to the History of Modern Science*:

> Objects in the field are not so much acted on by the field as they participate in it, and the action they experience expresses the effect they have on the distribution of force in the field, which obeys an overall principle of economy.[35]

The field is then constructed by the actions of objects and forces in the field, rather than imposing force upon the objects within it. Sinclair, consciously or unconsciously, adapts Faraday's conception of the field for the purposes of social and cultural critique. Sinclair's use of psychogeography, if it is indeed 'more than a metaphor', must be a practice, an active 'transmission of energy': a way of reading and rewriting the 'field', the spatial configurations of London.

The spatiality of the concept of 'field' is key to both Sinclair's poetic forms and to the 'site-specific' nature of his concerns. In this, Sinclair inherits the focus of Williams' *Paterson* and Olson's *Maximus* poems in elaborating a poetics which investigates space and place, a theme also taken up by fellow 'Revival' poets Lee Harwood (in such poems as 'Cable Street', collected by Sinclair in *Conductors of Chaos*) and Allen Fisher, whose *Place* series of poems and books chart south London (and particularly Brixton where Fisher lives). Peter Barry suggests 'seven types of continuity' which connect Sinclair to Fisher and others such as Aidan Dun, author of *Vale Royal* (1995). (Dun appears in Sinclair's *Lights Out for the Territory. Vale Royal* considers the 'psychogeography' of the St Pancras area of central London, a site to which Sinclair had also been drawn in the unfinished and unpublished *Red Eye* of the early 1970s, sections of which appeared in the *Grosseteste Review* and also in *Lights Out.*) Barry's seven types of continuity are: 'works of poetry on an epic scale'; a focus on the geography of London; a 'concern with mapping and re-mapping their territory in terms of such things as associated myths, historical traces, geo-physical forces'; a piling up of data and information; generic 'hybridity', mixing poetry, prose, diary extracts, jottings; an American poetic inheritance; and finally, an 'imagination of synthesis' in which discourses such as history, psychology and politics 'interact and interpenetrate'.[36]

Barry's categories are useful and give a shorthand analysis of Sinclair's emphases, but here I would like to emphasise the fourth and fifth 'continuities', the piling up of data and the generic hybridity. As I will explore further, later in this chapter, both *Lud Heat* and *Suicide Bridge* assume a rather fragmented form, analogous to Olson's 'open field' imperatives where the poem can import whatever it needs to into its structure, form following content. I would like to suggest that not only do Sinclair and Fisher propose a 'poetics of space' in terms of their site-specific texts, but the form of the poetic text itself becomes spatial rather than linear. This is particularly true of *Suicide Bridge*, where the traces of linearity discernable in *Lud Heat*'s summer of gardening disappear into myth, space and cosmic time. Not only does Sinclair exhibit a 'spatial turn' in terms of his interests, but also a turning to spatial form in his poetry. This perhaps helps to explain Sinclair's paratactic strategies in his writing, what

Barry describes as 'disjunctive, serial hits on successive targets, rather than constituting a flow, as if the lines are really end-stopped poetic images'.[37] Barry here sees a fundamental connection between Sinclair's poetic practice and his prose (fiction and non-fiction): that, in a sense, all Sinclair's writing aspires to the condition of poetry.

We noted in the Introduction that Sinclair's London can be characterised as a palimpsest; the same layering, or vertical/spatial textuality can also be ascribed to his poetry. If, as Peter Barry has suggested, that Sinclair's fictions lack narrative propulsion or forward drive, I would argue that rather than being a criticism of failure on Sinclair's part, this indicates Sinclair's investment in an Olsonian (or Poundian) poetics of form: it is not the 'metronome' of regular measure that organises the text but the spatial organisation of London, the city itself, that demands fragments, disjunctions, a series of 'hits' or sensations not unlike the 'shocks' that Baudelaire's *flâneur* experiences in the course of his strolls through Paris's streets, the 'shocks' symbolising the disruptive experience of modernity. The city's spaces themselves become a disjunctive series, 'piled up' on one another, rather than experienced as a temporally ordered and comprehensible map, panorama or tour. Tim Woods writes of Allen Fisher's *Place* that the poem 'reconfigures relations between spatial and temporal categories, pointing to an importance of place as an ontological category concealed in history or temporalisation'; by using a spatial poetics as well as a poetics of space, Fisher and Sinclair elucidate a 'counter-capitalist' re-establishment of spatial relations over temporal relations.[38]

Time and space: the fourth dimension

In H. G. Wells's *The Time Machine*, the Time Traveller explains the theoretical side of time travelling as follows: ' "Scientific people", proceeded the Time Traveller [. . .] "know very well that Time is only a kind of Space" '.[39] Time is the 'Fourth Dimension'. He goes on:

> It is simply this. That Space, as our mathematicians call it, is spoken of as having three dimensions, which one may call Length, Breadth, and Thickness, and is always definable by reference to three planes, each at right angles to the others. But some philosophical people have been asking why *three* dimensions particularly – why not another direction at right angles to the other three? – and have even tried to construct a Four-Dimensional geometry. Professor Simon Newcomb

was expounding this to the New York mathematical Society only a month ago.[40]

In *The Time Machine*, space and time are 'fixed', both static worlds to be explored. The Time Traveller seems to be able to move about in time without major disturbance either to the path of evolution or to historical 'time'. If we take further the metaphor of time as space, then for *The Time Machine*, time is an empty room. The Traveller can move about in it, observing and interacting with it, without disturbing its fabric. For C. Howard Hinton, the 'Fourth Dimension' is somewhat more etherial. Hinton plays a minor role, his son James more prominently, in *White Chappell, Scarlet Tracings*. C. Howard Hinton's conception of the 'fourth dimension' is what Bruce Clarke has described as 'an instantaneous connective space beyond material constraints'.[41] 'In Hinton's scientific cosmos', adds Clarke, 'to go behind the long chain of energic transformations is to emerge on the far side of the æther'.[42] Clarke shows that Hinton's speculations were plausibly grounded in James Clerk Maxwell's (then) current work on field physics, but in intention, go well beyond them. For reaching the fourth dimension was an act of mental discipline, brought about by strenuous mental exercise: 'The cognition of higher space called for and called forth a higher form of consciousness. Thus the individual pursuit of the fourth dimension was a moral act with collective evolutionary consequences'.[43] Time, in Wells, is the fourth dimension; for Hinton, the fourth dimension is a higher state of consciousness. In *Suicide Bridge*:

Skofeld reversed
          Olson's claim for Melville
    that he
'pushed back so far he turned time into space'
Skofeld pushed so fast
        he turned space into time

PLUS: 'intelligence' is a distortion of time[44]

The transposition between time and space – reading one in terms of the other – is confirmed later in the poem:

You don't need the Rutherford Institute, the Cavendish
or anything as vulgar as calculus
i.e. Lovecraft was *right*
        with his cod
    'post-Euclidean calculus'

his 'starry window'
          'shining trapezohedron'

pedants are outmanoeuvred
                if time is
in any way understood
          as an adjunct of architecture:[45]

Here, the higher form of consciousness is to understand that 'intelligence', human understanding, distorts time, makes it appear linear when in fact 'Past & present are coeval, equally radiant'.[46] Space is time, time is space; poetry brings forth (gives birth to) space-time, just as 'A Cosmogony for Hand & Hyle' begins with the beginning of space-time, where the 'mantled air divides'.[47] Sinclair calls up H. P. Lovecraft, the American writer of cosmological horror, as a comic authority to compromise the rational, science-based knowledge of the Rutherford Institute or the Cavendish Laboratory.

In 'The Enemy of the Stars', time is an 'adjunct to architecture' (echoing the Hawksmoor churches so vital to *Lud Heat*, which we will examine later). In 'A Biographical Sketch', the churches become 'a machine to understand/the stars/to mediate between worms & gods/a time platform'.[48] Through poetry, through myth, time may be understood as 'coeval' rather than linear, and 'history' or the past becomes immanent in the present. The churches are not the only time machines. If 'a poet is a time mechanic not an embalmer',[49] then the poem, the open field, becomes a time machine, where the forces of memory, control and language organise themselves into a coherent form: 'a place that is, literally/out of time'.[50] Robert Bond understands Sinclair, in *Suicide Bridge*, to offer 'a redemptive purpose to his treatment of an urban mythic forcefield'.[51] This redemptive purpose, as I understand it, has cosmological significance, which is why, partly, Sinclair has recourse to Blake's mythology. Seeing the universe whole, envisioning space-time rather than time and space, attempts to redeem the Blakean universe (our own) that is distorted by 'intelligence', divided, and subject to mechanism, domination and the violent mythic energy characterised as 'FASCISM'.

'The circuit completed'

Metaphors drawn from science are vital to *Suicide Bridge*. In *White Chappell Scarlet Tracings*, Sinclair incorporates a letter from the poet Douglas Oliver, who suggests that *Suicide Bridge*'s cosmological imaginings seem to represent 'more the creativities of the new sciences giving birth to phantoms more fit for our times' than a Christian cosmology.[52] Sinclair, in *The Verbals*, suggests that it was the influence of Jeremy Prynne (who had a typescript of Stephen Hawkings' *Large Scale Structures of Space-Time* on his desk when Sinclair visited him) that pointed him towards quantum physics.[53] Sinclair quotes from this very work in 'A Cosmogony for Hand & Hyle', the second piece, and first poem, in *Suicide Bridge*. The opening lines of the verse read:

> Hear it, mantled air divides   like a skirt
>   look down
> space-time, **M**
>   gravity, **g**
> causing light,
>   the life rush,
>   rattling, streaming,
>   mountain reflector of leaf & small stone,
> to deflect, bend inwards
>
> [. . .]
>
> singularities occur along the edge
> the birth, the notice, of Hand & Hyle[54]

'A Cosmogony for Hand & Hyle' begins at the beginning, the Big Bang, opening the cosmic narrative. This is the narrative not only of the universe, however, but of consciousness, in the form of two titanic figures, Hand and Hyle, whose birth is announced 'with roar of coal gas, diesel traffic,/the engines of annihilation', identifying them with earth, and more particularly, with humanity's mechanical inventions.[55] Curiously, this universal coming-into-being is identified with black holes, seemingly the cosmic end of being (space and time). Robert Bond reads the black hole as the symbol of an oppressive 'mythic forcefield' bearing down on London, citing these lines from Part 1 of 'A Cosmogony':

> This descends, is forced down
> On the neck of the city
> Is guided by the grid of the churches
> Is homed by 9th degree rituals
> By the promise of Mass Murder[56]

The black hole is the reverse image of the moon falling on to the spire of St Anne's, Limehouse, recounted in *Lud Heat*: 'February 4,

1974, and I endure an apocalyptic dream of the moon disk growing, crashing down on the city, burying itself in the tower of St Anne, Limehouse';[57] and also the 'sun surgery' or feverish heatstroke which afflicts the gardening persona in 'In the Surgery of the Sun'. Cosmological disaster gains astrological and symbolic significance in both texts, signifying the malign (occult) forces at work in London. If the black hole is a malign forcefield oppressing London, then its progeny, Hand & Hyle, are two evil demi-urges 'stalking' its streets.

The birth of Hand & Hyle is crucial to the mythic, or symbolic, project of *Suicide Bridge*. Hand & Hyle are 'characters' appropriated from Blake's *Jerusalem*. They are the twin progeny of the Universe, born from a black hole, at once Blake's two eldest sons of Albion, and Ronnie and Reggie Kray. With Coban, Hand & Hyle form an evil trinity in *Jerusalem*; here, they are twin malignant deities, presiding over the violence and evil abroad in the city. *Suicide Bridge* deploys paradoxical binaries in the service of its science/myth of births and deaths, and particularly uses the motif of the twin. The twin or double is found in *Suicide Bridge* and elsewhere in Sinclair's work. In 'Intimate Associations: Myth and Place', place is myth's 'Siamese Twin';[58] Stevenson's *Strange Case of Dr Jekyll and Mr Hyde* is a clear intertext for *White Chappell* (see Chapter 2 of this volume); and also in *White Chappell*, Dryfeld is reading *The Two, the Story of the Original Siamese Twins* when he decides (abortively) to commit suicide.[59] This latter reference begs the question: how can there be an 'original' (that is to say, a primary model or preceding subject) when the subject is already 'two'? This question is, of course, central to *Strange Case of Dr Jekyll and Mr Hyde*'s destabilisation of single subjectivity, and also to *White Chappell*'s insistence on the 'split' subject and bifurcated body. As we saw above, the imagination of the birth of the universe is itself predicated on division in *Suicide Bridge*: the 'mantled air divides'. Division, or the 'split', is a recurrent motif in Sinclair's early work.

Hutton and Slade (eighth and seventh sons), Skofeld (the ninth), Kox and Kotope (tenth and eleventh sons), and Peachey (the fifth son), are also taken from *Jerusalem* and rewritten for Sinclair's purposes, just as Blake had taken people involved in his trial for 'treasonous utterances'. (Kox and Skofeld were based on Blake's accusers.) Blake's practice parallels Sinclair's own, rewriting friends and acquaintances for textual purposes: in *White Chappell, Scarlet Tracings*, Martin Stone becomes Nicholas Lane; Brian Catling becomes S. L. Joblard; and the bookseller Driffield becomes Dryfeld. In *Suicide Bridge*, Blake's Hutton is transformed into a 'mad samurai', an assassin whose van disappears into the dockland mud 'like Janet Leigh's corpse-car in *Psycho*';[60] Slade is another killer, who runs up the River Lea (anticipating Sinclair's own symbolic journey in *London Orbital*) but is caught and killed by Hand & Hyle in 'Slade and the Tyrannicides', though his severed head 'speaks' the very last poem in the sequence. Both of these are in the section of *Suicide Bridge* entitled 'Victims', perhaps ironically commenting on their modes of life and death. Kotope and Peachey both appear in the 'Dupes' section. Kotope appears to be a rich, powerful seeker after knowledge; he is killed by 'Six Arabs on the Doorstep', but at least is afforded 'one final, animal vision of the city,/his body its body, flying'.[61] Peachey is another 'hit man', dispatched by Egyptian gods he erroneously calls forth. Like Michael Moorcock in the Cornelius stories, and in *Mother London* (1988), Sinclair seems particularly to locate London's mythic violence in the swinging/counter-cultural 1960s. We saw the importance of the connection between violence and the counter-culture, and Sinclair's reaction to/revulsion from it, in the Introduction. The last two pieces in the 'Victims' section, 'Victims: An Appendix' and 'Bad Magic, Bad Noise' are both rereadings of the Rolling Stones' free concert in Hyde Park: 'the shaman arouses, but does not/satisfy, can't get/the great lift,/emasculated by horse'.[62] Jagger here is the false shaman, the poem punningly indicating the impotence at the heart of counter-cultural 'revolution' in the form of sex, drugs and rock 'n' roll.

Sinclair turns to Blake's mythological treatment of London in order to collage a myth of a dominated Albion still gripped by 'mind forg'd manacles'. Blake's *mythos* provides a cultural and literary memory of resistance to configurations of power, and a rewriting of domination in overtly cosmological terms. *Jerusalem* is there to be appropriated: as Olson writes in 'Projective Verse', 'USE USE USE the process at all points'.[63] Once rewritten in this way, entered into the 'open field' of the poem, Sinclair can use Blake's vision for his own ends: to consider myth and the birth of myths, to consider London and the myths of London's birth. Geoffrey Ward, writing on Prynne, again provides an appropriate summary: 'Prynne's work entails a massive act of restitution, or a new constitution, of all language as open to use'.[64] Prynne's influence on Sinclair in this area can be traced throughout his work. It can be seen in Sinclair's use of language, and also in the redemptive purpose in Sinclair's writing noted by Robert Bond.

Myth and place

The centrality of division, the 'split', to Sinclair's work, and to *Suicide Bridge* in particular, indicates the Blakean 'stance towards good and evil' identified by Douglas Oliver, a division which itself indicates a dominated world.[65] Another of Sinclair's quotations from *Jerusalem* signifies both the strategy behind the deployment of 'new science' in *Suicide Bridge*, and also its identification with Blake's cosmology. It comes in 'Skofeld, Man of the East', the first poem in the final section of *Suicide Bridge*, 'The Older, Hidden Powers, the Secret Minds':

> Skofeld and Kox are let loose upon
> my Saxons! They accumulate a
> world in which Man is by his Nature
> the Enemy of Man, in pride of Selfhood
> unwieldy stretching out into Non Entity,
> generalising Art & Science till Art
> & Science is lost[66]

Skofeld and Kox are identified with Cambridge in *Suicide Bridge*, the location of both J. H. Prynne and of the Cavendish Laboratory, of Art (poetry) and Science (quantum physics). *Suicide Bridge*'s cosmological vision attempts to weld the two together, to poetise science and bring science into poetry. This is no banal attempt to heal C. P. Snow's 'Two Cultures', which diagnosed a dismissiveness towards science on the part of the British establishment, and attempted to set that hierarchy of value on its head; rather, its sets out the 'open field' as a means of exploring both art/poetry and science as ways of making meaning of the world. Both are, as versions of 'reality', myths.

As I stated above, 'Intimate Associations: Myth & Place', the first prose piece in *Suicide Bridge*, is central to this text, but also to the whole of Sinclair's project, and as such, is deserving of consideration at length. The piece begins with an injunction: 'Hands out of the entrails of time. Myths are lies', at once signifying Sinclair's conflicted and troubling understanding of the workings of myth.[67] Myths are 'lies' because they are a poetic/narrative means of understanding the world, and more particularly origins, for *Suicide Bridge* is dominated by death and (re-)birth. This mythicisation of origins is problematic for Sinclair, although, as we have already seen, the next piece, 'A Cosmogony for Hand & Hyle', itself begins with imagery of creation (the Big Bang). 'Intimate Associations' in fact supposes a development in the understanding of myth, organised through time. Sinclair posits an originary connection between the 'aboriginal', 'vegetal peoples' and land, given poetic shape by their creation myths: 'the erected land hurling star-sperm into the sky's belly'. Place becomes 'manifest in totemic animals', themselves ritually ingested 'as the living body of what the tribe is'; but when the connection between people and place is destroyed, 'Place . . . which is their own darkest, unspoken identification of self, is damaged beyond recognition & forced to find other, alien forms'.[68] Perhaps we should interrogate Sinclair's own myth of origins here, as it is *also* a creation-myth, a birth-myth, attempting to renarrate an understanding of myth itself through retelling in mythic terms. Sinclair is interested in 'mythogenesis', as Robert Bond calls it, but finds it impossible to escape the mythic structures of that which he is critiquing (through myth).

The next stage of the myth is 'myth as subversion'. In describing 'the men who wanted to maintain contact with the previous', Sinclair seems to characterise himself and others who wish to preserve the poetic, mythic understanding opposed to the scientistic knowledge that defines the world of Hand & Hyle.[69] However, Sinclair also understands that 'the need for the old myths is a confession of our failure to handle the world', and the recourse to myth and its energies can all too easily lead to 'FASCISM'.[70] Sinclair interestingly connects a 'lust' for place with colonisation, as if a European loss of connection to place results in the return of 'other, alien forms': 'Where there is unclaimed space, unwritten land, there is the quest, & there is mining, a sickly clawing, not only for minerals, crops, dead artefacts, but also for mythologies'.[71] Considering Sinclair's use of Egyptian hieroglyphs in *Lud Heat*, and 'Sumerian material' in *The Birth Rug*, a collection of poems, this constitutes a reflexive self-critique, and a conscious revision of the Olsonian poetic, problematising the freedom to 'USE' what is out there by introducing the idea of colonialism. Use can mean exploitation.

The interconnection of myth and place means that although the use of myth is problematic, it is also unavoidable, even necessary.

Penultimately, Sinclair turns to walking, central to his own imagination of place, his own rewritings of the myths of London: 'what
we walk is myth flattened into space'; 'place becomes active once
more & this is the purpose of the walk – to keep track open . . . to
bear witness'.[72] To walk, then, is to recover the connection between
myth and place. In bearing witness, the walking subject returns to
the condition of 'conduit' we found in Olson's poetics. The poet is
not an agent, but a 'witness', a transmitter of energies rather than a
creator of them. In Sinclair's myth of origins, the originator (the
poet) is erased, therefore perhaps avoiding charges of 'FASCISM'.
Finally, as is fitting in *Suicide Bridge*'s reiteration of the cycles of
birth, death and rebirth, 'Intimate Associations' turns to death: 'Place,
finally, can only be one thing: where you die'.[73] The end of 'Intimate
Associations' indicates the circularity that recurs in Sinclair's work,
from the end of *White Chapell, Scarlet Tracings*, where 'the circuit
[is] completed', to the walk around the M25 in *London Orbital*. Sinclair
writes:

> Your whole journey has been to find that place which you have dreamt,
> long before birth, glimpsed, snatched, visited – to find it, complete the
> story, which is the suicide bridge, which is the anticipation, sleep's rush
> on death, the forcing, the entry to something that is not yet, cannot yet
> be, known.[74]

Like Olson, Faraday, and C. Howard Hinton, Sinclair finally gestures
to the numinous, the 'fourth dimension', the space and time
unknown, where the discourses of 'reality' break down. Robert Bond
reads the 'suicide bridge' as a threshold, 'an achievable point of entry'
to a 'utopian not-yet', suicide becoming an act of willed transcendence
(and perhaps re-birth), echoing the terms of R. D. Laing's 'willed
self-liberation' we encountered in the Introduction.[75] Suicide and
sacrifice are connected in *Suicide Bridge* and elsewhere in Sinclair's
work, but most importantly for Sinclair, of course, are the 'sacrificial'
victims of the Whitechapel murders of 1888. We will consider this
in more detail in the next chapter. In *Suicide Bridge*, it is willed self-
destruction, however, rather than the sacrifice of others that results
in rebirth. London's mythic history, as used by Sinclair, is full of
violence, blood and sacrifice: the Whitechapel murders; Hutton, Slade,
Peachey and Kotope, the 'victims' and 'dupes', are sacrificed to the
malign energies of Hand & Hyle's London; and Bladud of Bath,
the tenth of the mythical kings of England, has a short poem-sequence

dedicated to him towards the end of *Suicide Bridge*. An Icarus-like figure, Bladud learned to fly, but crashed to his death onto Apollo's temple in Nova Troja (New Troy, or London). Bladud is part of the mythical genealogy of English kingship which traces the foundation of London to Brutus, son of Aeneas, another birth-myth of London and Albion.

In his quoted letter in *White Chappell, Scarlet Tracings*, Douglas Oliver considers that Sinclair, is letting his creativity flow out towards 'bad vortices', runs the possibility of an 'implication of at least some prurience', a prurience attached to reimagining violence and 'evil'. Oliver accepts Sinclair's response, that he must 'trust the process', the process of open-field composition in the service of opposition to control and power.[76] As I will argue in a later chapter, Sinclair's focus upon such figures as the Krays does run the risk of aggrandising their 'legend' at the same time as it tries to debunk it. Sinclair concentrates on the violence of individuals: murder rather than riot, although death through riot and urban disorder is at least as prominent in London's history as murder. Therefore, it is the Ratcliffe Highways murders, the Whitechapel murders and the Krays, which form the constellations of his particular cosmology, rather than the Gordon riots, the firing of Newgate prison, or the Brixton or Broadwater Farm riots of the 1980s. Mainly, one surmises, this is because riot is less individuated, therefore less immediately purposive, than murder; it is also less sensational, and as Sinclair is interested in the traces that such acts leave upon the symbolic fabric of the city, the more sensational the act, the more discernable its traces. In *The Verbals*, Sinclair describes the intention behind *White Chappell, Scarlet Tracings* as to enact a 'debate about the nature of pain', a pain inscribed upon the streets of Whitechapel; 'these crimes are horribly unappeased', he continues, 'and seem to dominate the territory'.[77] As will be argued in Chapter 7, Sinclair's poetry, fiction and documentary prose works intend not only to bring forth the forgotten histories of London, but to exorcise them.

Nicholas Hawksmoor: rewriting the city

In Michael Moorcock's book of interviews with Colin Greenland, *Death Is No Obstacle* (1992), he states:

> I started *Mother London* with a wish to write about my own experience of the world in my own city, and I wanted it to be a celebration of that

city. I wanted to write about the mythology of London, because that
had been my first impulse when writing the Cornelius stories too, and
I never thought I'd done it successfully there. I invented a mythology
more than I examined one.[78]

Michael Moorcock's confession, that he 'invented a mythology' rather
than examined one, can be fruitfully applied to Sinclair's own
reimagination of London and its myths. In the first section of *Lud
Heat*, 'Nicholas Hawksmoor, His Churches', Sinclair sets out what
has become his signature theme: the psychogeographic importance
of the eight churches designed and built by Nicholas Hawksmoor,
in and around the East End of London in the early decades of
the eighteenth century. Sinclair's 'psychotic geography' occults the
topographic arrangement of the churches, revising their places on
the map of London to indicate a magical dabbling in the space and
time of the city. (Peter Ackroyd's own appropriation of Sinclair's
speculations in 'Nicholas Hawksmoor, His Churches', *Hawksmoor*
(1985), goes further still. In *Hawksmoor*, which Sinclair somewhat
archly characterises in *Downriver* 'a celebrated "bestseller" that
attributed the most peculiar properties to local churches', Ackroyd
renames the architect 'Nicholas Dyer', collapses the late twentieth
century onto the eighteenth, and invents a fictitious addition to the
Hawksmoor churches, 'Little St Hugh'.) [79] Hawksmoor's project,
according to Sinclair, is to 'rewrite the city'; to turn the *'ugly*
inconvenient self destroying unwieldy Monster' into a 'regular and
commodious form'.[80] The alignments of the churches are read as a
deliberate 'geometry of opposition', an attempt to redivert the psychical
energies of the city from the configurations of power and oppression.[81]
David Cunningham suggests that *Lud Heat* 'remains determinedly
ambiguous as to whether these are Hawksmoor's own hidden designs
or the author's hyperactive imagination', but I would argue that
Hawksmoor's project is really Sinclair's own: to 'rewrite the city' by
imagining a mythic, geomantic, 'other' London that can be accessed
and used for the purposes of opposition to the forces of domination.[82]
Sinclair's use of 'geometry' returns us to Faraday and his 'lines of
force': Sinclair calls the Old Street obelisk a 'point of force'; and 'each
church is an enclosure of force'.[83] Faraday's science is occulted,
rewritten, as an interpretative and speculative tool to decode the
spatial organisation of urban life, an organisation Sinclair characterises as 'control-power, built in code force'.[84]

Where Sinclair's italicised quotation from Hawksmoor suggests a binary understanding of London – 'unwieldy Monster' as opposed to 'commodious form', order versus chaos – the inclusion of two diagrams (based on Catling's drawings) in 'Nicholas Hawksmoor, His Churches' suggest rather a realignment of forces, one order being supplanted by another. Myth imposes a narrative and poetic order upon the unknown/unknowable; Sinclair reorders material that is already present, releasing energies 'held prisoner in space and time', just as Olson and Prynne's poetics allow.[85] Sinclair not only sets out to 'reveal what was already pursuing an unseen life', but to reimagine it, rewrite it for purposes of critique or opposition. *Lud Heat* and *Suicide Bridge* are (complex) reorderings of myth, the spaces of London, and literary and cultural history. They are not 'chaotic', though their order is difficult to understand at times. These books are ordered, if we may return to Olson, according to the poetics of the open field.

Unlike *Suicide Bridge*, there is a kind of submerged 'narrative' in *Lud Heat*. Though regularly punctuated by prose 'essays' that set out Sinclair's imaginative terrain and poetic practice – in 'Nicholas Hawksmoor, His Churches', 'Rites of Autopsy' (discussed at greater length in the next chapter) and 'From Camberwell to Golgotha' – the majority of the poems and prose-pieces are organised around the experiences of a temporary gardener in the parks department of Tower Hamlets (the 'Dead Hamlets' of the subtitle). He joins the crew of the 'bothy' in the summer and early autumn of 1974, suffers hay fever and sunstroke, and mows the grass in and around the Hawksmoor churches of east London, particularly focusing on the church of St Anne's, Limehouse. These poems are clearly semi-autobiographical, cataloguing workmates, churchyard lunches, diary entries, to give a seemingly fragmented yet, taken as a whole, cohesive sense of the city and the summer. Throughout *Lud Heat*, the body is prey to the forces of the city. The narrator falls victim to sunstroke in 'In the Surgery of the Sun', his 'vertebrae a cage of burning wasps';[86] and in 'A Theory of Hay Fevers', 'disease [. . .] is a form of pure message', a somatic reaction to place: 'what you suffer is the place you choose to live'.[87] The body's allergic reaction to nature is, perhaps, the symptom here of the division between human and place diagnosed in *Suicide Bridge*'s 'Intimate Associations: Myth and Place'; the identification of body and land, human and place, is crucial to all of Sinclair's work. Hay fever becomes the index of the human body's estrangement from its own nature; the garden is a place of punishment.

Although the mythic elements in *Lud Heat* are less explicitly part of the textual fabric than *Suicide Bridge*, they are still present. The connection here is not to Blake; more appropriately, considering the centrality of the park and garden to the book, the main touchstone here is Milton. Edenic readings of the garden are put in play most clearly in 'Closed Field, The Dogs of the Moon'. The diary entry for 30 May reports the arrival of the dog handler, 'with tales of the brown sex police'.[88] The prurient dog handler describes a scene of *coitus interruptus* in a council tool shed. The dog handler tells of a man and a woman, both in their mid-fifties, discovered naked and evicted naked from the shed: 'As man & woman stumble into the yard. A Miltonic banishment'.[89] The parks and gardens of Tower Hamlets seem poor versions of Eden regained, but it is interesting how both Robert Bond and David Cunningham, in their analyses of *Suicide Bridge* and *Lud Heat* respectively, assert the 'utopian' impulse at work in Sinclair's remappings of London. Although *Suicide Bridge* and *Lud Heat* cannot reverse the fall, their imaginative reconfigurations of myth and the spatial orderings of power and control suggest an attempt to heal the fallen/falling world, and bring about a better one.

Lud Heat ends not with a walk, Sinclair's signature activity, but with a run, from Albion Drive to the Oracle Bunker, an old wartime gun emplacement on some waste ground near the Lea. 'Running the Oracle', the last prose-piece, begins at the turning of the year, with a journey to Ripon and northern England, then a return to London and its concerns. As in Blake's *Jerusalem*, London may be the primary site of Sinclair's investigations and imagination, but the state of Albion is his concern. Just as Coban, Skofeld and the other sons of Albion are related to parts of Britain, the ending of *Lud Heat* opens out from London to other parts of Britain, just as *White Chappell, Scarlet Tracings* will do with Sinclair's journey to the Essex marshes. *Lud Heat* does not end in enlightenment – the runner is 'an ignorant man, ground-held, muddy in motive' – but the book ends with a gesture of circularity and completion.[90] Where *White Chappell* finishes with the words 'the circuit completed', and *Downriver* echoes this figure negatively with 'my circuit was complete. I was back where I started [. . .] I had discovered nothing', *Lud Heat* ends with: 'so again we service the dead, complete the gesture, grasp at the arm raised in salute from the choked ground'.[91] In *White Chappell*, the 'circuit' between the 1880s and the 1970s is completed by Sinclair's journey to Sir William Gull's birthplace; at the end of *Lud Heat*, history, the body and the land are grasped together in one symbolic gesture.

Notes

1 Iain Sinclair with Kevin Jackson, *The Verbals* (Tonbridge: Worple Press, 2003), pp. 70–1.

2 Jonathon Green, *All Dressed Up: the Sixties and the Counterculture* (London: Pimlico, 1999), p. 140.

3 Michael Horovitz, 'Afterwords', in M. Horovitz (ed.), *Children of Albion: Poetry of the 'Underground', in Britain* (Harmondsworth: Penguin, 1969), pp. 316–77, p. 337.

4 Horovitz, 'Afterwords', p. 337.

5 Horovitz, 'Afterwords', p. 337.

6 Horovitz, 'Afterwords', p. 337.

7 Peter Barry, *Contemporary British Poetry and the City* (Manchester: Manchester University Press, 2000), p. 63.

8 Neil Corcoran, *English Poetry since 1940* (London and New York: Longman, 1993), pp. 164–5.

9 Sinclair with Jackson, *The Verbals*, p. 38.

10 Charles Olson, 'Projective Verse', in Paul Hoover (ed.), *Postmodern American Poetry: A Norton Anthology* (New York and London: Norton, 1994), pp. 613–20 (p. 614).

11 Iain Sinclair, *Lud Heat and Suicide Bridge* (London: Granta, 1995), p. 149.

12 Geoffrey Ward, 'Nothing but Mortality: Prynne and Celan', in A. Easthope and J. O. Thompson (eds), *Contemporary Poetry Meets Modern Theory* (New York and London: Harvester Wheatsheaf, 1991), pp. 139–52 (p. 146).

13 Sinclair, *Lud Heat and Suicide Bridge*, p. 136.

14 Sinclair with Jackson, *The Verbals*, p. 84.

15 Corcoran, *English Poetry since 1940*, pp. 174 and 175.

16 Corcoran, English Poetry since 1940, p. 175.

17 Corcoran, *English Poetry since 1940*, pp. 177–8.

18 J. H. Prynne, 'Moon Poem', *Poems* (Newcastle: Bloodaxe, 1999), p. 53, ll. 810 and 23–5.

19 Prynne, 'Moon Poem', ll. 34 and 36–7.

20 Prynne, 'Questions for the Time Being', p. 112, ll. 379; p. 113, ll. 49–51.

21 Prynne, 'Questions for the Time Being', p. 113, ll. 57–60; ll. 68–72.

22 John Bunyan, *The Pilgrim's Progress* (Harmondsworth: Penguin, 1986), p. 259.
23 Bunyan, *The Pilgrim's Progress*, p. 259.
24 Barry, *Contemporary British Poetry and the City*, p. 166; p. 167.
25 Olson, 'Projective Verse', p. 614.
26 Olson, 'Projective Verse', p. 614.
27 Olson, 'Projective Verse', p. 614.
28 Iain Sinclair, 'The Poet Steamed', *London Review of Books*, 26:16, 19 August 2004, 27–9, 28.
29 Olson, 'Projective Verse', p. 614; p. 620.
30 Michael Faraday, 'Experimental Researches in Electricity (1839–55) (1852)', in L. Otis (ed.), *Literature and Science in the Nineteenth Century: An Anthology* (Oxford: Oxford University Press, 2002), pp. 55–9 (pp. 55 and 57).
31 A. E. E. McKenzie, *The Major Achievements of Science* (New York: Simon & Schuster, 1973), p. 182.
32 McKenzie, *The Major Achievements of Science*, p. 182.
33 John Berger, 'The Moment of Cubism', in G. Dyer (ed.), *Selected Essays* (London: Bloomsbury, 2001), pp. 71–92 (p. 74).
34 Sinclair, *Lud Heat and Suicide Bridge*, p. 70.
35 M. Norton Wise, 'Electromagnetic Theory in the Nineteenth Century', in R. C. Olby, G. N. Cantor, J. R. R. Christie and M. J. S. Hidge (eds), *Companion to the History of Modern Science* (London and New York: Routledge, 1990), pp. 342–56 (p. 349).
36 Barry, *Contemporary British Poetry and the City*, pp. 165–6.
37 Barry, *Contemporary British Poetry and the City*, p. 176.
38 Tim Woods, 'Allen Fisher's *Place* Project and the "Spatial Turn"', *Parataxis* 8 (1996), 39–46 (43).
39 H. G. Wells, *The Time Machine* (London: Heinemann, 1911), p. 5.
40 Wells, *The Time Machine*, p. 4.
41 Bruce Clarke, 'A Scientific Romance: Thermodynamics and the Fourth Dimension in Charles Howard Hinton's "The Persian King"', *Weber Studies: An Interdisciplinary Humanities Journal*, 14:1, winter (1997), supplement to *ebr*, *Science Technology and the Arts* (accessed 7 June 2004). <www.altx.com/ebr/w(ebr)/essays/Clarke.html>, par. 12.
42 Clarke, 'A Scientific Romance', par. 11.
43 Clarke, 'A Scientific Romance', par. 2.
44 Sinclair, 'The Enemy of the Stars', *Lud Heat and Suicide Bridge*, p. 239.
45 Sinclair, *Lud Heat and Suicide Bridge*, p. 290.
46 Sinclair, 'Intimate Associations: Myth and Place', *Lud Heat and Suicide Bridge*, p. 148.
47 Sinclair, 'A Cosmogony for Hand & Hyle', *Lud Heat and Suicide Bridge*, p. 155.

48 Sinclair, 'A Biographical Sketch', *Lud Heat and Suicide Bridge*, p. 264.

49 Sinclair, 'Hutton: The Death', *Lud Heat and Suicide Bridge*, p. 218.

50 Sinclair, 'The Enemy of the Stars', *Lud Heat and Suicide Bridge*, p. 291.

51 Robert Bond, 'Suicide Bridge', *The Literary Encyclopaedia* (accessed 29 March 2004). <www.litencyc.com/php/sworks.php?rec=true&UID=10512>, par. 6.

52 Iain Sinclair, *White Chappell, Scarlet Tracings* (London: Paladin, 1988), p. 159.

53 Sinclair with Jackson, *The Verbals*, p. 100.

54 Sinclair, 'A Cosmogony for Hand & Hyle', pp. 155–6.

55 Sinclair, 'A Cosmogony for Hand & Hyle', *Lud Heat and Suicide Bridge*, p. 156.

56 Sinclair, 'A Cosmogony for Hand & Hyle', *Lud Heat and Suicide Bridge*, p. 158.

57 Sinclair, 'Nicholas Hawksmoor, His Churches', *Lud Heat and Suicide Bridge*, pp. 26–7.

58 Sinclair, 'Intimate Associations: Myth and Place', *Lud Heat and Suicide Bridge*, p. 149.

59 Sinclair, *White Chappell, Scarlet Tracings*, p. 145.

60 Sinclair, 'Hutton: The Death', *Lud Heat and Suicide Bridge*, p. 219.

61 Sinclair, 'Kotope, the Manner of His Dying', *Lud Heat and Suicide Bridge*, p. 185.

62 Sinclair, 'Victims: An Appendix', *Lud Heat and Suicide Bridge*, p. 226.

63 Olson, 'Projective Verse', p. 614.

64 Ward, 'Nothing but Mortality', p. 146.

65 Sinclair, *White Chappell, Scarlet Tracings*, p. 165.

66 William Blake, 'Jerusalem', *Complete Writings*, G. Keynes (ed.) (Oxford and New York: Oxford, 1966), p. 255: Ch. 2, Pl. 43, ll. 51–4.

67 Sinclair, 'Intimate Associations: Myth and Place', *Lud Heat and Suicide Bridge*, p. 147.

68 Sinclair, 'Intimate Associations: Myth and Place', *Lud Heat and Suicide Bridge*, pp. 147 and 148.

69 Sinclair, 'Intimate Associations: Myth and Place', *Lud Heat and Suicide Bridge*, p. 148.

70 Sinclair, 'Intimate Associations: Myth and Place', *Lud Heat and Suicide Bridge*, p. 149.

71 Sinclair, 'Intimate Associations: Myth and Place', *Lud Heat and Suicide Bridge*, p. 150.

72 Sinclair, 'Intimate Associations: Myth and Place', *Lud Heat and Suicide Bridge*, pp. 150 and 151.

73 Sinclair, 'Intimate Associations: Myth and Place', *Lud Heat and Suicide Bridge*, p. 153.

74 Sinclair, 'Intimate Associations: Myth and Place', *Lud Heat and Suicide Bridge*, p. 154.

75 Bond, Robert (2004a), 'Suicide Bridge', *The Literary Encyclopaedia* (accessed 29 March 2004). <www.litencyc.com/php/sworks.php?rec =true&UID=10512>, par. 7.
76 Sinclair, *White Chappell, Scarlet Tracings*, pp. 160, 159 and 160.
77 Sinclair with Jackson, *The Verbals*, pp. 115 and 116.
78 Colin Greenland, *Michael Moorcock: Death is No Obstacle* (Manchester: Savoy, 1992), p. 101.
79 Iain Sinclair, *Downriver* (1991) (London: Vintage, 1995), p. 98.
80 Sinclair, 'Nicholas Hawksmoor, His Churches', *Lud Heat and Suicide Bridge*, p. 14.
81 Sinclair, 'Nicholas Hawksmoor, His Churches', *Lud Heat and Suicide Bridge*, p. 15.
82 David Cunningham, 'Lud Heat', *The Literary Encyclopaedia* (accessed 29 March 2004). <www.litencyc.com/php/sworks.php?rec=true&UID= 3810>, par. 4.
83 Sinclair, 'Nicholas Hawksmoor, His Churches', *Lud Heat and Suicide Bridge*, pp. 16 and 20.
84 Sinclair, 'Nicholas Hawksmoor, His Churches', *Lud Heat and Suicide Bridge*, p. 21.
85 Sinclair, 'Nicholas Hawksmoor, His Churches', *Lud Heat and Suicide Bridge*, p. 38.
86 Sinclair, 'In the Surgery of the Sun', *Lud Heat and Suicide Bridge*, p. 107.
87 Sinclair, 'A Theory of Hay Fevers', *Lud Heat and Suicide Bridge*, p. 66.
88 Sinclair, 'Closed Field, the Dogs of the Moon', *Lud Heat and Suicide Bridge*, p. 43.
89 Sinclair, 'Closed Field, the Dogs of the Moon', *Lud Heat and Suicide Bridge*, pp. 43–4.
90 Sinclair, 'Running the Oracle', *Lud Heat and Suicide Bridge*, p. 141.
91 Sinclair, *Downriver*, pp. 67–8; Sinclair, 'Running the Oracle', *Lud Heat and Suicide Bridge*, p. 141.

2

Whitechapel autopsy:
an East End apocalypse

Haunted places are the only ones people can live in. (Michel de Certeau)[1]

Sinclair's first novel, *White Chappell, Scarlet Tracings* (1987, cited edition 1988), draws upon the events of the autumn of 1888, the 'Whitechapel Murders' of Jack the Ripper. It is also a consciously intertextual novel, drawing upon (amongst other things) Stevenson's *Strange Case of Dr Jekyll and Mr Hyde* and Conan Doyle's Sherlock Holmes stories (particularly *A Study in Scarlet*). It completes the first 'triad' of texts (*Lud Heat, Suicide Bridge* and *White Chappell, Scarlet Tracings*) and inaugurates the second (*White Chappell, Downriver* and *Radon Daughters*). As we saw in the previous chapter, in *White Chappell*, Sinclair refers to C. Howard Hinton's *What is the Fourth Dimension?*, which suggests that:

> We have got to imagine some stupendous whole *wherein all that has ever come into being or will come co-exists*, which, passing slowly on, leaves this flickering consciousness of ours, limited to a narrow space and a single moment, a tumultuous record of changes and vicissitudes that are but to us.[2]

As in *Suicide Bridge*, time here has a cosmological dimension, and echoes the emphases on cosmic time and limited human time, attempting to paint on both canvases simultaneously through psychogeography and myth. This explains the time-jumping structure of *White Chappell*: to explore the continuities of consciousness and 'force', the novel grafts the 1970s and 1980s onto the 1880s. Both *White Chappell*, and Alan Moore and Eddie Campbell's graphic narrative *From Hell* (1999), which is clearly indebted to Sinclair, reimagine the events of 1888. Both texts understand the 1880s to be the birthplace of the twentieth century, and the crucible wherein many of the myths of contemporary popular culture are forged. However, where *From Hell* sees our world as brought into being by the Whitechapel murders, *White Chappell* suggests, as we saw above, that 'we have got to imagine some stupendous whole *wherein all that has ever come into being or will come co-exists*' [Sinclair's italics].[3] This idea of temporal co-presence, or perhaps multi-presence, is one that informs the entirety of *White Chappell*; as Sinclair wrote in *Suicide Bridge*, 'Past and present are coeval'.[4] In fact, Sinclair deploys a metaphysic of topographic presence to underscore the mythic constructions of his narrative, one that can also be found in his collaboration with Rachel Lichtenstein, *Rodinsky's Room* (1999).

White Chappell, Scarlet Tracings: ghosts and presence

In western metaphysics, argues Jacques Derrida, a privileging of speech over writing, of the voice over text, makes the voice the embodiment of truth and of authenticity. In this phonocentrism, as he calls it, writing is seen to be derived from a pre-existing 'natural' form of communication, one which is prior to 'the fateful violence of the political institution'.[5] Because of this privileging of speech, 'what is written is always read as speech or the surrogate of speech'; this itself presupposes an origin and originator of that speech, both in a human subject and a legitimating order or structure.[6] For Derrida, this 'metaphysics of presence', the trace of the voice in the text (actually absent, but which is inferred by the reader in the text and then which displaces textuality itself) is found everywhere in post-Enlightenment discourse. This 'metaphysics of presence' is apparent in Sinclair's depiction of the city as an accretion or palimpsest of sign systems (as in *Lights Out for the Territory*, analysed in the Introduction to this book), the city as text, which in turn produces the 'third' presence, an authentic 'dream', 'voice' or expression of London. We will consider the concept of the 'third' presence or space further in Chapter 7. In his Introduction to the 2001 Penguin Classics reissue of *A Study in Scarlet*, Sinclair writes: 'The key Victorian fictions overlap, shadow each other, until their lead characters achieve an independent existence: they are part of the perpetual dream of the city'.[7] The character 'Sinclair' (a first-person narrator, like 'the Late Watson', who may or may not be the same character) explains further in *White Chappell*:

> Accepting the notion of 'presence' – I mean that certain fictions, chiefly
> Conan Doyle, Stevenson, but many others also, laid out a template
> that was more powerful than any local documentary account – the
> presences they created, or 'figures' if you prefer it, like Rabbi Loew's
> Golem, became too much and too fast to be contained within the
> conventional limits of that fiction. They got out into the stream of
> time, the ether; they escaped into the labyrinth. They achieved an
> independent existence.[8]

The presence of these mythic 'figures' is literally bodied forth, made
manifest and material, through the operations of language, narrative
and text. Not only is all time co-existent in space in this figure of
'presence', but Sinclair suggests that textual fictions impose their
existence onto space and time. Scrape the surface of one text, and
another is revealed beneath. We find intertexts throughout Sinclair's
fiction and non-fiction, and further signs of this in Chapter 7 of
White Chappell, where 'Sinclair' holds forth on Conan Doyle's *A
Study in Scarlet*. The first page of Conan Doyle's story is reproduced,
copied from another edition, but this version is 'treated' in the manner
of Tom Phillips's *A Humument* (1997). Here, as there, most of
the text is erased or overpainted to reveal an 'underlying' pattern of
words. This process reveals the textual substrata, the 'presence' which
haunts the text. 'Sinclair' reads this treated page as a direct but
subconscious commentary on the Whitechapel murders. Where, as
we saw in the Introduction to this book, in Sinclair's London place
itself becomes a text and reveals itself to the eye of the trained 'reader',
in *White Chappell* the reverse occurs. Text becomes a material space,
the 'underground' of which can be revealed by treating its pages,
disrupting the narrative to recover its 'hidden' message.

I wish to return here to the word 'haunts', because this has a
particular resonance within the recent study of Gothic fictions. Julian
Wolfreys, in his *Victorian Hauntings*, again adapts Derrida's figure
of the 'spectral' that we encountered in the Introduction to this book,
not to Sinclair but to an analysis of Gothic textuality. Wolfreys explains
the 'spectral' like this:

> The identification of spectrality appears in a gap between the limits of
> two ontological categories. The definition escapes any positivist or
> constructivist logic by emerging between, and yet not as a part of, two
> negations: *neither, nor*. A third term, the spectral, speaks of the limits
> of determination, while arriving beyond the terminal both in and of

identification in either case (alive/dead) and not as an oppositional or dialectical term itself defined as part of some logical economy.[9]

Spectrality then marks the limit of definition, a naming of that which cannot be named, a limit which is tropologically figured in Gothic texts as the ghost, double or the unseen. Wolfreys has also written directly on Sinclair, and here he suggests that in Sinclair's texts, the city becomes spectral: 'the spectral nature of the metropolis collapses any neat distinctions or oppositions between the real and the textual, the historical and the literal, walking and writing, witnessing and remembering'.[10] The insistent textuality of the city in *Lights Out for the Territory* then indicates the impossibility of figuring the city in textual form, but London itself haunts the texts just as Sinclair haunts its streets. Sinclair's desire to walk the streets of the city becomes, for Wolfreys, a desire to *know* London, and what is desired 'is so often described as a centre or a presence'.[11]

In Sinclair's texts, we also find a magical or metaphysical conception of writing and of imagination. As the character Hinton says in *White Chappell, Scarlet Tracings* in a letter to his sister, 'something *thinks* us, that's evident'.[12] The 'author' becomes merely a medium, attenuated out of existence, another trace in the matrix of textuality. For William Burroughs too, no words are 'owned' by writers. Burroughs is a writer whose influence on Sinclair's practice is profound, and Sinclair pays homage to him (as he does to J. G. Ballard in *Crash* (1999) and *London Orbital* (2002)) by making a pilgrimage to Lawrence, Kansas, Burroughs's final home: a photograph of Sinclair with Burroughs, and the first page of Burroughs's *Junky*, is reproduced in Sinclair's collaboration with Dave McKean, *Slow Chocolate Autopsy* (1997). Burroughs writes:

> Writers work with words and voices just as painters work with colors; and where do these words and voices come from? Many sources: conversations heard and overheard, movies and radio broadcasts, newspapers, magazines, yes, and *other writers*.[13]

Therefore, there is no creation, but only *re*creation; as in the concept of intertextuality, Burroughs saw the text as a 'tissue of quotations', an endlessly regressive chain of signifiers, with no beginning, and therefore no author. This was not only a conscious operation: the cut-up is a physical manifestation of an already-existing unconscious and linguistic process. Sinclair deploys this concept at the level of language, but also as a foundational assumption for his textual mythology: agency is continually displaced onto the acts of others, presence becomes absence. 'We have to settle ourselves into a text', Sinclair writes in *White Chappell*, nothing is written, everything is re-written. We are retrospective'.[14] This absence of agency (and authority) in the author is signified both through the conscious intertextuality of Sinclair's novel and statements such as this: 'Conan Doyle was taking down a form of dictation, accessing voices from a parallel universe (where they had always been present)'.[15] Although we can read this as a tongue-in-cheek reference to Conan Doyle's obsession with spiritualism, it is confirmed by this passage from *White Chappell*, which follows the reproduced page from *A Study in Scarlet*: 'Dictation at this speed takes the scribe, often under pressure of work or disease, so fast and so deep that he writes it before it happens, and by writing it he causes it to happen'.[16] The fictional text is dictation, transmitted from a numinous 'elsewhere'. Writing is inevitably Gothicised in this conception, becoming an occulted and mysterious practice, connected to the spectral or other. Wolfreys suggests that in Sinclair's texts, 'the artist is one possible figure of the spirit medium who might be attuned to the energy fields of London': the artist figures the 'ghost', and attempts to articulate the presence/absence of the city.[17] Curiously, this shamanistic idea seems to evacuate significance from Sinclair's own texts: they point to, and make meaning through, their intertextual connection with other works. Presence and absence is in fact a recurring thematic concern for Sinclair, and I will return to these issues in relation to *Rodinsky's Room* in a later chapter.

Not only do texts such as *A Study in Scarlet* express the culturally hidden, however; for Sinclair, they are prophetic. They prefigure *White Chappell, Scarlet Tracings* itself. Sinclair confesses that 'even though I had my title before I started to work . . . I was echoing the master'.[18] Art, writing or imagination, are recurrently figured in *White Chappell* as ' "tracings of unseen acts" ', the attempt to represent not only the unseen but the still to come.[19] J. G. Ballard is again a key influence here. One of Ballard's short-story collections is entitled *Myths of the Near Future*; and elsewhere, Ballard has explained his own intentions:

> The title *Myths of the Near Future* sums up what I think a lot of present writers . . . are concerned with: the mythologies of the future. Not myths that will one day *replace* the classical legends of ancient Greece, but *predictive mythologies*; those which in a sense provide an operating

formula by which we can deal with our passage through consciousness
– our movements through time and space.[20]

Predictive mythologies are, notably, imagined by Ballard in spatial
terms: they are a map, a way of orienting oneself in the future.
Ballard's model of predictive mythologies provides a key to understanding both *White Chappell* and *From Hell*. Investigating popular
mythologies and 'history', they are both investigations of the contemporary cultural landscape. Both *White Chappell, Scarlet Tracings* and
From Hell represent the Whitechapel murders as in some sense
prophylactic in intent, purposed to prevent as much as bring forth
a new state of being. In this they fail, for the murders cannot but
produce effects as much as forestall them. Our present 'haunts the
past' of the 1880s: the dominated space of contemporary London,
the violence and murder traced in the speculations of Sinclair and
Joblard, is the 'ghost of the future' that haunts the past of *White
Chappell*. In their narrative structures, the texts also demonstrate an
awareness that they are reproducing the myths of Jack the Ripper as
much as critiquing them. Both texts attempt to frustrate closure and
resolution, to disrupt the transmission of myth. *From Hell*'s narrative
is followed by an epilogue, a notes section and an appendix called
'Dance of the Gull Catchers' which suggests that all that has preceded
has been an utterly unreliable fiction. In the last chapter of *White
Chappell*, the narrator (perhaps 'the Late Watson', perhaps 'Sinclair',
and described in the third person in the first two paragraphs of the
chapter), finds himself in the salt marshes of north Essex, close to
the Gull family home. He discovers a barge like the one that Gull's
father owned:

> It is the shell of a great barge. Burnt out, charred, flaking; beams broken
> and twisted, grounded. In this drowned field, where water runs out, at
> this boundary, on the edge of things, between past and future. A spar
> goes down into the black silt, umbilical, connecting the hulk to this
> place. It is split, it is half of something.
>   I recognise it. And know that I have to write my way back to this
> moment.[21]

The reader will also recognise it, for a photograph of this barge is
placed on the title pages of books one and three of the novel. The
barge signifies an ending, for a barge had been the funeral pyre for
Gull's father earlier in the text, but the final image of conclusion is
paradoxical. Although the last sentence is 'the connection will be

made, the circuit completed', having to 'write my way back' suggests the beginning of a journey, not the end.[22] As we saw in the last chapter, the figure of 'circuits completed' is a recurrent one in Sinclair's work. The end of *White Chappell* does not offer closure, but sends us back to the beginning, and invites us to reread the text and complete the circuit ourselves.

White Chappell, Scarlet Tracings and *From Hell*

In *Textual Haunting*, Julian Wolfreys indicates the 'haunted' nature of books themselves. 'Books', he suggests, 'appear to have a material presence, without which anchoring that such materiality provides, our lives would assume a ghostly condition of impermanence'.[23] The act of reading is also spectral, bringing forth a 'presence' (in terms of narrative or character) that is textual (or absent). Books then exceed their own material form, are somehow occult objects, although in *White Chappell*, the dealings of the bookmen can in part be read as a satirical critique and indictment of commodity exchange, the hegemony of value. (In *London Orbital*, this becomes an invective against Blairite New Labour's insistence on 'best value' to the detriment of culture and society.) The 'spectral' act of reading clearly parallels Sinclair's conception of the characters of late-Victorian fictions getting 'out into the stream of time, the ether; they escaped into the labyrinth. They achieved an independent existence'.[24] Books are central to one of the three narrative threads of *White Chappell, Scarlet Tracings*, and indicate its emphasis on presence and absence, and the intersection of the material and textual throughout Sinclair's writings. The book is also connected to the body (as in the trope 'body of works', or the deployment of the word *corpus*). The body, the most material of objects, is also a fundamentally important figure for *White Chappell, Scarlet Tracings*, and for *From Hell*. It is on bodies that the narrative of the texts is literally and violently, 'traced'.

Rather than investigating (or celebrating) the enigmatic figure of Jack the Ripper, in *White Chappell, Scarlet Tracings* Sinclair uses the conspiracy-inflected version of Stephen Knight's *Jack the Ripper: The Final Solution* (1977) as a starting point for a fragmented meditation on the interaction between time and space, between history and place, focused not on the crimes themselves but on peripheral events and figures from the 'Ripper' narrative. Alan Moore and Eddie Campbell's *From Hell* (subsequently adapted in a screen version, directed by the Hughes Brothers and starring Johnny Depp) treats the events of 1888 much more directly, but draws upon the same sources and discourses as Sinclair and inhabits much of the same symbolic territory. Stephen Knight's *Jack the Ripper: The Final Solution* constructed a 'case' for Queen Victoria's physician-in-ordinary, Dr William Withey Gull, as the murderer. *From Hell*'s speculations concern a bastard royal child, attempted blackmail by five Whitechapel prostitutes, a Masonic cover-up, and a Victoria-sanctioned campaign of murder by Gull which carries apocalyptic overtones. As Judith Walkowitz notes in her illuminating study *City of Dreadful Delight* (1992), as a cultural event the Whitechapel murders drew upon several pre-existing threads in late-Victorian culture, most notably 'the grotesque female body . . . the labyrinthine city . . . [and] the mad doctor'.[25] To suggest Dr Gull as the perpetrator neatly splices all three discourses: a 'mad' physician, at the heart of a labyrinthine net of conspiracy, making monstrous (through murder and dissection) the female bodies of the five prostitutes. *White Chappell* also features Dr Gull, but as a boy; and the text's interest in bodies extends beyond the violence done to the five Whitechapel prostitutes in 1888. The dead body, and the concept of the autopsy, is one that will recur throughout the remainder of this chapter.

Dr William Withey Gull, the physician-in-ordinary to Queen Victoria who is the perpetrator of the Whitechapel murders in both *White Chappell* and *From Hell*, is a suggestive figure to focus a critique of discourses of power, gender and the city. Gull was an eminent physician in 'real life', doctor to the royal household. In *White Chappell*, Gull is introduced as a boy with rather disturbing insights. Discovered on a beach by a clergyman (who transplants him from his own family and social class – his father was a 'wharfinger' or boatman on the Essex lighters), the young Gull is already involved in inscribing his identity and story upon the landscape. Not quite literate, he has scrawled 'Aloga taimma a gaoow liifbb a baogy ho livin a haos', his transcription of 'Alongtimeagolivedaboywholivedinahouse', upon a slate found at the water's edge.[26] Questioned by the parson, the boy says he is 'Making a testa met', a 'testament . . . like the Old'.[27] Gull's testament is later completed in his apocalyptic violence, written upon the bodies of the five 'Ripper' victims. Interestingly, 'boy' is transposed into 'baogy' or 'bogey', Gull the bogeyman.

The mature Gull represents both the British political and medical establishment. Yet, transformed into the 'Ripper', Gull's surgical skills become monstrous travesties of themselves, exposing the violence done to the post-mortem body that is usually masked by medical discourse. *From Hell* makes much visual play with Gull's hands, often framed in the foreground of panels, directing the gaze of the reader towards the object of Gull's attention. They are, of course, both the instruments of healing and of dissection, of medicine and murder. The graphic novel is formatted in a regular nine-panel page, its symmetry often at odds with its visceral imagery. The final murder, of Mary Jane (or Marie Jeanette) Kelly, is the subject of the entirety of Chapter 10 of the graphic novel, and it is indeed an extremely graphic and disturbing rendering of a murder *as* autopsy, autopsy as murder. The line between the two becomes blurred. At one point, Gull, becoming progressively more deranged by the apocalyptic intent of his acts, hallucinates a public anatomy lecture, and discourses on the liver that he is extracting. 'Late as Hellenic times', he orates, 'it was believed to be the very centre of vitality, seat of the soul itself. Located underneath the ribs' caged lattice, pressed against the diaphragm's curved dome, it is a deep maroon in colour. It is divided, like the brain, in two great lobes, these being right and left'.[28] The violence done to the body in this murder-autopsy is savage and apocalyptic, intended to bring a new, cleansed world into being.

Gothic fictions and the disrupted body

Moore and Campbell portray this moment of apocalyptic and hallucinatory violence as a performance, and we should remember that the lecture is given in an 'operating theatre'. Dr Gull, like Jack the Ripper, is familiar with human anatomy, the product of hours spent at the dissecting table. The connection with the surgeon with the monstrous extends far back beyond 1888, however. Jonathan Sawday, in *The Body Emblazoned* (1995), notes the problematic position of dissection in the eighteenth and early nineteenth centuries. Taboos surrounding the dissection of the human corpse had prevented post-mortem examination for centuries (since the Roman times of Galen), and when used, were aligned with regimes of punishment. He explains:

> 'Penal dissection' – the codification by statute of a set of rules under which the corpse could be dismembered after death for the utilitarian investigation of the body's internal structure – is held to have begun, in England, with the passage of the infamous 'Murder Act' of 1752.

The overt context for the passage of the 1752 Act was a response to the perceived break-down in law and order on the part of the authorities. What was needed, it was felt, was a punishment so draconian, so appalling, that potential criminals would be terrified at the fate that awaited them in the event of their detection.[29]

The taboos surrounding the dissection of corpses meant that they were in short supply, and so criminals, already the subjects of capital punishment, were delivered into the hands of surgeon-anatomists as a further correction of their souls. In fact, such taboos surrounded dissection that the witnesses of a hanging would often physically battle with those appointed to take the body to the dissecting theatre, so that the body could be interred whole. The anatomist, Sawday argues, was often present at the execution itself, and that 'there was very little difference between the ritual of execution and the opening of the body to knowledge'.[30] The surgeons were identified with the executioners. Both dissection and execution were public spectacles; both were intended as part of a regime of punishment; in both, power and knowledge played upon the *body* of the subject. In *Suicide Bridge*, hanging and sacrifice are bound up with renewal or rebirth; autopsy rites are central to Sinclair's vision of the city in *Lud Heat*.

In a scene from Chapter 7 of *White Chappell*, two characters ascend to a preserved nineteenth-century operating theatre. Imagining the scene, the narrator describes the following:

> Long coated surgeons hack and cut, talking their virtuosity into the dry throats of the banked students. Splash the hands with water. A small looking-glass. Their own faces. Beards and teeth. The patients carried out. Performance concluded. The curtain of eyes.[31]

The theatre is a site for autopsy, the division and opening of the human body. The recurrent use of the word 'autopsy' (as in *Slow Chocolate Autopsy*) and the word 'forensic' in Sinclair's writings suggests a medico-scientific approach to myth and culture. The etymology of 'autopsy' also signifies another recurrent motif in Sinclair's texts, one indicated in the passage quoted above: vision. Autopsy derives from 'optics', from the Greek words *opsis* ('vision' or 'sight') and *autoptos* ('seen by oneself', a compound of *autos* and *optos*). An autopsy, then, as defined by Sinclair himself in *Lud Heat*, is 'the act of seeing with one's own eyes'.[32] The autopsy is an act of witness as well as a spectacle, emphasising the personal connection between spectator and event, between seeing and knowledge.

In a pivotal section in *Lud Heat*, Sinclair inserts a short essay called 'Rites of Autopsy', ostensibly a commentary on a film by the American filmmaker Stan Brakhage, but actually an investigation and explication of some of Sinclair's own recurrent images and ideas. The film, an experimental documentary:

> was largely shot at the Alleghany Coroner's Office on a Sunday morning in the Autumn of 1971. Sunday, the busy day of weekend suicide and mayhem, full house. Autumn, the time of equinoctial danger. Murder season, days of sacrifice.[33]

It is interesting to note that Sinclair studiously avoids the Americanism 'the Fall' to denote Autumn, thereby disabling the easy Miltonic/biblical puns that could be brought to bear. Instead, Sinclair once again connects suicide with sacrifice. The essay suggests that watching the film is an act of 'bearing witness to secret rites', rites connected with death and bodies.[34] The film makes one watch '*with our own eyes*', enforcing not passive consumption but participation in the rituals being filmed/represented.[35] To watch, 'to see with one's own eyes', is not unconnected with issues of power. Historically, power and knowledge was given expression through dissection, the making visible of the inside of the body, in medical discourse. Perhaps the most explicit demonstration of this doctrine comes from Xavier Bichat's *Anatomie générale* of 1801:

> What is the value of observation, if one does not know the seat of the disease? You can take notes for twenty years from morning to evening at the sickbed on diseases of the heart, lung, and stomach, and you will reap nothing but confusion. The symptoms, corresponding to nothing, will offer but incoherent phenomena. Open a few corpses, and immediately this obscurity, which observation alone would never have removed, will disappear.[36]

As Roy Porter suggests, 'here was the medicine of the all-powerful gaze'.[37] The autopsy, following swiftly on from death, was, in Bichat's rhetoric, the only true path of understanding the body. In life, the bodily symptoms were confused, incoherent, obscure – because not visible. In death, however, the body becomes open to the knife and the observation of the doctor. Explanation, understanding, knowledge, is elevated above cure. Porter notes a similar process to that suggested by Michel Foucault's concept of the panoptic regime: 'Clinical medicine aimed to be a science; it hinged on the "gaze" (clinical detachment), and was to be imbibed through the vigil of countless hours in the ward and the morgue'.³⁸ Dissection renders visible the hidden, reveals the disease beneath the skin, and asserts the mortality of the living body. This paradoxical connection between death and life is highly important to Sinclair's work. In 'Rites of Autopsy' we find Sinclair's insistent imagery of bodily bifurcation: 'Doctors are splitting the seconds of flesh, are cutting through the idea that the skin is a whole, one single garment, and not an infinite net of dividing events' also indicates that not the body is not only identified with space/place, but also with time: 'the body is a false cloak of minutes'.³⁹ Minutes and seconds also signify space or geography, of course, in terms of latitude and longitude, which particularly anticipates the centrality of Greenwich to *London Orbital* and *Sorry Meniscus*. 'Rites of Autopsy' denotes that death is surrounded by rituals that defer the horror of the spectacle of corporeality, the 'awful revelation of meat'; like Brakhage, Sinclair will force us to look.⁴⁰

The divided body in *White Chappell, Scarlet Tracings*

White Chappell, Scarlet Tracings has a tripartite structure, like Sinclair's later novels *Landor's Tower* (2001) and *Dining on Stones* (2004). Book One is entitled 'MANAC', Book Two 'MANAC ES CEM' and Book Three 'JK'. These are an invocation of the initials of the five Ripper victims (Mary Ann Nicholls, Annie Chapman, Elizabeth Stride, Catherine Eddowes, Marie Jeanette Kelly), and, importantly, not a commemoration of the person who perpetrated them. There are also three narrative threads, not two, as most critical commentaries have suggested. Sinclair himself confirms this in *The Verbals*: 'there are actually three elements in the book [but] that third element is sort of lost'.⁴¹ The first concerns Nicholas Lane, Dryfeld and the 'Late Watson' (the narrator), three booksellers who stumble upon a rare 'variant' of Conan Doyle's *A Study in Scarlet*; the second concerns 'Sinclair' and 'S. L. Joblard', a sculptor (based on Brian Catling), whose psychogeographic discussions take them across the symbolic and topographic spaces of Whitechapel; and the third is an oblique version of the 'Ripper' narrative, beginning with William Gull as a child, and narrating his development and later friendship with James Hinton, fellow surgeon and apocalyptic philosopher. Tripartite male relationships also structure the text: Lane, Dryfeld and 'the Late Watson'; Gull, Netley the coachman and the painter Walter Sickert (in Stephen Knight's version of the Ripper mythology); Sinclair,

Joblard and 'Mr Eves', a fellow Ripperologist; Sinclair, Joblard and
Frederick Treves (famous London doctor of the late nineteenth
century) in later chapters. When the relationship centres on only two
men (as in some scenes between Sinclair and Joblard, and between
Gull and Hinton) a third presence is always indicated. As the text
itself suggests, 'When two men meet a third is always present, stranger
to both'.[42] This third presence, here called up by the relationship
between the two men, is the evocation of the numinous figure of
Jack the Ripper, the 'authentic voice' of, or Gothic spectre haunting,
late Victorian Britain. This 'third presence' is most clearly indicated
in the section of the book where Hymie Beaker, immigrant Jewish
East Ender and concentration-camp survivor, is attacked by an
unknown assailant. Having seen (and disturbed) the elderly Beaker
earlier in the day, 'Sinclair' and Joblard later see a television news
report in which

> an identikit portrait of a man seen lurking, talking: horror hybrid, the
> features of myself and Joblard, blended. Gone out of human range.
> Where two men are.[43]

There is an overt allusion here to T. S. Eliot's *The Waste Land*
here, as we saw in the Introduction to this book. In *White Chappell*,
as in the figures of Rabbi Loew (and Treves's) Golem, or Stevenson's
Mr Hyde, a malignant entity is seemingly let loose to rampage across
the city, brought forth by occult forces. The idea of the 'third presence'
is also connected here to a kind of occult birthing caused by the
psychic connection between Joblard and 'Sinclair' and the forces
immanent in Whitechapel. Images of birth are recurrent in Sinclair's
texts, as we have seen with regard to *Suicide Bridge*, and here they
achieve a demonic otherness.

The images of bodily bifurcation that we encountered above in
'Rites of Autopsy' and Gull's description of brain and liver (in *From
Hell*) have a strong resonance for *White Chappell*. They repeat the
twin bodies, conjoined and interpenetrating, of Hand and Hyle that
are at the centre of *Suicide Bridge*'s creation myth. The first page of
the novel introduces Nicholas Lane, a bookseller, a character in a
parallel narrative in the text that describes the finding of a rare copy
of Conan Doyle's *A Study in Scarlet* and subsequent attempts to
transform this commodity into hard cash. Nicholas Lane is discovered
vomiting at the roadside:

> There is an interesting condition of the stomach where ulcers build like coral, fibrous tissue replacing musculature, cicatrix dividing that shady receptacle into two zones, with communication by means of a narrow isthmus: a condition spoken of, with some awe, by the connoisseurs of pathology as 'hour glass stomach'.[44]

The body here is described in terms of geography: the stomach divides into two 'zones', connected by an 'isthmus'. This image of bodily division is repeated insistently throughout the text, with the word 'split' occurring more than a dozen times, including the last page. The boyhood consciousness of William Gull himself speculates that 'There were more slates to be found along the shore. Their edges were sharp, you could cut the heads from fish. You could split your tongue if you licked them', and the image of the 'split tongue' is repeated later.[45] Both emphasise the connection between division (or violent incision) and language, and also deception, for 'split tongue' is akin to 'forked tongue'. Julian Wolfreys, in quoting Samuel Weber, indicates the importance of the word 'split' to Gothic texts and particularly to the figure of the double:

> The double is the ghostlike manifestation of *iterability*, which 'splits' each element while at the same time 'constituting' it through the split . . . the double, the *Doppelgänger*, is the most direct manifestation of this splitting, the *splitting image*, one could say . . . The paradoxical twist, however, is that according to the deconstructive graphics of simultaneity, any identity, including the self or the subject, is constituted only in and through this split, this doubling.

Weber's remark brings into focus the idea that doubling is not simply a rhetorical device but is the figure of haunting par excellence.[46]

Subjectivity is produced through doubling, then; self-identity is inextricably bound up with the double. The subjectivity of Gull is Gothicised through the deployment of the word 'split'. As in the 'case' of the respectable Dr Henry Jekyll and his double, Edward Hyde, the text makes manifest hidden desire through the figure of the *Doppelgänger*, a 'split' which assures the co-identity of subject and other, of Gull and Jack the Ripper. Gull is further implicated in split subjectivity in Sinclair's borrowing from the 'Ripper' mythology. A famous 'spiritualist', Robert Lees, at one point in the Ripper investigation in 1888 led the police to the house of a highly eminent surgeon. This house, Stephen Knight (and Moore and Campbell suggest) was that of Dr William Withey Gull. In *From Hell*, Gull's

wife, in high dudgeon, throws Lees and Inspector Abberline out of
the house and into disgrace. In *White Chappell*, however, once this
scene has occurred, 'Lady Gull' retires to 'her' bedchamber and reveals
the true identity beneath the robe:

> Wiping the mirror with a firm forearm, looks at herself, thick but
> unaroused, a knotted rope-end. Flattened nipples painted around with
> star-shapes, mapped skin: Sir William Withey Gull.[47]

This scene of disguise and masquerade is overlaid with transvestism
and the occult ('painted around with star-shapes'), complicating the
already troubled and split subjectivity of Gull. Hyde, the monstrous
Doppelgänger, becomes Lady Gull, the monstrously impersonated
wife.

In the word 'split', the violence of the autopsy and of the murder
is displaced onto images of somatic disruption, of the body divided
and divided against itself. Stevenson's *Strange Case of Dr Jekyll and
Mr Hyde* (1886), the key intertext here. In late Victorian Gothic, the
variant which Sinclair draws upon in *White Chappell*, the monstrous
lies not without, in ruined castles, marginal European spaces or
intruding into the shadows of ill-lit rooms; it is properly contained
within the space of the 'civilized', produced by it, coterminous with
it. Jack the Ripper, a mythic predator aligned with late Gothic figures
such as Dracula, returns the monstrous to the centre, but in Sinclair's
reading, Gull, unlike Dracula, bears no trace of atavism or racial
otherness. Gull, archetypally an establishment figure, disrupts constructions of good and evil, self and other, 'civilised' and 'monstrous'
upon which earlier Gothic fiction is founded, just as late Victorian
Gothic texts like *Strange Case of Dr Jekyll and Mr Hyde* disrupt
somatic and ethical boundaries.

Hyde is a recurrent figure in *White Chappell*, a body and an identity
monstrously produced or reproduced. Jekyll 'gives birth' to Hyde,
making manifest his desire; this conjunction of transgressive science
with monstrous (i.e., non-biological) reproduction draws upon
Frankenstein (1818, revised 1832), and is also a major motif in *White
Chappell*. In Book 3 of Sinclair's text, the historical figures of the
'Elephant Man' John Merrick, and his 'saviour' and doctor Frederick
Treves, are appropriated. Treves is recast as an occultist, 'breathing
life' into a Golem named Joseph who rampages around the East End.
Merrick, himself a symbol of the human made 'monstrous', is
identified with the Golem, a diabolic creation of the transgressive

doctor. In a curious scene at the end of Book 2 of *White Chappell*, Merrick is lifted onto the body of a semi-delirious girl, presumably to test the 'normality' of his sexual function, again raising the spectre of monstrous reproduction. (Earlier in the text, John Gull, William's father, 'split the eye of an egg' with his teeth, an image which overlays reproduction, vision and division.)[48] This inversion of the reproductive function is also found in Hinton's incestuous fantasy of flagellation with his 'sister' (sister-in-law) Caroline Haddon, and in Gull's post-mortem fantasy at the end of the penultimate chapter. Masturbating over some grapes, he fancies that '[f]rom this bowl his mother must eat. The taboo is broken. She will bear his child'.[49] (In contemporary Ripper mythology, Gull also drugs his victims with treated grapes.) This childlike misapprehension of the process of reproduction, and its investment in fantasy, recurs in the ambitions of the surgeons and doctors of *White Chappell*. Gull, defending himself, says:

> I have hacked out the infected womb that would have bred monsters. But my acts have failed. I did not see that they would *themselves* form the shape of a new myth, and that in removing the outline of the old fear I was planting a spoor of heat that would itself need to be brought to earth, chilled to immobility, stopped.[50]

The 'infected womb' is prostitution itself, another rendering of the body as metaphor for society. The prostitute, the diseased and 'fallen woman', is seen to be unfit for reproduction: the 'infected womb' will breed 'monsters'. Gull, the surgeon-executioner, perpetrator of apocalyptic violence, attempts to bring another, purer world into being through these 'sacrifices', an attempt which fails in both *White Chappell* and *From Hell*. In this sense, Gull and Hinton's messianic and apocalyptic project is a critical parody of mythologies which place bodily sacrifice at the centre of a narrative of rebirth. That, as Sinclair indicated in *Suicide Bridge*, leads to 'FASCISM'.

The bifurcated body in *White Chappell* signifies both psychological division and the fragmented state of London itself, 'split' by the Thames and between east and west. Judith Walkowitz suggests that London had been understood as a 'bifurcated city', east and west culturally and economically opposed: labour and capital, poverty and leisure, criminal and bourgeois, alien and nation. Franco Moretti, in his *Atlas of the European Novel 1800–1900* (1998), makes a similar argument about London's duality, which he diagnoses in Dickens's *Oliver Twist*.

Two half-Londons, that do not add up to a whole . . . It is Dickens' great
wager: to unify the two halves of the city. And his pathbreaking discovery:
once the two halves are joined, the result is *more* than the sum of
its parts. London not only becomes a larger city (obviously enough),
but a more *complex* one; allowing for richer, more unpredictable
interactions.[51]

As we noted in the Introduction to this book, contemporary formations
of urban space involve a double movement, between dispersal and
totality. The 'split' in London not only separates the city, then, but
also unifies it. The fantasy of the *flâneur*, as I suggested in the
Introduction, is of experiencing the city 'as a whole', the unifying
gaze of the male subject bringing the multiplicity of London or Paris
into an imaginary coherence. If, as Walkowitz argues about the
flâneur, 'the fact and fantasy of male bourgeois exploration had long
been an informing feature of nineteenth-century bourgeois male
subjectivity', then Jack the Ripper can be seen as a violent extension
of this fantasy of male agency and invisibility, of the sovereignty of
the male gaze and male desire, playing upon the bodies of women.[52]
  Women, excluded from Walter Benjamin's understanding of
Baudelaire's *flâneur*, are part of the spectacle rather than spectators
themselves, commodities rather than consumers, looked at rather
than looking. While there is no female *flâneuse*, there are women
who *do* stroll in the streets. Deborah Parsons, in her illuminating
study of walking and gender in *Streetwalking the Metropolis* (2000)
suggests the figure of the 'woman in the crowd', the *passante*, who
is the woman who passes by but is able to return the look of the
flâneur. Most apposite to the 'Ripper' mythology and to *White
Chappell* and *From Hell*, however, is the woman who walks for an
explicitly economic purpose: the prostitute or 'streetwalker'. While
the prostitute is neither *passante* nor *flâneuse*, her occupation of the
street can be seen as a direct challenge to the sovereignty of the male
flâneur. In the Whitechapel murders, her body (the commodity) is
subject to an apocalyptic violence which, in its conjunction of
millennialism and medicine, is also a means of bringing the divided
city back together again, to heal through dissection. Judith Walkowitz
again provides a clue to the use of the Ripper mythologies in *White
Chappell* and *From Hell*. In *City of Dreadful Delight*, she states:

> Inquest stories and depositions around Kelly's death provided fodder
> for the next one hundred years of conspiratorial theories, focused on

Kelly as the intended object of the Ripper's revenge, and as the centre of a set of interwoven relationships, linking high and low, East and West in class-divided London.[53]

This illuminates the insistent imagery of bifurcated bodies in *White Chappell* and the murder-autopsy imagery of *From Hell*. The Whitechapel murders do not only signify rupture and disruption to the social body of London, but they also provide a paradoxical textual space to heal that rupture. In staging the divided body, in representing the body taken apart and examined, the split is expelled and healed. The mesh of conspiracy brings together east and west London, Queen Victoria and the prostitutes, the surgeon and the murderer. The violence that heals is resolutely apocalyptic or even messianic. In *White Chappell*, the text suggests: 'What Hinton said, Gull did. Hinton claimed, "Prostitution is dead. I have slain it. I am the Saviour of Women"', a claim which corresponds to the intention of Gull's murder-autopsies.[54] Gull, the terminal *flâneur*, in fact brings a satanic apprehension of our world into being in *From Hell*. This is a grim joke at his own expense, for the apocalypse brings not revelation and the kingdom of heaven, but hell itself.

Notes

1 Michel de Certeau, *The Practice of Everyday Life* (Berkeley, CA and London: University of California Press, 1984), p. 108.
2 Iain Sinclair, *White Chappell, Scarlet Tracings* (London: Paladin, 1988), p. 112.
3 Sinclair, *White Chappell, Scarlet Tracings*, p. 112.
4 Iain Sinclair, *Lud Heat and Suicide Bridge* (London: Granta, 1995), p. 148.
5 Jacques Derrida, *Of Grammatology*, trans. Gayatri Chakravorty Spivak (London and Baltimore: Johns Hopkins University Press, 1976), p. 36.
6 Gayatri Chakravorty Spivak , 'Translator's Preface', in J. Derrida, *Of Grammatology*, trans. Gayatri Chakravorty Spivak (London and Baltimore: Johns Hopkins University Press, 1976), pp. ix–lxxxvii (p. lxx).
7 Iain Sinclair, 'Introduction' to Sir Arthur Conan Doyle, *A Study in Scarlet* (London: Penguin, 2001), pp. vii–xxi (p. xiii).
8 Sinclair, *White Chappell, Scarlet Tracings*, pp. 128–9.
9 Julian Wolfreys, *Victorian Hauntings: Spectrality, Gothic, the Uncanny and Literature* (Basingstoke: Palgrave, 2002), p. x.
10 Julian Wolfreys, *Deconstruction: Derrida* (New York: St Martin's Press; Basingstoke: Macmillan, 1998), p. 148.

11 Wolfreys, *Deconstruction: Derrida*, p. 147.
12 Sinclair, *White Chappell, Scarlet Tracings*, p. 29.
13 William S. Burroughs, 'Les Voleurs', *The Adding Machine: Collected Essays* (London: John Calder, 1985), pp. 19–21 (p. 19).
14 Sinclair, *White Chappell, Scarlet Tracings*, p. 64.
15 Sinclair, 'Introduction' to *A Study in Scarlet*, p. ix.
16 Sinclair, *White Chappell, Scarlet Tracings*, p. 61.
17 Wolfreys, *Deconstruction: Derrida*, p. 153.
18 Sinclair, 'Introduction' to *A Study in Scarlet*, p. xvi.
19 Sinclair, *White Chappell, Scarlet Tracings*, p. 148.
20 Re/Search, *J. G. Ballard*, 8/9 (San Francisco: Re/Search Publications, 1984), p. 42.
21 Sinclair, *White Chappell, Scarlet Tracings*, pp. 209–10.
22 Sinclair, *White Chappell, Scarlet Tracings*, p. 210.
23 Wolfreys, *Victorian Hauntings*, p. xi.
24 Sinclair, *White Chappell, Scarlet Tracings*, pp. 128–9.
25 Judith Walkowitz, *City of Dreadful Delight: Narratives of Sexual Danger in Late-Victorian London* (London: Virago, 1992), p. 191.
26 Sinclair, *White Chappell, Scarlet Tracings*, pp. 28 and 29.
27 Sinclair, *White Chappell, Scarlet Tracings*, p. 29.
28 Alan Moore and Eddie Campbell, *From Hell* (Paddington, Queensland, Australia: Eddie Campbell Comics, 1999), Ch. 10, p. 14.
29 Jonathan Sawday, *The Body Emblazoned: Dissection and the Human Body in Renaissance Culture* (London and New York: Routledge, 1995), p. 54.
30 Sawday, *The Body Emblazoned*, p. 80.
31 Sinclair, *White Chappell, Scarlet Tracings*, p. 64.
32 Sinclair, *Lud Heat and Suicide Bridge*, p. 54.
33 Sinclair, *Lud Heat and Suicide Bridge*, p. 57.
34 Sinclair, *Lud Heat and Suicide Bridge*, p. 57.
35 Sinclair, *Lud Heat and Suicide Bridge*, p. 57.
36 Quoted in W. F. Bynum, *Science and the Practice of Medicine in the Nineteenth Century* (Cambridge and New York: Cambridge University Press, 1994), p. 33.
37 Roy Porter, *The Greatest Benefit to Mankind: A Medical History of Humanity from Antiquity to the Present* (London: Fontana, 1999), p. 307.
38 Porter, *The Greatest Benefit to Mankind*, p. 312.
39 Sinclair, *Lud Heat and Suicide Bridge*, p. 58.
40 Sinclair, *Lud Heat and Suicide Bridge*, p. 54.
41 Iain Sinclair, with Kevin Jackson, *The Verbals* (Tonbridge: Worple Press, 2003), p. 114.
42 Sinclair, *White Chappell, Scarlet Tracings*, p. 36.

43 Sinclair, *White Chappell, Scarlet Tracings*, p. 97.
44 Sinclair, *White Chappell, Scarlet Tracings*, p. 11.
45 Sinclair, *White Chappell, Scarlet Tracings*, p. 29.
46 Wolfreys, *Victorian Hauntings*, pp. 14–15.
47 Sinclair, *White Chappell, Scarlet Tracings*, pp. 172–3.
48 Sinclair, *White Chappell, Scarlet Tracings*, p. 27.
49 Sinclair, *White Chappell, Scarlet Tracings*, p. 206.
50 Sinclair, *White Chappell, Scarlet Tracings*, p. 193.
51 Franco Moretti, *Atlas of the European Novel 1800–1900* (London: Verso, 1998), p. 86.
52 Walkowitz, *City of Dreadful Delight*, p. 16.
53 Walkowitz, *City of Dreadful Delight*, p. 218.
54 Sinclair, *White Chappell, Scarlet Tracings*, p. 113.

3

The widow; or, the critical baroque

It is impossible to outrage the baroque realism of the dying century. Imagine the worse, then double it. (Iain Sinclair)[1]

Introduction: the last of England

In the Introduction to this book, I argued that Sinclair's poetic and political trajectory in the late 1960s and the early 1970s can be understood, in part, through what Fredric Jameson has called a 'rupture' in the post-war socio-political landscape which took place between 1967 and 1973. This rupture inaugurates postmodernity: the society of the spectacle, the death of the subject, the waning or crisis in historicity. I also proposed that the so-called 'spatial turn' in critical theory (perhaps most notably in evidence in the work of Jameson and Foucault, but also found in the 'L. A. School' of urban geographers) was itself a symptom of this wider 'crisis in historicity'. Sinclair's own poetic practice, which turns from the 'documentary' text *Kodak Mantra Diaries* (1971) to *Lud Heat* (1975) marks Sinclair's own 'spatial turn', away from the quasi-revolutionary politics of the counter-culture and towards 'psychogeography'. Later in this chapter I will return to the wider implications of Sinclair's small-press publication activities in the period between *Suicide Bridge* (1979) and *White Chappell, Scarlet Tracings* (1987), with regard to the model of avant-gardist or oppositional modes of artistic and poetic practice that Sinclair models in *Downriver* (1991, cited edition 1995) and *Lights Out for the Territory* (1998). I will begin this chapter, however, with a contextualisation of the 'rupture' with regard to British post-war history and society.

In a 2004 article in the *London Review of Books*, Perry Anderson writes of a wave of books published in France which identified a crisis in French national identity: that the French nation-state (identified with a much larger idea or ideological project, namely 'the Republic') was somehow 'in decline'. While *'le declinisme'* was a new phenomenon, however, 'the whole controversy [seemed] like a rerun of long-standing debates on decline in this country', 'this country', meaning Britain. Anderson then gives a potted version of British decline:

> British diminution since the war has been a long-drawn-out process. But its starting point is clear: the illusions bred by victory in 1945, under a leader of 1914 vintage, followed virtually without intermission by the realities of financial dependency on Washington, austerity at home and imperial retreat abroad [. . .] Little alteration of political arrangements; moderate growth but still low productivity; pinched universities and crumbling railways; the unmoved authority of Treasury, Bank and City; an underling diplomacy. The record lacks high relief. The British way of coming down in the world might itself be termed a mediocre affair.[2]

The sense of 'decline', or, following Anderson, what I might here call 'declinism' (post-war Britain seen through the lens of what Patrick Wright, in *On Living in an Old Country* (1985), called an 'entropic view of history') can be found in many texts, from the political left and from the right.[3] Raphael Samuel, in *Island Stories: Unravelling Britain*, writes that 'No less striking than the collapse of British power, and this country's relegation to a second- or even third-class industrial nation, is the unravelling of any unitary idea of national character'.[4] Patrick Wright notes the 'rabid' nostalgia that imbues 'heritage' magazines of the 1980s such as *This England*, contrasting contemporary decline with an idealised pastoral 'Deep England'. 'Heritage' is, according to Wright, the corollary of an 'entropic view of history'; however, historians and political theorists from the left have also asserted Britain's post-war 'crisis' and diminution.

Tom Nairn, writing what Roger Luckhurst has recently called 'a series of emergency bulletins' between 1971 and 1977 (published in the Anderson-edited *New Left Review* and collected in *The Break-Up of Britain* of 1981), also diagnosed a British nation-state in 'crisis'.[5] In the slightly later 'The Crisis of the British State', published in the *New Left Review* in 1981, Nairn identifies both a structural diagnosis of decline and one that seems to indicate a particular crisis in the

1970s. The structural elements, writes Nairn, form a diagnosis of
the 'weakness of twentieth century British *society*':

> Economic collapse from a position of leadership to one of relative
> backwardness; its consequent loss of power and international prestige,
> and subservience to American aims; and its range of picturesque
> anachronisms, from the Windsor monarchy to the inimitable proletarian
> café.[6]

The 'decline, mediocrity and archaism' that Nairn sees as characteristic
of British society are, in his analysis, related to a structural problem
with the British nation-state – the United Kingdom itself. When
Nairn lists the symptoms of the current (late 1970s/early 1980s)
'crisis', its components are revealing: 'Ireland, mounting street
violence in the greater English cities, the disintegration of the Labour
Party (and hence of the old two-party stability), continuing separatist
agitation in Wales and Scotland, a renewed economic crisis *after* the
brief reprieve of North Sea oil'.[7] Two of the symptoms directly allude
to the 'break-up of Britain' which Nairn takes as his title and theme:
it is in fact a systemic failing of the legitimacy of the British nation-
state which relies not upon principles of democracy (Britons are
subjects not citizens) but an 'aboriginal sovereignty-myth: the 'Crown-
in-Parliament and the (literally) absolute authority of the latter'.[8] The
1970s 'crisis' of the British nation-state is then merely a reflection
of its bodged foundation: the 'break-up' is the ultimate political
consequence of the Acts of Union.

The 'acceleration' in the 'decline-spiral' is caused by what Nairn
calls 'the disintegration of Labourism'.[9] Like other analysts of post-
war Britain, Nairn posits an initial 'post-World War II consensus',
though he differs from other writers here in arguing not for some
kind of centrist (liberal, social-democratic) common ground between
Labour and the Conservatives (usually characterised by the word
'Butskellism' which conflates the names of two senior politicians
from the parties, Hugh Gaitskell and R. A. Butler), but for the
centrality of 'Labourism' to the post-war settlement. 'Labourism' can
be seen as a social-democratic impetus towards ameliorating the
harsher effects of capitalism through welfare programmes, free health
and education provision, and limited redistribution of wealth. In this,
he suggests that the defenders of the 'welfare state' and the 'Keynesian
compromise' from the right (or centrist) wing of the Labour Party
fought an increasingly doomed battle against 'economic breakdown

and reactionary assaults'.[10] Nairn sees the period 1964 to 1979 as crucial in the 'disintegration of Labourism', through the failures of two Labour administrations (1964–70, 1974–9); here we can connect what Fredric Jameson, in 'Periodizing the Sixties', pinpointed as the two rupture points (1967 and 1973–4) which inaugurate the era of postmodernity. Nairn suggests that in the periods 1964–7 and 1974–6 the 'modernization-dream' of Labourism 'crumbles into mere crisis-management, discrediting the progressives'.[11] The end of consensus, of the foundations of the post-war settlement, is often attributed to the coming to power of Margaret Thatcher and her monetarist policies in 1979; Nairn insists that it is the prior failure of a centrist 'Labourism' that creates the conditions for public support of right-wing reaction.

Alan Sinfield, in *Literature, Politics and Culture in Postwar Britain* (1989) comes to a similar diagnosis, but his terms are different. He suggests that 'welfare capitalism' dominates the post-war consensus, which he defines as a kind of corporatism in which 'the state takes on the running of the economy and the responsibility for social justice, and seeks, through a network of influence and control, to reconcile capital and labour by drawing them into the process of government'.[12] In Britain, argues Sinfield, welfare capitalism was 'doomed almost from the start because it requires a powerful commit-ment to social justice to secure popular co-operation'; unfortunately, the equation between 'social justice' and 'collective benefits' for society as a whole was undermined by the need to inculcate a culture of consumerism which ultimately rests upon 'competitive individu-alism'.[13] Sinfield connects this with the energies of the 1960s – consumption allied to 'disrespect for traditional authority' – to argue that Thatcherism is a completion of the project of the 1960s as much as it is a rejection of, and reaction to it. Sinfield locates the key points of crisis in 1968 ('when a considerable proportion of people became sceptical about the viability of social-democratic institutions') and 1976, when the then Labour Chancellor, Denis Healey, was forced to accept an economic austerity package as part of a financing agreement with the International Monetary Fund.[14] It is the failure of the post-war consensus, manifested in these two points of crisis, which, argues Sinfield, led directly to the election of Margaret Thatcher, whose political project it was to dismantle the vestiges of the post-war settlement.

The 'end of consensus' of the 1970s serves as the background for the 'savage comedy' of Sinclair's 1991 novel, *Downriver*. I suggested in the Introduction to this book that Sinclair's rejection of the politics of the counter-culture, and a move into the mythic, mirrors the failure of collective or revolutionary political practice, and a retreat into the discourse of the self. It also corresponds to the crisis in faith in 'social-democratic institutions' diagnosed by Sinfield as crucial to the end of consensus. It is no coincidence that the most widely quoted of all judgements upon Sinclair's work is that of Patrick Wright in *A Journey Through Ruins* (1993): Sinclair's 'symbolic mapping of London actually makes him less of an abracadabra man than a poet of the Welfare State, the laureate of its morbidity and failure'.[15] While the traces of the welfare state's 'morbidity' can certainly be located in the riven London of *Lud Heat* and *Suicide Bridge*, it is *Downriver*, which stands at the other end of the Thatcher era, which signifies Sinclair's return to a direct (rather than mythic) engagement with the political and cultural fabric of Britain for the first time since *Kodak Mantra Diaries*. That Sinclair turns to 'savage comedy', apocalyptic satire and Gothic overtones for his investigation of the matter of Britain, rather than returning to the 'documentary' form, perhaps indicates the traces of his rejection of a collectivist politics some twenty years after the event. It is not until 1997, with *Lights Out for the Territory* (which documents the bleakness of the Major years and was, ironically, Sinclair's commercial breakthrough) and 2002's *London Orbital* (for which see Chapter 6) that he returned to major works of non-fiction. Indeed, perhaps *Lights Out* seems more inflected by 'declinism' than *Downriver*: in his 1991 novel, Sinclair draws upon what he has characterised as the 'demonic' energies of Thatcherism to create a text of some force and energy.

Witness and agent

The form of *Downriver* itself reflects the 'break-up of Britain'. The text consists of twelve 'tales', which do not in themselves form a coherent narrative. While roughly mapped onto a journey down the River Thames (the river providing a kind of fluid backbone for the fabulations of the various tales), which ends in a pilgrimage to the Isle of Sheppey in Kent, at the mouth of the Thames Estuary, the tales feature a variety of characters and situations which explore the cultural and psychogeographic landscape of London after

Thatcherism. Robert Bond perceptively aligns the formal properties of *Downriver* with Sinclair's earlier poetic practice: the 'open field poetics' that we investigated in Chapter 1. Sinclair's 'open-field narratives', argues Bond, are put in the service of an exploration of 'London as a closed system', and are suffused by images of entrapment and enclosure.[16] It might be argued, therefore, that the form of *Downriver* deliberately resists totality, a totality that might be analogous to the closure of urban space in the era of postmodernity. In fact, Bond insists upon a 'dialectical relation between centralization and dispersal' in Sinclair's later works:

> The population dispersal – actual physical separation – effected by
> suburbanization is one sure sign of capitalism's exercise of its technical
> forces. Fractured communities model alienation in spatial form [. . .]
> Ejected from the centre, the dispersed community is re-formed in the
> pseudo-community of the housing or shopping development.[17]

The centralisation of power (in the hands of Prime Minister Thatcher and the Conservative Government) is mirrored in the Docklands developments of the late 1980s and 1990s: in Sinclair's analysis, this foreclosure of urban space is the imposition of an alienated and entirely artificial 'city of the future' onto the historical and lived space of London's eastern riverside, an imposition that displaces both the inhabitants and the history of London:

> The avenues! Treeless, broad, focusing on nothing. Dramatic perspec-
> tives leading to no revelation: no statues of public men, no fountains,
> no slogans. Nothing. No beggars, no children, no queues for buses.
> This city of the future, this swampland Manhattan, this crystal synthesis
> of capital, is already posthumous: a memorial to its own lack of nerve.
> It shudders and lets slip its ghosts. It swallows the world's dross. Isle
> of Dogs, receiving station of everything that is lost and without value.[18]

Curiously, the city of avenues that seems to be posited in opposition to the Docklands development is nothing other than that of the boulevards of Paris after the work of Haussman: itself a deliberate reordering of city space along ideological lines, overwriting that which was lived. In Sinclair's work, we can see the same emphases in a late 1990s text, *Sorry Meniscus* (1999) which fulminates against the Millennium Dome. There it is New Labour's project (inherited from the Conservative Major Government) that erases the social and historical particularities of Bugsby's Marshes and implants a simulacrum of lived space.

In the chapter 'The Isle of Doges (Vat City plc)' in *Downriver*, Sinclair gives his apocalyptic satirical imagination full reign. In it, Sinclair's own birthplace, South Wales, has been '"leased" to Onokura-Mishima Investments (Occidental)', and the Isle of Dogs sold to the Vatican (and nicknamed 'Isle of Doges' or 'Vat City'):

> This deregulated isthmus of Enterprise was a new Venice, slimy with canals, barnacled with *palazzi*, pillaged art, lagoons, leper hulks: a Venice overwhelmed by Gotham City, a raked grid of canyons and stuttering aerial railways.[19]

The pun Dogs/Doges, and the references to a Gothicised/Gothamised Venice, indicate that what is at the heart of Sinclair's satire here is power, temporal power transformed (as elsewhere in his writings) into occult forms. Several characters (such as the artists Imar O'Hagan, a version of the real-life Gavin Jones) decide to embark on a 'hero-voyage' by coracle to try to penetrate the mysteries of a secret ceremony that 'is intended to halt time, wound its membrane and give them access to unimaginable powers'.[20] The group of men eventually comes to witness a sexualised power-ritual that owes everything to the imagination of Dennis Wheatley.

The imagined presence of Stephen Hawking at this ceremony, however, indicates a return here to the concern with myth and space-time that was found in *Suicide Bridge*: Hawking intones '"Space-time has no beginning, no end. There was no moment of Creation. The boundary condition of the Universe is that it has no boundary [. . .] Imag mag mag inary time is sss real ti ti time"'.[21] Time itself begins to disintegrate at the end of Hawking's pronouncements, the language fragmenting into dissonant parts. The ceremony is then an intervention into space-time, and another of the characters who witness the event, Davy Locke, suggests that:

> You realize that we may actually have been flung back into an ahistorical anomaly: a confirmation of Hawking's absence of boundaries, a liquid matrix, a schizophrenic actuality that contains the fascinating possibility of finding ourselves placed in post-modern docklands and *quattrocento* Florence, *at the same time*.[22]

As we saw in the last chapter, Sinclair often uses a model of imagination infecting reality and even temporal causation (the writer works ahead of the events she or he is transcribing): here, '"If the imagination is primary, then anything we can imagine must lie in wait to ambush us"'.[23] It is important to note how Sinclair here stresses the responsibility of the writer for his or her own fictions, that the active connection between the imaginary and the real enforces a sense of the consequences (ethical, actual, fantastical) of writing. If the ceremony in the Docklands is intended to release occult powers and make monsters manifest, in some senses this stands as a symbol for the act of imaginative writing itself, and the monsters released are Sinclair's own.

The issue of writerly agency is one that has occupied critics of the novel. Robert Bond argues that 'the novel's concern with the constricting nature of naturalistic method is also driven by Sinclair's awareness of the contemporary writer's lack of social agency';[24] David Cunningham persuasively argues that what is 'perhaps unique about *Downriver* is the text's own immanent registering of the dangers involved' in witnessing the 'darkly disturbing world depicted' in the novel;[25] Rachel Potter asserts that 'there is an almost obsessional reflex concerning the status of the witness as a fictional device'.[26] To witness is to be present, and to record what transpires; however, it seems to preclude intervention into the events represented. As the narrator writes of the occult ceremony in 'The Isle of Doges', 'We could see everything, but we were powerless; we could not intercede'.[27] Ultimately, in the final chapter of the novel, the narrator ('Sinclair') turns over the role to one of the characters, the sculptor S. L. Joblard (based on Brian Catling) who appears in this text as he had in *White Chappell, Scarlet Tracings*. The narrator does this by letter (again a displacement of agency), in which he writes:

> I can't carry on; or, rather, I can participate, provoke the action, but I cannot report it. For a whole dreary catalogue of reasons, this has become impossible. Anything I touch transforms itself into a fresh metaphor for pain and anguish, burns those around me, leaves me unharmed. I want to offer you the protection of the narrator's role.[28]

Joblard understands this refusal of the narratorial role to be a piece of 'cheap trickery', as of course Sinclair (the author) narrates through one of his fictional characters who does not have autonomy from his fiction (and in fact performs a near-identical role to the narrator 'Sinclair').[29] Why then this gesture? Rachel Potter entirely distrusts it. She argues that Sinclair's writing 'is a slum-tourism, an occult-tourism' which, in representing the 'journeying witness to the physical and cognitive realities of the place, he is firmly placed as a voyeur'. Potter's argument that 'Sinclair is not willing to take possession of the horror' he depicts in his novels seems to run directly counter to the 'obsessional reflex' with the act of witness she notes in *Downriver*, and to the reading I offer above of the writerly responsibility with regard to the imaginative 'monsters' that are manifested at the end of 'The Isle of Doges' chapter.[30] Clearly, Sinclair's 'letter' to Joblard indicate his awareness of the problematic relation between event and writing, and awareness that infuses his thinking throughout Sinclair's texts. If the turning-over of narration to Joblard is in some sense an abdication, it is also an acknowledgement of the responsibility of the writer not merely to 'report' but actively engage – to 'participate', to 'provoke' – that returns *Downriver* once again to the oppositional practice of the counter-culture.

The problematic of agency indicates an anxiety about the relationship between the kind of avant-gardism represented by countercultural artistic or poetic practice, and the possibility of intervening in a wider social or cultural matrix through reaching a broader audience. In *The Verbals*, Sinclair notes the difficulties faced by those artists and poets he prizes with regard to audience, and in a sense, his 'Return of the Reforgotten' projects indicate Sinclair's willingness to try to help others to reach the wider audience he achieved with *Lights Out for the Territory* and *London Orbital*. Where Allen Fisher and Brian Catling have become professors (Catling at the Ruskin School of Art in Oxford), Sinclair notes, Barry McSweeney 'drank himself to death, basically. Wanting an audience, which another culture would have given him'.[31] Robert Bond has argued that Sinclair, in *Downriver*, represents 'an artistic anti-economy economy' where artists 'market their art internally, if at all'.[32] The unfortunate emblem of this lack of complicity with the market forces is the poet Nicholas Moore, who is at the centre of the chapter 'The Guilty River' in *Downriver* (which immediately follows 'The Isle of Doges'). Moore, once well known in the 1930s, descends into obscurity and neglect; a dialogue between 'IS' and the poet Peter Riley is reported in which Riley's encounter with the old and infirm Moore, holed up in entropically disorganised rooms near Orpington in Kent, reveals the fate of the neglected modernist. The narrator embarks on a kind of pilgrimage to (the now-deceased) Moore's house, but can find no entrance, and no resolution to the poet's exclusion. Twice the text refers to Moore's 'exile': once as 'sentimental exile' in comparison with the Cambridge spy Guy Burgess in Moscow, and also as a 'condition of exile'. 'If the culture at large refuses to imagine your existence', writes Sinclair, 'how strong is the impulse to spit in its eye? Or: do you stick modestly to your last and wait (to the death) for a tap on the window?'.[33] The motif of exile is strong in Sinclair's writings about the 'Reforgotten' poets and artists; we shall return to it in the next chapter.

Here, though, I would like to question the idea of an avant-gardist artistic practice successfully forming some kind of 'anti-economy', in opposition to the dominant form of commodity exchange which is symbolised in the Docklands development. As the fates of McSweeney and Moore attest, an art without an audience ultimately proves self-negating. The logical end-point of such a poetic practice is that the most valuable art is one that has no audience at all. As I have suggested above, Sinclair's activities in texts such as *Lights Out for the Territory* indicate that he wants to bring artists he understands to be important to wider attention. In fact, Sinclair's own poetry of the output of the 1980s, self-published through his own 'Hoarse Commerce' press, dwindles to print runs in two figures. *Fluxions* of 1983 was printed in an edition of twenty-one; *Flesh Eggs and Scalp Metal* (1983) in an edition of twelve; *Autistic Poses* (1985) just eleven copies. The punning title of the desk-top 'press' Sinclair published them under indicates that these texts were themselves outside a system of monetary exchange, 'given away' to confirm their non-commodity status. As Sinclair notes, however, in the 1980s he gave himself over to the 'quasi-literary' activity of bookdealing, which would eventually provide him with some of the material for *White Chappell, Scarlet Tracings*. Somewhat ironically, of course, bookdealing places the material object of the book at the very centre of an economic system of commodities and monetary exchange. Sinclair's own example therefore indicates that the artist's exclusion from a capitalist economy is, in fact, the end of artistic production rather than a form of opposition to that economy.

Sinclair's later career seems to negotiate between the poles of non-complicity with commodity exchange and the need to find a wider audience to keep the means of artistic production open. Sinclair's return to the 'documentary' form in *Lights Out for the Territory, London Orbital* and *Edge of the Orison* has in fact gained him a much wider audience than either his fiction or (particularly) his poetry. Since 1997, Sinclair has mixed fiction with major publishers (*Landor's Tower* and *Dining on Stones*) with non-fiction (*Rodinsky's Room, London Orbital, Edge of the Orison*), and with occasional, more experimental texts (*Liquid City, Sorry Meniscus, Dark Lanthorns, Saddling the Rabbit, White Goods*) which are often companion pieces to major works and are published by small presses, such as Goldmark or Etruscan Books. While there is often a convergence of theme or concerns between 'major' and 'small press' texts, Sinclair's decision to publish in this way certainly indicates a sense of the necessity of audience to maintain himself as a writer. Through bookdealing or through publishing deals with such 'major' and mainstream houses as Penguin, Sinclair's work emphasises the necessary connection between complicity and agency that we can find as early on in Sinclair's work as *Downriver.*

The skin floor

Docklands, in *Downriver*, is 'posthumous', a necropolis devoted to capital. Where, in *Lud Heat*, the alignments of the Hawksmoor churches symbolise malign control over urban space, here the Docklands developments become yet another occult intervention into the fabric of London, distorting the city and expelling its citizens. The emphasis upon ruptures in the fabric of 'space-time' symbolise the 'break-up' or 'disintegration' of the social fabric of Britain, and more particularly London, after the end of consensus. The disruptive economic energies that 'welfare capitalism' was instituted to protect its citizens from, in Alan Sinfield's terms, find full expression in the Docklands.

In *Future Tense* (1990), Robert Hewison identifies the changes in the cultural fabric of Britain during the 1980s, and includes Sinclair in his analysis in a chapter called 'The Last of England', which is taken, like my own section title in this chapter, from Derek Jarman's film of the same name. In *The Last of England* (1987), Jarman filmed in the then-derelict Royal Victoria Docks (the setting for *Downriver's* 'The Isle of Doges'), to create an apocalyptic vision of a Britain taken over by balaclava-helmeted gunmen, a Britain characterised by urban decay and violence, by dispersal and displacement: a Britain whose decline is in the terminal stage. Jarman's apocalyptic vision of Britain after the end of consensus finds its analogue in Sinclair's *Downriver:* as Hewison notes, it is at the eastern edge of the city, where post-industrial decay becomes an 'enterprise zone', that the effects of the raw edge of capital can be seen.

Hewison takes as his symbol of the 'private enterprise regeneration' of the Docklands the area now known as 'Tobacco Dock' in Wapping. In an echo of the work of Mike Davis, whose *City of Quartz* (1998) catalogued the privatisation of public space in downtown Los Angeles in the 1980s, Hewison suggests that the conjunction of warehouse and shopping mall (the 'regenerated' use of the post-industrial space) is 'where nineteenth and twenty-first century space meet . . . in the creation of defensible space'.[34] This privatised space is itself 'post-Modern pastiche', using iron gazebos, a portcullis, a clock tower; but what this reinvention masks is the history of the building, and of the Docklands, itself. This finds its apogee in 'Henry's Bar' which presents itself as floating free from history, 'neither in the present nor the past'; the bar appears in the guise of 'the conservatory of some late-Imperial outpost, with wicker chairs, potted ferns, coloured glass partitions, brass ceiling fans'. Tobacco Dock becomes a simulacrum of history, an artificial or imaginary space which, in Hewison's words, 'denies the old by a inserting a new fabric that itself denies that it is new'.[35] What we have in Tobacco Dock is no longer history, but 'heritage'.

Patrick Wright, in *On Living in an Old Country* (1985), exposes the discourse of 'heritage' in a Britain 'in decline'. In fact, he asserts that 'the definition of heritage has been expanded in the recent sense of decline': what I have earlier called 'declinism' and 'heritage' are connected in Wright's argument in depending upon a shared 'entropic view of history'.[36] This view of history is a nostalgic and in some senses reactionary one, in that it views modernity with suspicion and distaste, and looks backward to a kind of golden age 'heritage England' that is entirely imaginary. Wright's analysis of the discourse of 'National Heritage' is pertinent to the regeneration of Docklands and Tobacco Dock in particular:

> National Heritage involves the extraction of history – of the idea of historical significance and potential – from a denigrated everyday life and its restaging or display in certain sanctioned sites, events, images and conceptions [. . .] Abstracted and redeployed, history seems to be purged of political tension: it becomes a unifying spectacle, the settling of all disputes.[37]

History becomes a spectacle and a commodity, one with an ideological function: to mask the conflicts of material history and replace it with a dehistoricised space of consumption, in which heritage is itself consumed. This is symbolised, for Robert Hewison, in Tobacco Dock, whose very name enacts a masking of history: the warehouse was once known as 'the skin floor'.

Hewison only obliquely refers to the economic and political structures which are the foundations of the mercantile trade that constitutes the material history of the Docklands: that 'the skin floor' is a site of empire. The presence of 'Henry's Bar' repeats the masking of history by 'heritage', where the fact of empire becomes merely decor. Hewison's own language self-consciously takes on the language of empire and colonisation: 'Next to the heart of a major European capital lay a new Australia ripe for colonization. But Docklands had its unseen aborigines', who are dispersed by the intrusion of the new city of capital.[38] Sinclair himself, in *Downriver*, refers to the inhabitants of east London as 'aboriginals'. In 'The Case of the Premature Mourners', the penultimate chapter, Sinclair presents the fate of unwanted others in imperial London: 'Dissenters and criminals (marginal to the needs and legitimate desires of the state) were once spilled into the wilderness of an unmapped world: where they fought for breath with savage aboriginals'.[39] Here, Sinclair signifies a basic equivalence between British 'undesirables' transported to the margins of empire, and the 'savage aboriginals' whose very presence is masked by (and often physically eliminated by) the intrusion of the colonial subjects. In the final chapter, Joblard and Sinclair journey to the Isle of Sheppey, where London's displaced make a home: 'Leysdown on Sea is the ancestral dreamsite of a Lost Tribe: all the aboriginal cockney characteristics, celebrated in fiction and song, have migrated here'.[40] Curiously, the Kent coast close to the mouth of the Thames estuary is where another 'exile' resided, one I have already mentioned: Derek Jarman, who famously tended his garden in Dungeness. In *Downriver*, this, though, is a forced migration; the Last Londoners exist in a kind of displaced netherworld at the mouth of the Thames, a terminal point for the city's working class.

The presence of colonial discourse, shared by Sinclair and Hewison, points towards a major intertextual presence in *Downriver*, that of Joseph Conrad and most particularly *Heart of Darkness*. (Hewison's phrase about 'the heart of a major European capital', cited above, could also be seen as a kind of allusion to Conrad.) Docklands is a contemporary 'heart of darkness' on the eastern edge of the city, 'one of the dark places of the earth' in Conrad's phrase.[41] Where Marlow tells his tale upon the *Nellie*, moored in the 'lower reaches of the

Thames', Sinclair and his confrères embark on journeys downriver, towards Tilbury and ultimately to Sheppey. Where Conrad relocated the 'heart of darkness' from the margins of empire to the imperial capital – the Thames 'seemed to lead into the heart of an immense darkness' in the famous final phrase of the novella – Sinclair and Hewison seem to indicate that the Docklands development is in itself a kind of colonialism.[42] This connection is made explicit at the end of the first chapter of *Downriver*, where the sculptor Joblard puts together a montage of twelve postcards (not coincidentally the same number as the chapters of the novel) from the imperial past. These are entitled 'Joblard's HEART OF DARKNESS'.[43] The text describes each card in detail, tableaux which represent scenes from African colonialism, including hunting, ivory poachers, and exoticised 'natives' and 'cannibals'. Sinclair stresses the German or Dutch provenance of the cards, signifying their connection to the Belgian colony of the Congo which is the destination of Marlow's journey in *Heart of Darkness*. However, at the end of the sequence of cards, Joblard notes that only one had been sent by post, and not from Africa to England, but from London (particularly Leytonstone in the East End) to Africa: 'Nothing could match the mysteries shrouding the heart of Leytonstone'.[44]

In *Heart of Darkness*, Marlow talks of the 'many blank spaces of the earth', unmapped or uncolonised areas that 'got filled in since my boyhood with rivers and lakes and names'.[45] The 'blank spaces' themselves legitimate colonisation, for they rest upon the assumption that there are no 'aboriginals' inhabiting the space, only an empty resource-field to exploit. The Docklands development, characterised as 'riverside opportunities' by Sinclair, itself reimagines the Docks as a 'blank space', in which any remaining 'aboriginals' can be displaced to Sheppey or beyond. Another, equally famous, passage from *Heart of Darkness* illuminates *Downriver*'s imagination of the 'regeneration' of London, particularly in the chapter 'The Isle of Doges':

> The conquest of the earth, which mostly means the taking it away from those who have a different complexion or slightly flatter noses than ourselves, is not a pretty thing when you look into it too much. What redeems it is the idea only. An idea at the back of it; not a sentimental pretence but an idea; and an unselfish belief in the idea – something you can set up, and bow down before, and offer a sacrifice to.[46]

The centrality of dispossession to colonialism could not be more plain. Crucially, the narrator Marlow ends the passage with a reference to sacrifice, a sacrifice in the name of the 'civilising' idea that informs the reality of colonial dispossession and destruction. *Downriver* consistently refers to sacrifice and suicide, associated with the river. In the second chapter, Dr Adam Tenbrücke, the owner of a 'shelf of Conrads', later chains himself to the riverside and drowns himself. In 'The Isle of Doges', the magic ritual is meant to be sealed by sacrifice; and there are references to the *Princess Alice* riverboat disaster throughout the text, in which dozens of people drowned when a pleasure cruiser sank on the Thames in the 1880s. These literal sacrifices symbolise the elimination of the lived everyday space of the Docklands dwellers in the name of 'development', just as the victims of the 1888 Whitechapel murders in *White Chappell, Scarlet Tracings* are sacrificed to the occult forces that deform the fabric of London.

In *Downriver*, there are traces of a reverse colonisation which Peter Brooker, writing in *Modernity and Metropolis* (2002) finds troubling. In 'The Isle of Doges', 'Mother London' (a reference to Michael Moorcock) is described as 'splitting into fragments, the overlicked shell of a chocolate tortoise'. The 'occult logic of "market forces" dictated a new geography', one in which the city is riven along ethnic or communal lines.[47] The section Brooker finds especially disturbing runs as follows:

> Banglatown, as it was vulgarly called, replaced the perished dream of Spitalfields. The 'born-again' Huguenots dumped their Adam fireplaces, and ran. The stern fathers of the One True Faith sent columns of black smoke twisting skywards as they redressed the violations of culture of drunkards and apostates that surrounded them. Vulture priests, percolating hatred beneath their turbans, bearded in a nest of absolutes, spittle their chanting congregation with infallible accusations.[48]

Brooker argues that Bangladeshis are 'as if invisible' in Sinclair's fiction, and Bengalis, when represented, shown negatively. While not accusing Sinclair of racism, Brooker does assert that *Downriver* falls prey to the power of 'whiteness' (articulated by Richard Dyer) as a representational figure 'whose apparent transparency is the very sign of its undeclared but hegemonic ethnicity', and suggests that Sinclair's texts betray 'the continuing, unresolved relations of Islam and the West'.[49] Brooker should probably write what he really means here, and directly accuse Sinclair of racism. The passage I have quoted certainly seems inflected with Islamophobia, and the clause 'vulgarly called', which might offer a reading in which the foregoing is the discourse of the 'vulgar' rather than the narrator, is too slight to really bear the weight of this (generous) interpretation. More likely, I would suggest, is that this passage shows the traces of the then-recent *fatwa* issued against Salman Rushdie (an 'apostate') after the publication of *The Satanic Verses* (1989), Rushdie's own mythic and apocalyptic fabulation on London and its ethnic tapestry. It is important to stress, in Sinclair's defence, that later texts seem particularly impelled towards investigating the ethnic history of the East End, but Brooker is accurate in his judgement in that Sinclair's focus is away from the South Asian inhabitants of Brick Lane and its environs, and more towards the vanishing Jewish culture of Whitechapel, of which David Rodinsky is an emblem. This vanishing itself allows it to be read as a sign-system of traces, rather than confronted as a living space.

What connects the erasures of history under the sign of 'heritage', the sense of British 'decline', and a concentration upon the spaces of London is what Roger Luckhurst, following Paul Gilroy and Ian Baucom, terms 'post-imperial melancholy'. This accompanies the 'diminution' of British life we found at the beginning of this chapter identified by Anderson, Nairn and others. Luckhurst notes that 'Baucom isolates a narrative of English identity in the promise of a *locale*, the "auratic", magical place, which gives its occupants a sense of belonging'.[50] This gives another sense, perhaps more troubling, to the discussion of Sinclair's psychogeographic project, which I analysed in detail in the Introduction to this book. 'Post-imperial melancholy' is a symptom of the changes in British society which incur Sinclair's invective. Psychogeography, in re-enchanting 'locale', may be an expression of the very things Sinclair critiques. While I would defend Sinclair from charges of racism, ethnicity is certainly a problem in *Downriver*'s critique of Britain in the 1980s. By the time of Sinclair's *Edge of the Orison* (2005), Sinclair has come under critical scrutiny for a 'nostalgic' sense of opposition to contemporary Britain, which would ultimately align him with the anti-modernity 'deep England' heritage enthusiasts who are, in fact, the focus of pointed satire in Sinclair's work. It must be admitted that the sense of loss which accompanies the erasures of communal and cultural history, particularly in Sinclair's non-fiction, could easily shade into the nostalgia that is a symptom of contemporary cultural conditions.

Mark Rowlinson, in his essay 'Physical Graffiti', certainly implies that Sinclair is complicit in what he critiques:

> London, it would seem, is subject to two modes of privatisation, one involving the accession of free-market economics of the former role of politics in the capital, the other associated with the born-again *flâneurs* haunting Dalston Junction or Greenwich Reach, who are to be met as the diviners of intricate urban visions, strangely evasive about their subjectivity, in books that tap into the London that does not meet the casual eye.[51]

As I noted above, in the tension between witness and agency in *Downriver*, Sinclair deliberately complicates any sense that he might stand outside the structures he satirises; he is already, unavoidably complicit with capital and with exploitation.

The widow

The subtitle of *Downriver* is 'The Vessels of Wrath'. The novel is, in itself, such a vessel. The satire or 'savage comedy' in the novel is in the service of an angry critique of the policies of Margaret Thatcher, and a grotesque caricature of the then prime minister as 'the Widow', a monstrous tyrant. I will return more directly to the figure of Thatcher shortly, but *Downriver* is not alone in this period in reimagining London in satirical, critical or apocalyptic terms: Jarman's *The Last of England*, Rushdie's *The Satanic Verses*, the Stephen Frears/Hanif Kureishi film *Sammy and Rosie Get Laid* (1987) and even Hewison's critical book *Future Tense* draw upon what Sinclair calls the 'Thatcherite explosion' in *The Verbals*. Ironically, the destructive energies of Thatcherism provided the material for Sinclair's most exuberant novel. Just as we will see that *London Orbital* is presented as an attempt to undo the malign influence of the Millennium Dome, Sinclair characterises his project in *Downriver* as intending to counter the 'demonic' influence of Margaret Thatcher herself. The imagination of London (in *Downriver*, in Moorcock's *Mother London*, in *The Last of England*) becomes a means by which to resist the ideological and physical reinvention of the city symbolised in the Docklands.

Roger Luckhurst, in 'The contemporary London Gothic and the "spectral turn"', also suggests that Sinclair's writing be considered a form of Gothic. Luckhurst suggests that the Gothic provides particularly 'resonant ways of apprehending contemporary London'.[52]

The reason for this attraction to the Gothic for contemporary writers is as follows: 'So etiolated is any idea of a metropolitan public sphere that we have turned instead to private experiences of hidden routes, secret knowledges, flittering spectres, the ghosts of London past'.[53] The Gothic is then not only a form in which to explore the occulted cultural landscape of contemporary London, it is also a symptom of the closure of the public sphere made concrete in the privatised space of Canary Wharf. Luckhurst also notes a particular problem with Gothic fictions and their ability to marshal a coherent political critique of the present: 'the unstable valences of the London Gothic . . . often flip fantasies of persecutory tyranny into a nostalgia for those very spaces of unregulated violence or disorderly conduct'.[54] This, I would suggest, is produced by the energies of Thatcherism which, I stated above, provides the energy behind what is the most exuberant of all of Sinclair's texts. What haunts the London Gothic is, then, the spectre that had haunted London for much of the last two hundred years: the mob. The mob is the seeming inverse of, but in fact supplement of, the violence of state power. Sinclair confesses as much in *The Verbals* when he states that Thatcher 'wanted to destroy the power of London, the mob, which finally through the Poll Tax riots brought her down'.[55] *Downriver*, therefore, is much a product of the Thatcher era and its energies as it is a rejection of, or negation of it. Alan Sinfield argues that 'the larger danger of Thatcherism lies not in its moments of triumph, but in its eventual failure to satisfy or control the emotions it arouses'.[56] In the occult language of *Downriver*, it is the demons, the 'vessels of wrath', which Thatcherism lets loose which finally bring about her end in unlicensed violence (the poll tax riots), and this violence is itself anticipated and repeated in the apocalyptic visions of the 'Last of England' texts.

The figure of Margaret Thatcher herself, in the guise of 'the Widow', is at the centre of the satire in *Downriver*. The Widow is a caricature but also a figure of monstrosity: 'The Widow was a praise-fed avatar of the root-Maria from *Metropolis*: she looked like herself, but too much so'; 'She was padded like a Dallas Cowboy . . . Her head was unnaturally tilted (as if she had been wrongly assembled after a motorway pile-up)'.[57] Both of these quotations emphasise monstrosity through the mechanical: not just barely female, the Widow is barely human. The majority of the narrative in which the Widow figures concentrates upon the construction of a vast statue to commemorate 'the Consort', 'a scaffolded Colossus' whose size merely indicates the 'naked hubris' of the venture and of the Thatcher period as a whole.[58] Curiously, Sinclair twice emphasises royal significations with regard to the Widow; the 'Consort' clearly refers to Prince Albert, whose death provoked a long and very public period of mourning in the household of his own widow, Queen Victoria. Perhaps more pertinently, Sinclair reinvests one of the sites in his own personal mythology, St Anne's Limehouse, as 'her personal shrine': 'She'd outmanoeuvred [Prince Charles], shifted the axis downstream: stuffing Wren's overloaded Roman bauble by rededicating Nicholas Hawksmoor's unfrocked riverside monster, "that masterpiece of the baroque"'.[59] The symbolic and occulted power of Sinclair's own *Lud Heat* is then negated within the novel by the Widow herself: 'Time has, she has discovered, this marvellous facility for civilising the most recalcitrant material'.[60] The use of the word 'civilising' is crucial here; the rededication of St Anne's is another form of colonialism, overlaying a real history with a simulacrum of heritage.

Spectacle is crucial to the 'reign' of the Widow. This is emphasised in 'The Isle of Doges' by the vast apocalyptic ritual that takes place at the Victoria Docks (a not insignificant location), and also by the connections Sinclair asserts between the Widow and Queen Elizabeth I. The Widow imagines journeying down the Thames by barge (a satirical echo of the journeys made by 'Sinclair' and his companions elsewhere in the novel):

> In viceregal splendour, turn with the tide, disembark at dawn, or make a progress, a torchlit procession, with heraldic beasts, courtiers, cameramen, brownsnouts . . . The whole gaudy epic (a pastiched version of Rubens's 'Arrival of the Queen at Marseilles', made suitable for family viewing) would be slapped down on previously primed canvas, by an official War Artist, and hung in the National Gallery before she had finished her second gin and french. Get your heritage in first.[61]

The Widow then accrues the signs of royalty about her to create a simulacrum of 'tradition' and 'power', the archaic traces of the British nation-state which Tom Nairn identified as being a sign of 'decline'. Thatcherism, of course, is presented by Sinclair and the others writers I have discussed in this chapter as both a symptom of, and a completion of, the 'end of consensus' of the disintegration of 'welfare-capitalism'. The domination of a communal ethos by aggressive individualism finds its motto in the words of the Widow: '"I can only echo the words . . . of Captain Robert . . . Falcon Scott.

'For God's sake look after . . . our own people. That has always been
. . . and remains . . . our first principle. Looking after our own
people"'.[62] Scott, symbol of sacrifice made in the name of the spirit
of the British empire, is invoked, but his words are heavily ironised.
'Our own people' surely encompasses the British but not the colonial
subjects that made up most of empire; similarly, the meaning of the
last sentence stresses not paternalism, but a divisive privileging of
certain social and economic groups at the expense of others.

A speech made by the Widow at the inauguration of 'prison hulks'
(a vaunted return to 'Victorian values') allows Sinclair to expose the
radical disturbance to the fabric of Britain that underpinned
Thatcherism: not conservative, but radical in an entirely malign way.
' "History has been conquered," ' she intones, ' "The future is whatever
We believe it to be!" ':

> A prison is a state of mind. And, unlike our opponents – who are
> fettered in ritual dogmas – *We* sincerely believe that We can *all* be
> released from outmoded concepts of state care. And, in good faith, We
> make you this offer: let every man become his own warder, protecting
> the things he loves best: his *family*, his *home*, his *country*. Then, and
> only then, will We discover what *true* freedom means.[63]

As Robert Bond has noted, *Downriver* is suffused with images
of spatial enclosure. What the Widow's speech here indicates is a
closure of ideology: British subjects are indeed 'fettered', prisoners
of a state of mind. This state of mind encourages the belief that it
is only in subjection that true freedom can be gained (signified in
the conservative ideological triad of family, home and country). It is
only when Londoners and Britons embrace the 'mind forg'd manacles'
(to quote Blake's 'London') that they achieve the 'freedom' granted
to them by the Widow and her imperatives, the 'freedom' of consumerist choice, the freedom to live outside (or after) the 'safety net' of the
welfare state. In *Downriver*, there is, it seems, neither material and
physical freedom, nor freedom from the ideological imperatives of
Thatcherite consumer capital.

This does not mean, however, that *Downriver* is a despairing fiction;
it is filled with anger, with energy, and was, after all, published not
during Margaret Thatcher's premiership but after her fall. In this
chapter, I have considered whether artistic practice can form a kind
of resisting 'anti-economy' to the enclosing and deforming principles
of capitalism, and found this argument wanting; however, it is worthy

of note that the final journey in *Downriver* is beyond the city, suggesting a space outside rather than an ultimately imprisoning and all-encompassing spatial and ideological closure. The last pages of the novel find Joblard, turned narrator, sitting watching a cricket match on the Isle of Sheppey while the sun sets. The Isle of Doges, emblem of the erasures of history and lived space under capitalist conditions, is opposed to the Isle of Sheppey, ambivalent place of escape but definitely outside the confines of Thatcher's London. Joblard finally achieves a state of mental quiet, a meditative calm that undoes the energies of the economic 'storms' of the 1980s:

> I am without desire, and outside time . . . I want to come back to this place, to bring my family, my children, but I don't want to be here now. I must ring the ladies of Eastchurch for a cab to ferry me out. Until that arrives I'll just sit here, and keep my eyes firmly closed. [64]

The final words of the novel are in fact 'A HAPPY ENDING?'.[65] This place of meditative quiet is an escape, albeit a temporary one, but at least opens the possibility of happiness, if nothing more.

Notes

1 Iain Sinclair, *Downriver* (1991) (London: Vintage, 1995), p. 357.
2 Perry Anderson, 'Dégringolade', *London Review of Books*, 26:17, 2 September 2004, 3–9 (p. 3).
3 Patrick Wright, *On Living in an Old Country: The National Past in Contemporary Britain* (London and New York: Verso, 1985), p. 73.
4 Raphael Samuel, 'Unravelling Britain', in A. Light with S. Alexander and G. S. Jones (eds), *Island Stories: Unravelling Britain, Theatres of Memory Volume II* (London and New York: Verso, 1998), pp. 41–73 (p. 43).
5 Roger Luckhurst, *Science Fiction* (Cambridge: Polity), p. 173.
6 Tom Nairn, 'The Crisis in the British State', *New Left Review* I/130, November–December (1981), 37–44 (37–8).
7 Nairn, 'The Crisis in the British State', p. 37.
8 Nairn, 'The Crisis in the British State', p. 38.
9 Nairn, 'The Crisis in the British State', p. 38.
10 Nairn, 'The Crisis in the British State', p. 40.
11 Nairn, 'The Crisis in the British State', p. 39.
12 Alan Sinfield, *Literature, Politics and Culture in Postwar Britain* (Berkeley and Los Angeles: University of California Press, 1989), p. 278.
13 Sinfield, *Literature, Politics and Culture in Postwar Britain*, p. 279.
14 Sinfield, *Literature, Politics and Culture in Postwar Britain*, pp. 279 and 282.

15 Patrick Wright, *A Journey through Ruins: A Keyhole Portrait of British Postwar Life and Culture* (London: HarperCollins, 1993), p. 258.
16 Robert Bond, *Iain Sinclair* (Cambridge: Salt, 2005), p. 135.
17 Bond, *Iain Sinclair*, pp. 181 and 176
18 Sinclair, *Downriver*, pp. 276–7.
19 Sinclair, *Downriver*, pp. 263 and 265.
20 Sinclair, *Downriver*, p. 283.
21 Sinclair, *Downriver*, p. 287.
22 Sinclair, *Downriver*, p. 297.
23 Sinclair, *Downriver*, p. 297.
24 Bond, *Iain Sinclair*, p. 133.
25 David Cunningham, 'Downriver', *The Literary Encyclopaedia* (accessed 29 March 2004). <www.litencyc.com/php/sworks.php?rec=true&UID=5531>, par. 3.
26 Rachel Potter, 'Culture Vulture: The Testimony of Iain Sinclair's *Downriver*', *Parataxis* 5 (1992–3), 40–8 (43).
27 Sinclair, *Downriver*, p. 289.
28 Sinclair, *Downriver*, p. 376.
29 Sinclair, *Downriver*, p. 380.
30 Potter, 'Culture Vulture', pp. 43 and 44.
31 Iain Sinclair with Kevin Jackson, *The Verbals* (Tonbridge: Worple Press, 2003), p. 139.
32 Bond, *Iain Sinclair*, pp. 157 and 158.
33 Sinclair, *Downriver*, p. 316.
34 Robert Hewison, *Future Tense: A New Art for the Nineties* (London: Methuen, 1990), p. 82.
35 Hewison, *Future Tense*, p. 84.
36 Wright, *On Living in an Old Country*, p. 72.
37 Wright, *On Living in an Old Country*, p. 69.
38 Hewison, *Future Tense*, p. 80.
39 Sinclair, *Downriver*, p. 336.
40 Sinclair, *Downriver*, p. 397.
41 Joseph Conrad, *Heart of Darkness* (1901), Paul O'Prey (ed.) (London: Penguin, 1989), p. 29.
42 Conrad, *Heart of Darkness*, p. 121.
43 Sinclair, *Downriver*, p. 25.
44 Sinclair, *Downriver*, p. 29.
45 Conrad, *Heart of Darkness*, p. 33.
46 Conrad, *Heart of Darkness*, pp. 31–2.
47 Sinclair, *Downriver*, p. 265.
48 Sinclair, *Downriver*, p. 265.
49 Peter Brooker, *Modernity and Metropolis: Writing, Film and Urban Formations* (Basingstoke: Palgrave, 2002), p. 103.

50 Luckhurst, *Science Fiction*, p. 173.
51 Mark Rawlinson, 'Physical Graffiti: The Making of the Representation of Zones One And Two', in S. Onega and J. A. Stotesbury (eds), *London in Literature – Visionary Mappings of the Metropolis* (Heidelberg: Universitätsverlag C. Winter, 2002), pp. 233–53 (p. 243).
52 Roger Luckhurst, 'The contemporary London Gothic and the Limits of the "Spectral Turn"', *Textual Practice*, 16:3, December (2002), 527–46 (541).
53 Luckhurst, 'The Contemporary London Gothic', 541.
54 Luckhurst, 'The Contemporary London Gothic', 540.
55 Sinclair, with Jackson, *The Verbals*, p. 135.
56 Sinfield, *Literature, Politics and Culture in Postwar Britain*, p. 307.
57 Sinclair, *Downriver*, pp. 220 and 255.
58 Sinclair, *Downriver*, p. 254.
59 Sinclair, *Downriver*, p. 221.
60 Sinclair, *Downriver*, p. 221.
61 Sinclair, *Downriver*, p. 221.
62 Sinclair, *Downriver*, p. 255.
63 Sinclair, *Downriver*, pp. 336 and 337.
64 Sinclair, *Downriver*, p. 407.
65 Sinclair, *Downriver*, p. 407.

4

Internal exiles

As we have seen throughout this study, Iain Sinclair's work places a great investment in the figure of the outsider. In his 'Introduction' to the poetry collection *Conductors of Chaos*, which concentrates on 'Neo-Modernist' British and American poets, whose work appears largely outside the mainstream even of poetry publication, he writes that:

> the work I value is that which seems most remote, alienated, fractured. I don't claim to 'understand' it but I like having it around. The darker it grows outside the window, the worse the noises from the island, the more closely do I attend to the mass of instant-printed pamphlets that pile up around my desk . . . Why should they be easy? Why should they not reflect some measure of the complexity of the climate in which they exist?[1]

We find here the traces of Romanticism: these poets are, in a sense, contemporary Britain's 'unacknowledged legislators'. Their avant-gardism (their 'difficulty') is a direct reflection of the world and times in which they live. Their 'fractured' forms are in actuality a kind of mimesis, a representation of the fractured social, economic and political landscape of modernity. The Romantic poet most alluded to in Sinclair is not P. B. Shelley, however, it is William Blake, particularly *Jerusalem*, whose apocalyptic imagination of London and Albion (echoed in Sinclair's own Albion Village Press) recurs in several texts, particularly in lines about 'the Isle of Leutha's Dogs'. In Sinclair's 2005 non-fiction text, *Edge of the Orison*, he turns from Blake to John Clare, the later Romantic poet, whose own outsider status was assured by his provinciality (he was from Northamptonshire) and by a personal history of incarceration for the symptoms of 'madness'. *Edge of the Orison* is a quotation from Clare's work, and Sinclair's walk within it retraces Clare's 'Journey Out of Essex', when the poet absconded from his place of confinement and set out for home.

Sinclair's emphasis, in the quotation above, on the connection between the poet or artist and the cultural landscape against which, and in which, they work, repeats the importance of small-press publication I noted in Chapter 3, where Sinclair's own history of '*samizdat*' or '*hors commerce*' publications explicitly places the art work outside of systems of commodity exchange or consumerism. Like the poetry in *Conductors of Chaos*, the 'difficulty' of locating a fugitive publication is repeated in the 'difficulty' of its form; for both, work is necessary. Simple consumerism is compromised. (Of course, there are ironies attending the republication of small-press works in a Picador collection.) In *Lights Out for the Territory*, Sinclair revised a piece which he had written for the catalogue of an exhibition held at the gallery of Mike Goldmark (publisher of the limited editions of Sinclair's books) in Uppingham, Rutland. This piece evolved into the chapter 'The Shamanism of Intent' and is named after the title of the exhibition. Shown in the exhibition were works by artists

> so stubborn, so ruinously estranged from the tribe, that their outcast status was something more useful than a disguise, a horn mask. Is it too preposterous to think of this delusion – that work is capable of re-enchanting place – as a reality, a significant marker on the chart of our culture?[2]

Again, we find the outcasts engaged in matters absolutely fundamental to the very culture that excludes them (or that they are estranged from): the 're-enchantment of place'. We can also see how these artists, so characterised, might sit very well with Sinclair's own emphases on the material effects of symbols, through occulted or magical power: 'lines of force', countered by the mythological texts of *Lud Heat*, are analogous to the work of the 'shamanic' artists Sinclair catalogues and celebrates.

Once again, then, we find Sinclair turning to the rhetoric of the occult, the non-material, the numinous, as a means by which to posit a counter-project to the prevailing cultural, economic and societal conditions. In 'The Shamanism of Intent', he stresses once more the connection between Thatcher and Thatcherism, and the works of the artists he prizes, just as he had done in *Conductors of Chaos*:

> The Bird-Mother [a figure of evil and death appropriated from Mircea Eliade's *Shamansim: Archaic Techniques of Ecstasy*], a necklace of

skulls in her yellowing, equine teeth, returns from the battlefield, some
lost bog in the South Atlantic, ordering the tribe to rejoice. Celebrate
death. Drum with scattered bones. The Bird-Mother cannot sleep. We
are the residue of her waking nightmares, we are her pain. Out of rage
and confusion, whisky fumes, fantasies of revenge, emerges the radiant
City: Docklands.[3]

This passage anticipates the rhetoric of Sinclair's excoriations of the
Millennium Dome and other intrusions into the historical and lived
fabric of the city, and also echoes the connection between Thatcher
and the occult that was found in *Downriver* (and in Sinclair's
pronouncement, in *The Verbals*, that Thatcher's reign constituted a
case of 'actual demonic possession'). Just as the malign influence of
the Dome is countered by Sinclair's project to walk the M25 counter-
clockwise, the artist-shamans reflect the disturbed fabric of 1980s
and 1990s Britain while attempting to intercede against it.

It is not the officially sanctioned 'high' culture that, for Sinclair,
can form some kind of countervailing discourse, or even redemptive
act, against the malign forces he sees to be at work in contemporary
Britain. It is in the outsider or 'outcast', in the disinherited, unre-
garded, marginal figures like Gavin Jones and Brian Catling that
such counter-projects may be seen to be operating. Sinclair writes:

> Certain artists – the ones you came across by accident, working their
> own turf – began to look strange, otherworldly, out of it . . . The will
> to continue, improvise upon chaos, could be defined as 'intent': a
> 'sickness-vocation', as Eliade has it, an elective trauma. The health of
> the city, and perhaps of the culture itself, seemed to depend upon the
> flights of redemption these disinherited shamans (there were women
> too, plenty of them) could summon and sustain. They were associated
> in my mind with other avatars of unwisdom: scavengers, dole-queue
> antiquarians, bagpeople, out-patients, muggers, victims, millennial
> babblers.[4]

'Avatars of unwisdom' relates this list of the marginal to the 'mad
visionary' that I diagnosed as being a central figure in Sinclair's
thinking in the Introduction to this book, and the counter-cultural
ideas about marginality and artistic vision influenced by R. D. Laing.
In the figure of John Clare, another 'mad visionary' (like Blake) and
socially excluded artist (like the 'shamans of intent'), Sinclair finds
another, earlier version of this figure. The shamans take the 'sickness'
of contemporary Britain upon themselves and redeem it through
their art, according to Sinclair, but the implication of 'elective trauma'

is that such a position involves suffering, neglect, and marginalisation. Sinclair's project in *Lights Out for the Territory* (which was Sinclair's breakthrough into mainstream success) is then to redeem these figures by bringing them to a wider audience, to heal the suffering that they choose (Christ-like) to endure for our sake.

To return the marginal to the centre, if that is Sinclair's project here, is somewhat paradoxical, as Sinclair suggests that it is the very marginality of these poets and artists that he values: 'I don't claim to "understand" it but I like having it around' is what he wrote of the poets represented in *Conductors of Chaos*. Sinclair's own intention to bring what he calls the 'pre-forgotten' or 're-forgotten' writers and artists to greater light is, surely, laudable, for as I noted in Chapter 3, Sinclair himself has experienced what happens to the poet when his audience shrinks to a dozen readers (who receive the publication as a gift). In the film *The Cardinal and the Corpse*, and in *Lights Out for the Territory* and elsewhere, Sinclair celebrates lost or forgotten writers, from the Victorian writer W. Pett Ridge to William Hope Hodgson, author of *The House on the Borderland* (for which Sinclair wrote an afterword to a paperback edition of 1989); from Alexander Baron, author of London proletarian novel *The Lowlife* (for which Sinclair also wrote an Introduction to another paperback reprint), to Derek Raymond (aka Robin Cook), who wrote a series of dark detective fictions and whose last, valedictory public reading is described in *Lights Out*.

One of the ironies that surround Sinclair's celebration of the 're-forgotten' writers is that it involves a parallel process to the literary judgement that had excluded them from critical attention in the first place. As Rod Mengham notes, '[Sinclair's] relentless mythologizing of forgotten and re-forgotten writers is nothing if not the setting up of an alternative canon'.[5] An 'alternative canon' itself returns marginal writers to the centre of attention, perhaps undoing the very status from which they derive their creative power. *Conductors of Chaos*, for instance, collects poetry originally published in the small-press editions that Sinclair professes to find so stimulating, and returns them to a consumerist economy (of reading). If Sinclair wants to bring to a wider public writers whom he considers considerable but undiscussed, he must select them from the critical abyss, and in that selection neglect others. This is unavoidable, of course, but Steve Pile notes the same process of selection operating when Sinclair walks to uncover lost or forgotten histories. Pile writes:

Sinclair himself is drawn to talk only about particular things, to trace only specific histories . . . Sinclair is fascinated with those exciting tales of the underworld, of leftist revolutionaries, of artists, writers and film-makers, but not with stories about those mundane trips to the shops with the kids in tow or the difficulty of using public transport when you're sick and tired.[6]

The argument may seem somewhat obvious and banal, but I think Pile has highlighted a crucial point in Sinclair's work: that his own writing becomes an authoritative guide to an 'other' London, a forgotten or occluded London; but that forgotten London is only one of very many. Pile is right to note that in Sinclair's texts, the 'real' London (opposed to the official) lies not in the banal, everyday existence of its denizens, but in the visionary 'dispossessed'.

One of the living writers Sinclair celebrates is Michael Moorcock, who, in *Rodinsky's Room*, is described as 'another exile; the great Londoner, memory conduit, had shifted himself [to Texas]'.[7] Moorcock actually does live in Texas: he is seen in his home in the Petit–Sinclair film *Asylum*. However, the motif of exile is a recurrent one in the figures that Sinclair investigates, the 'outsiders'. In *Edge of the Orison*, we find the same figure of exile in relation to the spaces of Clare's life and death. In Northampton library, Sinclair discovers a death mask of the poet which, like the objects found in Rodinsky's room, is: 'A confirmation of absence. The municipal shrine is a secondary imprisonment, keeping the poet in Northampton, along with his papers, his much-travelled library . . . The books travelled, as he did, into a definitive exile'.[8] Death is the final exile for Clare, but alienated and incarcerated far from his home, Clare himself suffered a form of 'internal exile' for long periods of his life. This idea of 'internal exile' is prefigured earlier in the text, where Sinclair writes of Northborough, the village in which Clare once lived now 'heavy with absence. Of all the cemetery villages encountered on our walk out of Essex, this is the paradigm. Internal exile as a prelude to the Big Sleep'.[9] Internal exile is a form of life-in-death, a condition of marginalization and suffering.

Rodinsky's Room

In *Rodinsky's Room* (1999), Sinclair's collaborative text with Rachel Lichtenstein, issues of exile, marginalisation and suffering are located in the history of the Jewish East End. The East End, on London's own margins, plays a special role in Sinclair's imagination of London: as site of the Whitechapel murders and therefore crucible of the Jack the Ripper myth (which Sinclair appropriates in *White Chappell, Scarlet Tracings*); home and 'manor' of the Krays, the underside of 'Swinging London', who appear as 'Hand and Hyle' in *Suicide Bridge*; and as Sinclair's locale, his familiar terrain, where he has worked and walked for over three decades. The East End's proximity to the City is also of symbolic interest for Sinclair. In *Lud Heat*, the Hawksmoor churches of the East End are Masonic, occult realignments of space and history. It is worth noting, however, that by 2005's *Edge of the Orison*, Sinclair states:

> I repudiated the notion of Nicholas Hawksmoor . . . as a member of an occult elite. London is a body kept alive, energised by complex lines and patterns that can be walked, built upon: celebrated on exploited. The reality is democratic, anyone can play.[10]

Sinclair has clearly become aware of criticism of his project as a kind of obscure, elitist semiology of adepts, which I have argued in earlier chapters is an effect of the occult discourse Sinclair deploys in his early work. In a radio programme broadcast in 2003, called 'The Devil's Architect', Sinclair goes even further:

> I don't think for a minute that Hawksmoor himself was some sort of occultist, or had some kind of dark theory of history that we wanted to enact. But I think unconsciously or consciously he sort of understood that the element of London that works is this Manichean division between darkness and light. It really defines the city. There's always been the need to make money, the need to be brutal about how you make money, and then having done so, create some structure that will allow the light in, and his churches shine, and they're built on darkness, and that kind of schizophrenic element has never been better defined. And so the churches are a constant provocation to the imagination of writers of fiction and haunters of the city.[11]

His 'democratic' emphasis on walking the city, and the Hawksmoor churches merely a 'provocation' to London writers, is an interesting turn away from the very material that, partly through its popularisation in Peter Ackroyd's *Hawksmoor* (1985), has become a signature element in the wider appreciation of Sinclair's work.

As I noted in my chapter on *Downriver*, Sinclair seems particularly attuned to the history of the Jewish presence in Whitechapel, to the detriment of later immigration from the Indian subcontinent.

Sinclair's attraction to the Jewish community is accompanied by a sense of loss, even nostalgia, though the history of the East End is one of repeated (even cyclical) immigration. The Jewish community actually supplanted the Huguenots that had arrived there earlier. Peter Ackroyd, in his *London: the Biography* suggests that:

> It has often been suggested that the East End is a creation of the nineteenth century; certainly the phrase itself was not invented until the 1880s. But in fact the East has always existed as a separate and distinct entity [. . .] The presence of 100,000 Jewish immigrants, in Whitechapel and in Spitalfields, only served to emphasise the apparently 'alien' quality of the neighbourhood. They served also to reinforce that other territorial myth which clung to the East End. Because it did indeed lie towards the east, it became associated with that larger 'east' which lay beyond Christendom and which threatened the borders of Europe [. . .] The East End was in that sense the ultimate threat and the ultimate mystery. It represented the heart of darkness.[12]

The East End was seen as different, 'alien'. William Fishman, who has chronicled the history of the East End in several books, in *East End Jewish Radicals* (1975) outlines the growth of anti-Semitism in the last decades of the nineteenth century. He writes:

> The earliest official outburst against aliens is observed in the *Pall Mall Gazette* (February, 1886) which referred to 'A *Judenhetz* brewing in East London', deduced from a letter it had received warning its readers that 'the foreign Jews of no nationality whatever are becoming a pest and a menace to the poor native East Ender'.[13]

The East End has been London's other, the site of repeated immigration: alien, marginal, criminal, not-British, and inhabited by a strange and dangerous 'multitude' which threatened to 'swamp' the centre. Conversely, in contemporary popular culture, there is an ideological construction of a 'native East Ender', white and working class. It exists in the problematic representation of ethnic difference in the BBC soap-opera *EastEnders*, in the sentimentalisation of white working-class culture evident in the cult of the gangster, and the continuing myths of the Kray brothers. It is noteworthy that the second chapter in *Lights Out for the Territory* deals with the funeral of Ronnie Kray, Sinclair retracing the path of the funeral cortege to compromise the route. Like his 'incisions' into the psychogeographic landscapes of the City, Sinclair's retracing of the route of the funeral cortège is an attempt to expose and disrupt these myths. He is not complicit with what he calls 'Kray Kulture', but I would argue that his investigations of London's history in *Lights Out for the Territory* and elsewhere, in its recapitulation of the myths of London's gangland, calls into being, as much as it tries to destabilise, popular images of the East End as a last repository of 'authentic' working-class (white) culture. In his defence, Sinclair's conception of London as palimpsest explicitly includes the East End's history of cyclical immigration. *Dark Lanthorns* (1999), a limited-edition Goldmark text which features a dust jacket that mimics the *London A–Z* owned by David Rodinsky, is another set of 'excursions' into London's forgotten territories. Sinclair revisits the walks that Rodinsky himself performed, as they are traced in Rodinsky's *A–Z*. Here again forgotten history – the 'lost' narrative of the reclusive Rodinsky, his family, and the fate of the Jewish East End – are revivified, given new life, through another exercise in mapping.

In *Rodinsky's Room* (1999), Sinclair's collaborative text with Rachel Lichtenstein, issues of exile and otherness find an emblem in the obscure personal history of a man who 'disappeared' from the upper rooms of the Princelet Street synagogue in Whitechapel in 1969, David Rodinsky. The room, in the state of chaos and disrepair that it was left in by Rodinsky, becomes the site of a kind of archaeological investigation. Lichtenstein catalogues and preserves the objects in it, and *Rodinsky's Room* (which is presented in the form of alternating essays or chapters by Lichtenstein and Sinclair) narrates the history and aftermath of a phenomenon which, for a time, had become something of a cult. (Rodinsky's room can also be found in the pages of Patrick Wright's *A Journey through Ruins*. As 'Frederik Hanbury', Wright appears in disguise in *Downriver*, where he visits Rodinsky's room with the narrator. The rooms are also mentioned by Robert Hewison in *Future Tense*. See Chapter 3 of this book.)

Rodinsky's Room is not an entirely successful collaboration, although it is interesting to note that in *Liquid City* Sinclair calls *Rodinsky's Room* 'Rachel Lichtenstein's book', for which he contributed 'speculative essays'.[14] This disavowal of authorship marks out the problematic position of Sinclair's contribution to the project, one that I will discuss below. Lichtenstein's chapters follow a chronological course, charting her growing obsession with Rodinsky. This quest – for Rodinsky's identity – is mapped onto a journey of self-discovery for Lichtenstein, one which involves a recuperation of her own Jewishness. Susan Alice Fischer suggests that *Rodinsky's*

Room is as much autobiography on Lichtenstein's part, as biography of Rodinsky: 'Her passion is necessarily autobiographical, not only to learn what became of David Rodinsky, but to find herself and her creative vision'.[15] The implication here is that Lichtenstein finds Rodinsky a useful vehicle for self-expression; not that Lichtenstein uses the figure of Rodinsky in a cynical or selfish way, but that the narrative of 'discovery' of the secrets of the room are necessarily a kind of self-examination and self-fashioning. In the course of the 'autobiographical' narrative, Lichtenstein (who changed her name back to the Jewish 'original', from 'Lawrence', the one adopted by her immigrant forebears and the surname of her parents) undergoes a process of conversion to orthodox Judaism, in Israel. Her journey, incorporating visits to Israel and then to Poland, where her ambition to recover the site of the original *shtetl* in Georgia is frustrated, is a search for origins. In the early chapters, the plainness and directness of her writing contrasts strongly with Sinclair's, and lends a sense of authenticity to her struggle to rediscover lost Jewish histories of the East End (and later eastern Europe). These histories have not been 'lost': they were destroyed, erased, by Nazi genocide and by the still-evident anti-Semitism of Poland and elsewhere; and they have been overwritten by the 'development' of Whitechapel and the East End in the name of late-capitalist 'urban renewal'.

At first, the chapters written by Sinclair seem trivial or inauthentic next to Lichtenstein's writing. Her voice is one that demands we partake of her quest for origins, for identity, for 'truth'. What Lichtenstein wants to know is what happened to David Rodinsky, in his life and his death. The search is rooted in history. It is a detective story of sorts, piecing together 'Rodinsky' from the clues of his room and from her investigations into the cabbalistic traditions of rabbinical Judaism. Rodinsky, Lichtenstein argues, seemed so odd, was finally transported to Longrove asylum in Epsom, because his activities were ultimately untranslatable to the mores and assumptions of contemporary London life. (Languages and translation are a dominant theme of the book.) Rodinsky was a rabbinal scholar *manqué*, argues Lichtenstein, displaced to the East End.[16] His story is then exemplary for the Diaspora, in which 'traditional ways of life' are either lost or misunderstood, sacrificed to 'assimilation' (Anglo-Jewry) or othered as alien and incomprehensible (the Ashkenazim of Whitechapel).

Such simple binaries obscure the complex relationship between Sephardic and Ashkenazim, between Anglo-Jewry and Russo-Polish

Jews. William Fishman, in *East End Radicals*, quotes from the *Jewish Chronicle* of August 1881:

> They [the immigrants] retain all the habits of their former home and display no desire to assimilate with the people among whom they dwell. They appear altogether to forget that in accepting the hospitality of England, they owe a reciprocal duty of becoming Englishmen.[17]

The attitudes displayed here express anxiety over the future of Anglo-Jewry itself, and expose the precarious position of even a community which had 'assimilated' itself and become 'English'. The Sephardic community had learned to speak the language of the other, not of the coloniser, but of a capricious people and state which – for the present – tolerated the presence of that community. This seems no defence against renewed prejudice. The insular and self-protecting Ashkenazi communities left pogroms and found the East End ghetto. Little wonder then that there was a reliance upon the traditions and language that they brought with them. Fishman argues:

> They sought freedom and found it within the limits of old restrictions [. . .] They were still, though with less physical danger, confined within the bounds of the ghetto. Nostalgia for their Russian and Polish homelands (the *heim*) persisted among a people in self-confessed exile (*goles*).[18]

Note again the trope of exile. It is curious that the nostalgia of the homelands that Fishman elaborates in the Jewish community of the East End finds an analogue in *Rodinsky's Room*: Lichtenstein travels to Poland to try to discover where Rodinsky's family travelled from. For Lichtenstein, though, the journey is one to find origins (of Rodinsky's and her own sense of self-identity) rather than one of nostalgia. It is, however, in some sense a journey 'home' for Lichtenstein.

Lichtenstein's assumption is that one can piece together who 'David Rodinsky' was from the evidence that he left behind, both in the room in the Princelet Street synagogue and in the official records that she mines. The quest for Rodinsky, of course, must lead to his grave, and it does, over which Lichtenstein utters the *kaddish*, the Jewish prayer for the dead. This pronouncement is the final performative act for the book, finally bringing 'David Rodinsky' into being, if only in his grave. (It is noteworthy that in the book *Rodinsky's Room*, Lichtenstein only discovers a small tin plaque, pushed into the grave as into a plant pot, which bears his name and dates. In the

Sinclair–Petit film *London Orbital*, there is a large marble gravestone.
As Sinclair's text of *London Orbital* reveals, it was Lichtenstein herself
who commemorated the grave with a headstone.) The quest for Jewish
identity, one of the 'occluded histories' which make up a large part
of Sinclair's œuvre, invites our sanction and our approval, bringing
with it the significations of genocide and persecution. Rodinsky
becomes an emblematic (and problematic) Jewish victim, one of
London's lost.

Rodinsky's Room, I would argue, offers the reader a 'trap'. This
is a word that Sinclair uses to describe Rodinsky's room itself. In
Downriver, Sinclair writes:

> Now I began to understand the nature of the trap [. . .] There was
> nothing astonishing in the disappearance of this man. He could not
> be more available. It was all still here: the wrappings, the culture, the
> work he had attempted, his breath on the glass – and even, if we carried
> it away, his story. We could provide the missing element, fiction, using
> only the clues that Rodinsky had so blatantly planted.[19]

The 'trap' in *Rodinsky's Room* is to validate Lichtenstein's narrative
of the 'discovery' of the 'identity' of 'David Rodinsky'. The letter that
Sinclair quotes from Brian Catling is more nearly correct: it is
addressed to 'Rodinski', the name scored through, erased, placed
under *sous rature*.[20] This is correct because there is no such person
as 'David Rodinsky'. The 'identity' that Lichtenstein recovers is a
construct, a meticulously researched fabrication. This is not to say
that it is false or a lie. However, we must be sure to remember that
'David Rodinsky' is not coterminous with the man who actually lived
there, whoever he may have been. Lichtenstein reconstructs presence
from the room's absences, from its clues and its semiotic ghosts.
Sinclair, rather, is interested in the absence. His *London Review of
Books* article on the phenomenon was called 'The Man Who Turned
Himself Into A Room', emphasising both the importance of transformation rather than stability of identity and that there is no longer
any 'Rodinsky' *there*.

Although Sinclair's comments on Lichtenstein's work sometimes
seem redundant, he is right to suggest that the room was waiting
for the one person who would 'put it all together', to reconstruct
'Rodinsky'. His own attempts are, in the end, frustrated. His idea to
have a collection of 'Rodinsky stories' is a self-confessed failure. He
takes Michael Moorcock to see the rooms and to gauge his reaction,

but Moorcock is inscrutable: 'Moorcock could make of it what he liked. All or nothing. That was his affair. But it was the finish for me. I abandoned any notion of collecting Rodinsky stories'.[21] Little wonder: once Lichtenstein is part of Rodinsky's story, there is no need for anyone else. Her dogged pursuit of the 'real' 'Rodinsky' invalidates, usurps, erases, renders inauthentic, all other versions. The quest is not explicitly tyrannical or exclusionary, but once it brings in the history of the Jewish Diaspora, a history of persecution and genocide, then all other narratives are undermined. There is no way that any other narrative would have the power or authenticity of the one of Jewish 'homecoming', of the search for identity and lost histories.

To compensate, Sinclair brings in myths from Eastern Europe and Jewish culture, such as the golem or the *dybbuk*. Rodinsky himself becomes a golem, roaming the city.[22] Sinclair's emphasis on absence (that of Rodinsky, particularly) has a thematic and structural parallel with the book itself: where Lichtenstein's chapters are presence-full, Sinclair evacuates from his own 'essays' (i.e. his word for his contribution, which signifies an 'attempt', self-cancelling and unfinished) anything but signs, imported myths, responses from other writers which are not responses, such as those of Moorcock. At one point Sinclair confesses: 'By seeing how the room affected other people, I would perhaps discover what it meant to me'.[23] Perhaps he feels that his own responses are, in some sense, placed next to Lichtenstein's, invalid. He cannot call up presence but merely point elsewhere, to the absence which is the room, or to figures which are themselves insubstantial (the golem and *dybbuk*). In a sense the book is about failure, the inability to successfully marry two very different projects, two different 'readings' of the room: presence and absence, identity and 'Rodinsky'. Christopher C. Gregory-Guider, in a very interesting article on the text, notes that 'a tension mounts over the course of *Rodinsky's Room* as Sinclair's attempts to maintain the otherness of Rodinsky's story [Rodinsky as absence or unfathomable mystery] begins to contrast with Lichtenstein's ongoing demystification of Rodinsky's life'.[24] It is this tension, I would suggest, that ultimately causes the text to fall apart, its irreducible incoherence a product of two irreconcilable understandings of the meaning of the room and of Rodinsky himself. As Sinclair notes of his own meditations, at the end of the chapter in which Gregory-Guider finds 'their most metaphorically-rich expression': 'Rachel Lichtenstein was wearied by these notions'.[25]

In *Lights Out for the Territory*, Sinclair describes Lichtenstein
as 'an artist who specialised in not-forgetting', an 'archivist of the
unconscious'.[26] Many of Sinclair's own projects involve memorialisation (such as the 'reforgotten' writers, or *Edge of the Orison*'s
combination of John Clare's journey and Sinclair's wife Anna's
own family history) and he is drawn to the works of others that are
involved in the same process. Ultimately, Rodinsky's room becomes
a kind of memorial to the man who inhabited it, and to the Jewish
community that has now largely left Whitechapel. *Rodinsky's Room*
documents the process of this memorialisation. Rachel Whiteread's
House, the controversial sculpture sited next to an East London park,
is one of the central works that Sinclair considers in *Lights Out for
the Territory* because of its attempt to memorialise, to make concrete,
the traces of the interior of a house that was no longer standing. It
signified the lost houses and communities of London, but Sinclair
seems to distrust it. In fact, he writes: '*House* was a concept, the
human elements were the flaws: it was the husk of an idea, extin-
guished in execution. The sooner it was disposed of the better: only
then could it work on memory, displacing its own volume'.[27] It is
only in the demolition of the sculpture, when *House* itself turns into
memory, that it passes beyond official culture (the Turner Prize, the
art establishment) and into something of value. As Rod Mengham
argues, 'this form of remembering is validated only if it is unofficial,
antinomian, iconoclastic. Civic memory is derided, official memorials
regarded as symptoms of a collective amnesia'.[28] The status of this
remembering is troubling, however, for Sinclair's project in the texts
I have discussed in this chapter is to recover the very memories that
have been lost or erased over time. It is only in Sinclair's own texts,
published by mainstream publishers and accessible to a wider public,
that they find some kind of acknowledgment and continued existence.

Notes

1 Iain Sinclair, 'Introduction', in I. Sinclair (ed.), *Conductors of Chaos: A
Poetry Anthology* (London: Picador, 1996), pp. xiii–xx (p. xvii).
2 Iain Sinclair, *Lights Out for the Territory: 9 Excursions in the Secret
History of London* (London: Granta, 1998), p. 239.
3 Sinclair, *Lights Out for the Territory*, p. 240.
4 Sinclair, *Lights Out for the Territory*, p. 240.

5 Rod Mengham, 'The Elegiac Imperative' [Review of *Lights Out for the Territory* and *Liquid City*], *Kenyon Review*, 23:1, winter (2001), 173–7 (177)

6 Steve Pile (2002), 'Memory and the City', in J. Campbell and J. Harbord (eds), *Temporalities, Autobiography and Everyday Life* (Manchester: Manchester University Press), pp. 111–27 (p. 122).

7 Iain Sinclair and Rachel Lichtenstein, *Rodinsky's Room* (London: Granta, 1999), p. 270.

8 Iain Sinclair, *Edge of the Orison* (London: Hamish Hamilton, 2005), p. 219.

9 Sinclair, *Edge of the Orison*, p. 70.

10 Sinclair, *Edge of the Orison*, p. 294.

11 'The Devil's Architect', broadcast 29 May 2003, BBC Radio 4.

12 Peter Ackroyd, *London: The Biography* (London: Chatto & Windus, 2000), pp. 675 and 679.

13 William J. Fishman, *East End Jewish Radicals 1875–1914* (London: Duckworth, 1975), p. 69.

14 Iain Sinclair and Marc Atkins, *Liquid City* (London: Reaktion, 1999), p. 223.

15 Susan Alice Fischer 'A Room of Our Own: Rodinsky, Street Haunting and the Creative Mind', *Changing English: Studies in Reading and Culture*, 8:2, October (2001), 119–28 (122).

16 Sinclair and Lichtenstein , *Rodinsky's Room*, p. 314.

17 Fishman, *East End Jewish Radicals*, p. 67.

18 Fishman, *East End Jewish Radicals*, p. 92.

19 Iain Sinclair, *Downriver* (1991) (London: Vintage, 1995), p. 136.

20 Sinclair and Lichtenstein, *Rodinsky's Room*, p. 260.

21 Sinclair and Lichtenstein, *Rodinsky's Room*, p. 272.

22 Sinclair and Lichtenstein, *Rodinsky's Room*, p. 180.

23 Sinclair and Lichtenstein, *Rodinsky's Room*, p. 257.

24 Christopher C. Gregory-Guider, 'Sinclair's *Rodinsky's Room* and the Art of Autobiography', *Literary London* 3:2 (2005) (accessed 1 December 2005), <www.literarylondon.org/london-journal/guider.html>, par. 22.

25 Gregory-Guider, 'Sinclair's *Rodinsky's Room* and the Art of Autobiography', par. 20. Sinclair and Lichtenstein, *Rodinsky's Room*, p. 200.

26 Sinclair, *Lights Out for the Territory*, p. 232.

27 Sinclair, *Lights Out for the Territory*, p. 233.

28 Mengham, 'The Elegiac Imperative', p. 176.

5

The visual text

Was a marriage of convenience between literature and cinema possible?
(Iain Sinclair)[1]

Although I have written previously in this book about mapping the
city, in Sinclair's texts actual maps are rare. Rather, Sinclair narrates
space through the structure of the walk. As I suggested in Chapter
1, Sinclair's texts tend towards spatial organisation. His poetry is
intensely imagistic, his prose paratactic. Significations pile up in
layers, words cancel the previous one or meanings are accreted.
Sinclair's prose fictions, to which we will return in Chapter 7, are
particularly prone to a form of 'semantic drag', a retardation of the
syntactic and narrative flow caused by the brilliance of the individual
sentence, and Sinclair adopts several strategies to ameliorate the
effects of this 'drag', which we will investigate later.

Maps and diagrams

The 'spatial organisation' that I diagnosed in the Introduction and
Chapter 1 of this study does have a more direct relevance to Sinclair's
books, however. I have deliberately used 'book' rather than 'text' in
the preceding sentence, for a recurrent (yet hardly remarked upon
critically) motif in Sinclair's work is the importance of the book as
a visual object, signified by effects of typography, illustrations and
other visual material, photographs, diagrams, and in the limited
editions of Sinclair's texts produced by Goldmark, additional
holographic or other inserted material. (In *Dark Lanthorns*, this is a
piece of printed paper which approximates the wrapper of a bar of
chocolate with some written directions on the reverse.) Initially, one

might assert two possible influences upon this recurrent motif. The first is Sinclair's own productive practice, and the history of his own publications: his first book, *Kodak Mantra Diaries*, was self-produced (under the name 'Albion Village Press'), as were *Lud Heat*, *Suicide Bridge* and several subsequent 'chapbooks' or booklets during the 1970s and 1980s. As I argued in Chapter 3, there is a political or ethical significance to this self-publication, as the texts self-consciously assume a counter-cultural position, outside of mainstream publication and distribution (and, as some of the 1980s booklets were given away in editions of a dozen or so, also outside a system of monetary exchange). Sinclair's self-produced texts are carefully designed to be objects in their own right: *Kodak Mantra Diaries*, for instance, is spiral bound in a very unusual format (long and thin, 15 inches long by 5'/2 inches wide), and there is important visual material included in the Albion Village Press versions of both *Lud Heat* and *Suicide Bridge* which is not reprinted in the more widely available Granta paperback edition of both texts.

Another possible initial influence on an emphasis on the book as a material object is Sinclair's history as a dealer in books. *White Chappell, Scarlet Tracings* includes, as one of its three narrative threads, the story of Nicholas Lane, Dryfeld and 'the Late Watson', and the trouble surrounding the acquisition of a rare edition of *A Study in Scarlet*. We can also find allusions to the world of the bookdealer in other novels like *Downriver* (where Dr Adam Tenbrücke collects Conrad) and *Radon Daughters* (where one of the narrative threads concerns a manuscript 'sequel' to William Hope Hodgson's *The House on the Borderland*). The bookdealing trade is one where the materiality of the book, its condition and provenance, are more important than the words that are contained within it. The material book then becomes a commodity. Considering the limited editions of Sinclair's books published by Goldmark (some signed by the author), how Sinclair's books are designed and produced seems consistently to assert their material status.

In this chapter I will consider the visual apparatus of Sinclair's major works, including *Slow Chocolate Autopsy* (which contains 'graphic stories' in collaboration with Dave McKean), and also Sinclair's films with Chris Petit. In *The Verbals*, Sinclair indicates that he has always been interested in cinema, and particularly filmmaking, having attended a film school in London and then taught film in an art college in Walthamstow (where Brian Catling was one of his students). In Chapter 2 I noted the importance of Stan Brakhage's films to the idea of autopsy ('seeing with one's own eyes') in *Lud Heat* and *White Chappell*, and in this chapter I will investigate the importance of the visual and cinematic further. Not only is Sinclair interested in the formations and deformations of urban space; not only is his poetry organised spatially as an 'open field'; but the space of the page, the space of the book, is a vital element in understanding Sinclair's writing practice.

As I noted above, maps are rare in Sinclair's texts. Maps proper only appear in *Slow Chocolate Autopsy* (where they are integrated into the complex texture of McKean's panels) and in *Dark Lanthorns*, where the entire book mimics the *London A–Z* that was found in the abandoned room of David Rodinsky, the emblematic Whitechapel figure Sinclair also writes of in *Downriver* and *Rodinsky's Room*. In *Dark Lanthorns* Sinclair traces (and retraces) the relationship between map and walking, using the journeys Rodinsky himself marked on the *A–Z* to attempt to reconstitute the conditions of Rodinsky's life, and Rodinsky's London. Rodinsky's maps are not just plans of the city, but inscriptions of urban trajectories. The space of London is revisited by walking it, and the journeys are inscribed (literally) on the map and, by extension, on the material fabric of the city itself. Sinclair attempts to summon the lost presence of Rodinsky (emblematic of the lost Jewish presence in Whitechapel) by revivifying his walking practices, quasi-magically invoking him through an urban ritual based upon journeys inscribed on Rodinsky's map.

Franco Moretti, in his book *Atlas of the European Novel 1800–1900* (1998), offered an entertaining and illuminating set of analyses of novels and stories of the nineteenth century, illustrated by and generated by maps. He writes, as a theoretical justification for his project:

> What do literary maps allow us to see? Two things, basically. Firstly, they highlight the *ortgebunden*, place-bound nature of literary forms: each of them with its peculiar geometry, its boundaries, its spatial taboos and favorite routes. And then, maps bring to light the *internal* logic of narrative: the semiotic domain around which the plot coalesces and self-organises.[2]

The maps in Moretti's book are fascinating in what they reveal, but his cartographic method is problematic. As Ania Loomba notes, 'Maps claim to be objective and scientific, but in fact select what they record and present in specific ways, which are historically tied with colonial enterprises'.³ As an analytical tool for the literary critic, then, maps must be treated with caution. Maps are not neutral, nor blank spaces of textual criticism. In three later articles (later collected into *Maps, Graphs, Trees*, 2005) Moretti delves deeper into the conceptual underpinnings of his cartographic methods. In the second of the articles (published in the March–April 2004 volume of *New Left Review*) Moretti notes a criticism made of his *Atlas of the European Novel* by the Italian geographer Claudio Cerreti, who pointed out:

> how patterns entail a Cartesian reductions of space to extension, where 'objects are analysed in terms of reciprocal positions and distances . . . whether they are close or far from each other is something else'. But this, he goes on, is not really geography: this is geometry; just as the figures of the *Atlas* are not really maps, but diagrams. The diagrams *look* like maps, yes, because they have been 'superimposed on a cartographic plane': but their true nature emerges unmistakeably from the way I analyse them, which disregards the specificity of the various locations, to focus almost entirely on their mutual relations.⁴

A diagram, in Moretti's terms, is then a 'set of relations', whereas a map is a 'cluster of individual locations'. Moretti is attracted to diagrams, he confesses 'because for me *geometry "signifies" more than geography*' (Moretti's emphasis).⁵

This tension between map and diagram is also in evidence in Sinclair's work. On the back cover of the dust jacket of *Dark Lanthorns* – a book designed to mimic the look of a late 1960s *London A–Z* streetmap – there is a reproduction of a map of the London Underground system. This design classic, a rounded rectangle at the centre of a system of arteries and veins, is faded, the ink blurred with damp. The print, blue-black on white (rather than the now more familiar colour reproduction), is indistinct, the lines receding beneath surface like veins below the skin, the names of the stations lost. The basic shape, if not the stations themselves, is legible, however, and indicates one of the ways in which Londoners (and visitors to London) orient themselves. The first maps of the underground followed lines of geography; the current design is geometrical, space and distance compressed, London given comprehensible form in one diagram. This London Underground, an abstraction of the network of tunnels and stations that make up the transport system, is not a 'true' representation of the city, but allows the traveller to see a totalised (and therefore entirely comprehensible) map of its design. The relations between the lines and stations is more important to the design, because far more comprehensible, than an adherence to actual locations of Underground stations on a topographic map.

However, it might be more illuminating to suggest that the map is a kind of diagram, than placing the two in binary opposition; a very complex diagram, but one that necessarily involves reduction, abstraction and extension on a flat, Cartesian plane. The map corresponds to 'real', physical space, but it is not that space, only a reduced (and therefore legible) representation of it. In Sinclair's hands, maps do indeed reduce the city to 'significant pattern', whether that is the letters V, O and X inscribed on London by Sinclair's walks in *Lights Out for the Territory*, or the recapitulation of Rodinsky's walks in *Dark Lanthorns*, or what we shall move on to now, the organisation of the East London Hawksmoor churches in *Lud Heat*. In the Albion Village Press edition of *Lud Heat*, a 'map of the 8 great churches' is drawn by Brian Catling. This map is indeed reduced; physical elements present are the Thames, River Lea and Limehouse Cut; Victoria Park and Gospel Oak, St George's Field and Tower Hamlets Cemetery; and all other features are human-made buildings and monuments, such as the Hawksmoor churches, the Tower, William Blake's house and Cleopatra's Needle. The sketchy nature of this map, which has lots of white (or blank) space, emphasises the relations (triangulations, 'lines of influence, the invisible rods of force') between the churches, and completely erases the lived space of London itself. The dotted lines between the churches make these lines of force visible and comprehensible. The font affects an Ancient Egyptian look, as does the title emblem, and representations of the Eye of Horus and the god Anubis. The font and pictorial elements emphasise the occult design of the map, and the malignant power of the location of the churches. The map articulates the space of London in a very different way to the rest of *Lud Heat*: where the poems and prose is difficult, obscure, mythic, the map provides a comprehensible, simple diagram.

The version of the map in the Granta edition of 1998 is different to the Albion Village Press edition. In fact, it is attributed to one 'Brian McKean', a curious conflation of Brian Catling and Dave McKean which is, probably accidentally, of a piece with the split and diffused subjectivities of many of the characters in Sinclair's texts. While McKean's map is similar to Catling's original, there is a lot less white space, as the map is compressed to fit the smaller paperback size; the script is larger; and contains greater use of black (in the triangle shapes that indicate the churches, and in the head of Anubis). Overall, though clearly hand-drawn, McKean's map exhibits a more polished and professional appearance, as one might expect from a graphic artist and mainstream press. Curiously, though more visually striking, McKean's map is less comprehensible because of compression; some of the very minor features on the Catling map (such as 'Old Bethlehem Hospital') are given greater prominence, and some things added. The large white spaces of Catling's map emphasise the relations between the churches in a simple diagrammatic way, a manner that is somewhat complicated by the increased legibility of other features in the later map.

Why does Sinclair use such a diagram? It is important to note that not all of the visual material present in the Albion Village Press edition of *Lud Heat* (such as reproductions of engravings of St Anne's, Limehouse, or photographs of a younger Sinclair at work in the grounds of the church and elsewhere) is present in the Granta reprint. It is therefore significant that Catling's map (and two others, one of St Anne's, and another of a wartime bunker) is redrawn for the 1998 edition. Glyn White, in *Reading the Graphic Surface*, offers an explanation:

> A rather more common feature of critical works is to fix ideas by presenting them as diagrams, attempting to use the graphic surface [the face of a page of printed text] to impose a hierarchical order on language, communication, literature and psychology . . . [A]s Bennington argues, the ultimate effect of such diagrams is to acknowledge that 'one cannot formulate everything in a logic but at most in a graphic'. When the graphic surface is used as a theoretical limit, and anchoring device, it is not surprising that some critics fail to see its possibilities in fiction.[6]

Just as Booth's map fixes space, White argues that diagrams 'fix ideas', makes them concrete and comprehensible, and places them in a defined hierarchical order. Perhaps most illuminating is the quotation drawn from Geoffrey Bennington: that what cannot be formulated in logic and language may possibly be done in a visual representation. Just as I have noted throughout this study that Sinclair often gestures outside of the material towards the transcendent, the graphic or visual element of Sinclair's texts then gesture towards what cannot be communicated through language. (The hieroglyphic elements of Ancient Egyptian found in the *Lud Heat* maps also signify the concept of a pictorial communication, different to a language of signs.)

Modernism, space, aura

I have noted above that Franco Moretti uses a diagrammatic (or geometric) mapping of fictional texts in order to decode the relations between the spaces and of those texts. Moretti prefers 'geometry' because its relational emphasis provides more 'meaning' than topographic location. Sinclair's own conception of urban space is itself geometric. The very first line of *Lights Out for the Territory* is: 'the notion was to cut a crude **V** into the sprawl of the city, to vandalise dormant energies by an act of ambulant signmaking'.[7] Sinclair is interested in the actual, topographic fabric of London, but the centrality of the map/diagram to both editions of *Lud Heat* signify a crucial investment in a symbolic and diagrammatic reordering of London's spaces (and therefore 'dormant energies'). In his essay 'The Moment of Cubism', John Berger explores the spatial emphases of this critical mode of modernist art. He writes: 'The metaphorical model of Cubism is the *diagram*: the diagram being a visible, symbolic representation of invisible processes, forces, structures. A diagram need not eschew certain aspects of appearances: but these too will be treated symbolically as *signs*, not as imitations or re-creations'.[8] Cubism is, to an extent, mimetic, but representations of the 'real' appear as signs of underlying or invisible forces and structures. Berger could have been writing about Sinclair's representations of space. This quotation certainly seems to indicate, as I argued in Chapter 1, the traces of modernism in Sinclair's poetic practice (although as I suggested in the Introduction, Sinclair's 'spatial turn' can also be aligned with the phenomenon of postmodernity). Cubism, Berger argues, 'broke [the] continuity' of illusionist, representational pictorial space in order to force the viewer's gaze 'on the picture surface, aware once more of two-dimensional shapes on a two-dimensional canvas or board'.[9] Cubism is therefore estranging, forcing a consciousness of the picture as an art object rather than as a representation of an object or 'real' space. The pictorial space of illusion is broken down.

According to Glyn White, play with the 'graphic surface' of literary texts also causes estrangement. Whereas, in a conventional text, 'to create the internal world of the text, we have [as readers] to enter the graphic surface', forgetting or suppressing the textuality and materiality of the reading experience in order to immerse in narrative and world, 'texts featuring graphic disruptions of conventional layout demonstrate their materiality'.[10] We have seen in an earlier chapter how the material object of the book is a recurrent motif in Sinclair's texts, but here I would like to stress the importance of estrangement from the 'graphic surface' in the reading experience of Sinclair's texts. It is, in fact, analogous to the brilliance of language at the level of the sentence or line that creates 'semantic drag', at the expense of narrative propulsion in Sinclair's prose fictions. Reading Sinclair's texts are 'difficult' in the way that viewing a Cubist canvas is 'difficult', in that the texts deliberately refuse to offer the reader the pleasures of immersive representation. The actual space of the text on the printed page is self-consciously organised and demonstrates that organisation consistently to the reader (unlike in mainstream texts, where textual layout is 'naturalised' through use of typographic conventions). In *Lud Heat*, the section 'The Vortex of the Dead! The Generous!' contains a poem in the shape of a downwards-pointing arrow; in *Dining on Stones*, sections of the novel are presented in different fonts to signify their provenance. (Two 'stories' by a character, Marina Fountain, are presented in the textual fabric in courier font. These are in fact reprinted from earlier Sinclair texts.)

The estranging textual and graphic devices are analogous to the attempt Sinclair makes throughout his work to 'see with one's own eyes', without the deforming lenses of ideology, control or merely habit. Julian Wolfreys, in an article which analyses the visual and graphic strategies of Sinclair's texts, argues that:

> Such techniques, adapted to writing and the representation of London, inform all of Sinclair's major publications, whether presented exclusively the presentation of words in prose or poetry, or whether accompanied with photographs, photomontages, or illustrations produced by a number of media. Sinclair's text is inescapably graphic.[11]

For Wolfreys, typographic and visual strategies of Sinclair signify, in the forms of the texts themselves, the 'graphic interruptions that mark and write the city topographically and historically'.[12] The spatial form represents the occluded fabric of power and control of London itself. While making the reader conscious of the 'invisible rods of force' at work in the fabric of London, Sinclair's texts also demand a self-conscious and active readership, participating in reimagining and re-enchanting London through a non-immersive experience of the text. Robert Bond also suggests that Sinclair encodes a pecu-liarly self-conscious mode of reception. Through discontinuity and montage-like textual effects, Bond suggests, Sinclair effects a kind of 'interruptive meditation', an estrangement by which the ideological flow of contemporary lived experience is ruptured and the 'real' perceived anew. I will return to the importance of cinema below, but would here emphasise the again the importance of a modernist artistic practice in the form of cinema as montage: the collision of two shots, two images, to produce meaning for the estranged, self-conscious viewer.

An emphasis on the materiality of the book is vital to understanding the visual and graphic structures of Sinclair's texts. Glyn White deploys the idea of 'aura' with regard to the art object developed by Walter Benjamin. Benjamin, in 'The Work of Art in the Age of Mechanical Reproduction' suggests that the work of art in the period before mechanical reproduction was suffused by an inimitable presence in time and space, its specific history, and changes to its physical condition. This 'authentic' art object is possessed of 'aura', a kind of value crated by its uniqueness and authenticity.[13] In the age of reproduction, this 'aura' is dispelled, but Benjamin celebrates the liberating possibilities of this change rather than lament the loss of the authentic. White applies the idea of 'aura' to the material object of the book:

> The medium of print is inherently mechanically reproducible and had been in widespread use for three centuries when Benjamin was writing (as he knew well). The novel, which developed as a printed form, has thus never held the same type of aura as painting, a fresco or sculpture, because by its very nature it is not unique. The loss of aura from the work of the author begins with its publication, and thus only original manuscripts may be invested with this quality.[14]

It is worthy of the note that a crucial plot device in Sinclair's *Radon Daughters* is a manuscript of a 'sequel' (written before the original) to Hope Hodgson's *The House on the Borderland*, a manuscript that is appropriated by a rather dubious secret state operative named Drage-Bell. (In *The Verbals*, Sinclair reveals that the genesis of the publication of *Radon Daughters* came about through a publisher proposing to Sinclair that he should write such a 'sequel', to a book that ends with the destruction of the universe. *Radon Daughters* was the result of this proposal.) This manuscript certainly has 'aura': it is possessed by the Cambridge academic Simon Undark (a version of the poet and don J. H. Prynne) and coveted by Todd Sileen, the one-legged pedestrian and X-ray addict, a quasi-magical or totemic object. Elsewhere in his works, Sinclair incorporates the manuscript or typescript into the visual texture of the book: the cover of *The Verbals* overlays Sinclair in the crypt of St Anne's, Limehouse with a reproduction of a marked-up transcript of part of the interview; in *Slow Chocolate Autopsy*, Sinclair's script is incorporated into the graphic story 'The Double Death of the Falconer' by the artist Dave McKean. The machinery of production, and the 'authentic' or 'original' object, is introduced into the visual patterning of the book itself.

Crucially, though, I would argue that 'aura' is central to the small-press publication of much of Sinclair's later poetry, his self-published volumes *Kodak Mantra Diaries*, *Lud Heat* and *Suicide Bridge*, and also the limited Goldmark editions of books that accompany the publication of Sinclair's major texts by mainstream publishers. These texts much more nearly approach the status of 'work of art'. Editions are numbered, signed by Sinclair, and some contain unique holographic or other inserted material. This mode of publication returns writing to a kind of artisanal activity and renders the physical, material object of the book a unique work rather than mechanically reproduced commodity. These texts then gain some of the 'aura' lost in the age of modernity.

A diagram of the visual

As we can see in Table 1, which lists the visual components of Sinclair's texts, up to 1999's *Sorry Meniscus*, black and white reproduction of illustrations and photographs predominates. After 1999's BFI Modern Classic essay on David Cronenberg's *Crash*, which, like the rest of its series is filled with colour stills (and is printed on glossy paper), colour reproduction predominates. The means by which photographs are reproduced also changes, from being integrated into the text itself (printed directly on to the page) to becoming colour plate sections, bound separately to the written text. We can conclude that the higher quality production of Sinclair's books, with colour reproduction of the visual material predominating, alters the relationship between photographic image and text, until 2005's *Edge of the Orison*, which returns to an 'integrated' layout.

A further conclusion can be drawn from Table 1 about Sinclair's chosen collaborators. The first is Brian Catling, Sinclair's most important early collaborator, who provides the visual material in the Albion Village Press editions of *Lud Heat* and *Suicide Bridge*. The second major collaborator is Marc Atkins, the photographer who acts as a kind of ambulatory Boswell in *Lights Out for the Territory*. His photographs are central to the visual texture of Sinclair's books from the 1995 Vintage paperback reissue of *Downriver* to the dust jacket of 2002's *London Orbital*. Atkins's photographs not only provide additional visual information for the reader, as carefully composed 'art works' they stand in opposition to Sinclair's own snapshot 'logging' of various walks that he uses later as an aide-memoire when writing. Atkins's photographs aestheticise the city, particularly in the collaborative work *Liquid City*. The relation between Atkins's photographic images and Sinclair's words changes in each text, and is particularly self-consciously presented in *Liquid City*. The importance of Catling and Atkins is to the presentation or visual texture of the books as material objects; their visual sensibilities become encoded into the fabric of Sinclair's work, and their images vital to the way in which the texts work upon the reader.

In 'The Photographic Message', Roland Barthes analyses 'traditional' and 'contemporary' usages of text and image. He writes:

> The image no longer *illustrates* the words; it is now the words which, structurally, are parasitic on the image [. . .] Formerly, the image illustrated the text (made it clearer): today, the text loads the image, burdening it with a culture, a moral, an imagination.[15]

Barthes considers newspaper or magazine publication more than book illustration here, but his insights into the relationship between image and text are worthy of consideration. His emphasis on the caption, a text which determines the meaning of the image through linguistic connotation, is important to an analysis of photographs in Sinclair's books. Ironically, this is because the photographs in all but the BFI *Crash* have no captions. Where, in Barthes' analyses, the binary of text and image form a hierarchy – one determines, or is parasitical upon, the other – in Sinclair's *Crash*, and in *Liquid* City, the text and the image represent the same space, the same experience, but differently. The text does not attempt to comment on, or determine the meaning of the photograph, nor does the image 'illustrate' the text or provide the same information in a different form (as the diagram/map of *Lud Heat* does). As Barthes himself notes,

Table 1

	Year/Publisher	Integrated photos	Integrated illustrations	Diagrams	Section title photos	Section title drawings/paintings	Bound-in plates	Graphic stories	End-paper illustrations (HB only)	Other	McKean	Catling	Atkins
KMD	1971 AVP	B/w											
LH	1975 AVP	B/w	*	*						'found' plates of St Annes, Blake, Typography		*	
SB	1979 AVP	B/w	*			B/w						*	
LH & SB	1995 Vintage Granta			*						Effie Paleogou photo on jacket	*		
WCST	1987 Goldmark				B/w					Rigby Graham frontispiece John Bellany painting on dustjacket			
WCST	1988 Paladin									Richard Parent cover painting			
D	1991/1995 Vintage												
RD	1994 J. Cape				B/w								*

SCA	1997 Phoenix		B/w	B/w	*		Graphic stories + Cover	*
LT	2001 Granta							
DoS	2004 Hamish Hamilton				*	Typography	Dustjacket	
LOFTT	1998 Granta			B/w				*
SM	1999 Profile	B/w						*
Crash	1999 BFI	Colour				Film stills		
LC	1999 Reaktion							*
RR	1999 Granta			Colour				
DL	1999 Goldmark		Colour			Emma Matthews Maps, loose insert		*
LO	2002 Granta			Colour	*	Renchi Bicknell	Dustjacket	*
WG	2002 Goldmark		Colour			Emma Matthews		
EotO	2005 Hamish Hamilton	B/w						

there is never a real incorporation [between text and image] since the
structures of the two structures (graphic and iconic) are irreducible
[. . .] It is impossible [. . .] that the words 'duplicate' the image: in the
movement from one structure to the other second signifieds are
inevitably developed.[16]

In *Liquid City*, text and image generally stand in semi-autonomous
relation even though they present the same subject(s): 'Drif and
Martin Stone' is accompanied by a shot of Stone; Sinclair's poem 'A
Serious of Photographs' is accompanied by shots of electricity pylons
on the Isle of Grain in the Thames estuary. Rarely does Sinclair
describe or analyse one of Atkins's photographs, though he does
in 'The Synagogue' and '*Rodinsky's Mirror*'. Sometimes (as in 'the
vegetative Bunyan') an Atkins shot is the starting point for one of
Sinclair's own meditations or mini-narratives. In these, text and image
stand in dialectical relation, one causing a dynamic in the other.

Slow Chocolate Autopsy

In 1997, Sinclair published *Slow Chocolate Autopsy* in collaboration
with Dave McKean. It is a collection of short pieces connected through
the device of a recurrent character, Norton. The stories range from
the death of Christopher Marlowe in a Deptford tavern, to the
decapitation of a football fan in order for his own head to be used
in a game of 'hardball', to a visionary tale narrated from the point
of view of minor gangland villain (and Kray brothers' victim) Jack
'The Hat' McVitie. Most of the pieces were published elsewhere
prior to their collection in *Slow Chocolate Autopsy*, and Sinclair
himself confesses in *The Verbals* that the book was put together quite
quickly and is one of the more minor works in his œuvre. As such,
it has suffered from critical neglect, as only Julian Wolfreys article
'Londonography; Iain Sinclair's Urban Graphic' (2005) deals with
the text in any detail. It is important, however, for three reasons: it
is the first major appearance of 'Norton', who, as 'Andrew Norton',
reappears in *Landor's Tower* and *Dining on Stones* as a fairly
transparent alter-ego for Sinclair himself; second, the text contains
four 'graphic stories' in collaboration with McKean, the first (and so
far only) excursion by Sinclair into this field (whereas McKean has
a long and distinguished history in the graphic novel); and third, the
production of the text is self-consciously announced by Sinclair in
the 'Acknowledgements' as a kind of companion piece or parallel

work to the Sinclair–Petit film *The Falconer*. One of the graphic stories is in fact entitled 'The Double Death of the Falconer', and takes elements from the narrative of the film, including representations of the artist and filmmaker Peter Whitehead (who had made the film *Wholly Communion*, about the Albert Hall Poetry Reading in 1965, which I mentioned in Chapter 1). Whitehead was a consistent figure in the British counter-cultural scene of the 1960s, and is represented in the film as a kind of shaman, obsessed with the symbols of falconry.

In 'The Double Death of the Falconer', Whitehead is represented by 'Peter Pytchley', an artist who suffers a heart attack and whose identity is 'absorbed by Alan Wolfehead, his body double'.[17] Wolfehead is a 'pulp-fiction anti-hero' and secret state 'spook', stretched out on a hospital gurney, who directs his 'daughter' Frankie Lux to 'tag', 'hook' and 'lock up' Norton. She follows Norton to the National Portrait Gallery where an exhibition by 'Axel Turner' (a version of Marc Atkins) is taking place. Present in the background of the frames in the hospital is 'Olga', Wolfehead's 'angel of death', a kind of double or fetch, a motif emphasised visually by two overlapping panels at the top of the ninth page of the story, where Wolfehead's speech balloon runs into and interlaces with Olga's. Frankie meets Norton at a book signing at the London bookshop 'Murder One', at which William Burroughs's last book *My Education: A Book of Dreams* is being promoted. (Burroughs returns right at the end of *Slow Chocolate Autopsy*, in pages which follow the 'Acknowledgements' and which are not connected to any story in the text. The front cover of the Ace Double edition of Burroughs's *Junky* – then published as *Junkie* under the pseudonym of William Lee – is reproduced opposite the first page of Chapter 1 of *Junky*, which is superimposed upon a photograph of Sinclair standing next to Burroughs in front of the latter's white clapboard house in Lawrence, Kansas. Where *Kodak Mantra Diaries* commemorates Allen Ginsberg's impact upon the counter-culture in London, and his importance to Sinclair personally, here we find an oblique homage to Ginsberg's friend and another major, though less acknowledged, influence on Sinclair's work.)

In the story, Norton sports a black goatee beard (which he later doffs then puts back on again, signifying his fluid subjectivity through masquerade) and clutches a skull and glass of red wine. He pitches a book project to Frankie – 'Send me your best dream, your worst nightmare' – as, one suspects, a kind of pick-up, although we later see the book project being downplayed by a publisher's representative with the phrase 'Strictly anthology rates on this one'. Norton then follows Frankie down the Charing Cross Road, literally: McKean uses the *London A–Z*, flattened into a perspectival plane, on which to place the two figure in sequential panels. They literally 'walk the map'. Once at the gallery, Norton dons the goatee once more, and declaims 'Give us a quid. A quid for a dream'. There are echoes here of both *Hamlet* and *Richard III*; the skull, a symbol of mortality, prefigures Norton's fate. He stares at one of Turner's portraits, which is actually a distorted version of the face of Sinclair taken from the photograph with William Burroughs. When Frankie photographs Norton, however, which is intercut with Wolfehead's unheard interdiction 'No!', Norton dissolves. Kneeling, clutching his head, the skull dropped mid-air (or floating) beside him, he says: 'Help me. My fucking face is melting'. Above him on the page, Olga stands in a triptych of panels as the angel of death, Egyptian-goddess be-winged. Norton is revealed to be Wolfehead's own double: at the bottom of the page, Wolfehead lies back on the gurney, staring blankly, the edge of the drawing burnt paper; on the facing page, a similarly burnt sheet contains the image of a silhouette marked on the floor, smoke rising. Whether it is Norton or Wolfehead that has dissolved is unclear. The final image of the story returns to one at the top of the first page, a photocopy of Battersea Park from the *A–Z* overdrawn with pencilled trees and two small figures. One says to the other (who is presumably 'Turner'/ Atkins): 'The Pytchley story's dead in the water. They say it's all been done before. Sorry, son, but it's back to the walks and the obit snapshots'.[18] The story is circular, and finally makes a self-conscious joke about Atkins's own 'entrapment', not inside the space and time of London, but as a collaborator in Sinclair's book projects.

It is important to stress the complex visual overlaying and hybridity of McKean's work in *Slow Chocolate Autopsy*. Julian Wolfreys emphasises McKean's analogous visual practice of what he calls the 'chorography' of Sinclair's texts, chorography being an Elizabethan term that denoted 'the various historical, folkloric, and cultural resonances which could be unearthed in one location'.[19] Wolfreys describes McKean's work thus:

> In a number of montages that gather together photographs, film-stills, fragments of type, pen and pencil drawings, maps and etchings, McKean projects uncanny chorographical forms that serve to figure London and particular strands from the history of its decomposing identity.[20]

McKean's work is, in fact, a kind of compressed compendium of many of the graphic and visual devices Sinclair uses throughout his own texts. Note again the importance of the word 'montage', as we found above in Robert Bond's conception of Sinclair's 'interruptive' intent. As Wolfreys himself argues, a key phrase in *Slow Chocolate Autopsy*, found in the graphic story 'The Griffin's Egg', indicates the centrality of montage (as a collision of images) to this text in particular, and Sinclair's work as a whole: 'Stick any two postcards to a wall and you've got a narrative'.[21]

The visual text

Slow Chocolate Autopsy is, as Wolfreys notes, neither novel, nor graphic novel, nor short-story collection or sequence, but a hybrid of all three. This hybridity makes *Slow Chocolate Autopsy* a difficult text to approach as whole, because it resists coherence. Consistency is achieved partly through the recurrence of McKean's artwork, as he produces title pages to the text-only stories that connect visually to the four collaborative graphic stories in the book. *Slow Chocolate Autopsy* is, however, an experiment in what I have taken as my epigraph to this chapter, 'a marriage of convenience between literature and cinema'. *Slow Chocolate Autopsy* cannot be cinema, of course, but McKean's densely compacted artwork approaches the visual richness of the moving image; it is itself a form of 'montage'.

Sinclair has himself returned to cinema since the late 1990s. His first collaboration with Chris Petit, *The Cardinal and the Corpse* (1993) is a semi-documentary film that elaborates upon the 'refor-gotten' writers that Sinclair is at pains to promote, writers such as William Hope Hodgson, mentioned above, or then-living writers such as the crime novelist Derek Raymond (Robin Cook). Petit directed from Sinclair's script. Subsequent films *The Falconer* (1998), *Asylum* (2000) and *London Orbital* (2003) are co-directed by Petit and Sinclair, and edited by Emma Matthews. *The Falconer*, whose visual texture attests to the input of McKean, is presented as a Burroughsian text. An opening title declares 'A film I which nothing is true and everything is permitted', while on the soundtrack song lyrics insinuate 'It's only a movie'. The film is narrated in thirteen parts, and features Peter Whitehead at its centre. The narrative framing device involves a photographer, one Françoise Lacroix, who is employed as a researcher, to 'log' an archive of videotapes which propose Whitehead as the 'spook's spook', involved with MI5 and the secret state; as an occultist who attempts to bend the universe to his will; as a survivor of the 1960s; as a terrified loner; as a kind of psychological or actual vampire; and ultimately as a kind of narcissistic self-mythologiser whose impenetrable matrices of lies, half-truths and semi-legendary stories infect the very fabric of the film. Whitehead is not a double or split subject, but a multiple one, presenting one of a wardrobe of possible selves at any one time. The invocation of Burroughs, that 'nothing is true and everything is permitted', signifies that the film presents this multiplicity and inconsistently quite deliberately and self-consciously. As with the estranging function of the graphic and visual devices I noted earlier, *The Falconer* refuses immersion, and its fragmentary form ultimately refuses narrative, in order for the viewer to be brought forth as a self-conscious decoder rather than passive consumer.

As I have intimated, *The Falconer*, as a film, is also infected with text and textuality. There are thirteen intertitles, and the texture of the film itself is made up of layers: film, video, CCTV footage, irises or frames, photographs, still images, text, scratches or abrasions, and non-synchronous audio. In *Asylum*, the next collaboration, the complex visual texture is reduced to a science fiction-inspired frame story in which the film itself is made up of found 'tapes', and rather curious CGI sequences that punctuate the film. These are investigated to uncover 'the cultural memory of the race', as a female voice-over narration declares. Sinclair himself also provides voice-over narration in *Asylum* and talks of memory as a resource: the entire film self-presents as 'a film about memory, exile and madness'. The science-fiction frame-story is somewhat apocalyptic, suggesting some kind of image-virus (again, shades of Burroughs) has brought about the necessity of this investigation into 'cultural memory'. Where, in *The Falconer*, Whitehead relentlessly self-presents at the centre of the film, here Sinclair himself performs a kind of self-conscious (and self-parodic, perhaps) 'routine' about the Green Way, while Michael Moorcock – said to 'embody a thousand years of London's literary history' – is located in exile in Texas, though his footage is much more documentary in tone and his presence far less performative. Again, identity is in flux in *Asylum*, and the film as a whole a rather oblique take on the importance of memory that can be found more urgently in other Sinclair texts. The recurrent presence of footage taken from a car in motion does, however, anticipate the much more substantial *London Orbital* film.

I have noted elsewhere in this study that the sequence of Sinclair's publications has operated since the mid-1990s on a kind of 'twin track' strategy. Mainstream publications are often accompanied by small-press volumes that approach the material in a different way; the prime example is *Dark Lanthorns* and *Rodinsky's Room*. I have suggested here that the films also stand in relation to literary texts, such as *The Falconer* and *Slow Chocolate Autopsy*. For *London Orbital*, there are two texts of the same name: the book, and the film. This might suggest that the film of *London Orbital* is a kind of film version of the book, even a kind of adaptation, but in fact this is not so. Both texts stand alone as very different meditations on similar material (though both also are connected to *Sorry Meniscus* and *Crash*). I will treat of the thematic content of both film and book in Chapter 6, but here will sketch the particular motifs and techniques which make the film *London Orbital* the most effective of all of the Petit–Sinclair collaborations.

The motif of identity and split subjectivity, recurrent throughout Sinclair's texts, is handled in *The Falconer* through the multiple self-presentation of Whitehead, and the destabilisation of 'truth' and 'reality'. In *London Orbital*, the 'split' is manifested both in the visual image – split-screen visuals are used particularly effectively – and through the use of two voice-over narrators, Petit and Sinclair. Where the book concentrates on Sinclair's counter-clockwise walk around the 'acoustic footsteps' of the M25, the film's focus is upon footage taken from a car driving around the motorway. Sinclair's walking project attempts to undo the malign influence of the Millennium Dome; Petit's driving project deftly imitates the state of fugue that descends upon the motorway driver, with slightly defocused video photography and jump-cuts between different parts of the motorway expressing disorientation and dislocation. The sound stage is also used in a highly effective manner: Petit deploys 'found' radio phone-in dialogue, looping electronic pulses and beats, and a recurring 'Arabic' or Middle Eastern-influenced percussive track to provide a kind of formal coherence and patterning to the seemingly (and deliberately) endless driving footage. The footage and the soundtrack loops, just like the M25 itself, but ultimately provides order rather than disorientation.

The most affecting images are from Sinclair's own 8mm silent 'home movie' footage taken in the late 1960s and early 1970s. More recent Sinclair texts, such as *Edge of the Orison* (2005), have shown a marked and deliberate strategy to insert Sinclair's own personal history, personal or familial memories into his texts. His meditations on time, loss and memory gain a particular emotional resonance and urgency when expressed through the placing of footage of Sinclair's wife, Anna, as a young woman on the streets of London, directly into the texture of the film. If, as Petit's narration suggests at the end of *London Orbital*, 'we become lost' through a cultural system of erasure and overwriting (finding its symbol in the M25), then Sinclair's imagery of Anna is a concrete manifestation of 'memory'. She is not lost, nor is this image of the past, and nor are we if we record, log, remember. What we must do, Sinclair suggests, is to preserve the archive, of our own lives, and of our own communities.

Notes

1   Iain Sinclair, *Lights Out for the Territory: 9 Excursions in the Secret History of London* (London: Granta, 1998), p. 274.
2   Franco Moretti, *Atlas of the European Novel 1800–1900* (London: Verso, 1998), p. 5.
3   Ania Loomba, *Colonialism/ Postcolonialism* (London: Routledge, 1998), p. 78.
4   Franco Moretti, 'Graphs, Maps, Trees: Abstract Models for Literary History – 2', *New Left Review* 26, March–April (2004), 79–103 (95).
5   Moretti, 'Graphs, Maps, Trees', p. 96.
6   Glyn White, *Reading the Graphic Surface: The Presence of the Book in Prose Fiction* (Manchester and New York: Manchester University Press, 2005), p. 42.
7   Sinclair, *Lights Out for the Territory*, p. 1.
8   John Berger, 'The Moment of Cubism', in G. Dyer (ed.), *Selected Essays* (London: Bloomsbury, 2001), pp. 71–92 (p. 84).
9   Berger, 'The Moment of Cubism', pp. 84–5.
10 White, *Reading the Graphic Surface*, pp. 20 and 18.
11 Julian Wolfreys, 'Londonography; Iain Sinclair's Urban Graphic', *Literary London* 3:2 (2005) (accessed 1 December 2005). <www.literarylondon.org/london-journal/julian.html>, par. 2.
12 Wolfreys, 'Londonography', par. 3.
13 Walter Benjamin, 'The Work of Art in the Age of Mechanical Reproduction', in Hannah Arendt (ed.), trans. Harry Zohn, *Illuminations* (London: Fontana, 1992), pp. 211–44 (pp. 213–14).

14 White, *Reading the Graphic Surface*, p. 24.
15 Roland Barthes, 'The Photographic Message', *Selected Writings*, S. Sontag (ed.) (London: Fontana, 1983), pp. 194–210 (pp. 204 and 205).
16 Barthes, 'The Photographic Message', p. 205.
17 Iain Sinclair with Dave McKean, *Slow Chocolate Autopsy* (London: Phoenix, 1997), p. 116.
18 Sinclair with McKean, *Slow Chocolate Autopsy*, p. 131.
19 Wolfreys, 'Londonography', par. 7.
20 Wolfreys, 'Londonography', par. 20.
21 Sinclair with McKean, *Slow Chocolate Autopsy*, p. 88.

6

Driven to the margins

Iain Sinclair begins *London Orbital: A Walk Around the M25* (2002) with the following: 'It started with the Dome, the Millennium Dome'.[1] In 1999, Sinclair had published *Sorry Meniscus*, a small text which outlines two visits Sinclair made to the Dome in the years preceding its opening, in 1997 and 1999. Sinclair's publications (not least in the *London Review of Books*, who arranged the visits), on London spaces and literatures, seemed to make him an apt choice to assess the impact of the Dome. He could hardly have been expected to be uncritical of the project – which he characterises as a 'classic Tory scam' appropriated by New Labour as a 'blank canvas' on which to project 'stunning images, product placement, faces of the plastic gods' – but in retrospect, the Dome seems to have had an extremely perturbing effect on Sinclair's map of contemporary London.[2]

One must wonder why the Dome seems to tax Sinclair so much (other than the sense that it is literally *taxes* in their millions of pounds which underwrote its construction, running and disposal. In *London Orbital* Sinclair notes that the Dome cost '£80 a minute to the taxpayer').[3] In psychogeographical terms, the Dome is a kind of intervention in the spatial fabric of London, a deforming presence that attests to the imperatives of power and capital that are the foundations of Sinclair's opposition to New Labour. In terms of the cultural and social history of London's civic spaces, however, perhaps the Dome is not so anomalous after all. In *Sorry Meniscus*, Sinclair paraphrases the discourse of New Labour publicists when rationalising the Dome to the public: 'They said the Great Exhibition was a waste of money. They said the Festival of Britain wouldn't pull the punters. This is a signal to the world: we can transform vision into reality in the shortest possible space of time. Give us the bread and we'll give you the circuses'.[4] In calling up the Great Exhibition of 1851 and the 1951 Festival of Britain, also located on the south bank of the Thames, Sinclair indicates that the Dome is part of what Tony Bennett has called the 'exhibitionary complex' that determined the form and purpose of the rise of public museums and exhibitions in the second half of the nineteenth century. Using Foucault's ideas of panoptic space, Bennett argues that the Great Exhibition

> brought together an ensemble of disciplines and techniques of display that had been developed within the previous histories of museums, panoramas, mechanics' Institute exhibitions, art galleries, and arcades. In doing so, it translated these into exhibitionary forms which, in simultaneously ordering objects for public exhibition and ordering the public that inspected, were to have a profound and lasting influence on the subsequent development of museums, art galleries, expositions, and department stores.[5]

Museums and galleries, once opened to the public, had a regulatory or disciplinary effect on the behaviour of the London crowd. The combination of spectacle and surveillance, a museum architecture which allowed both the crowd to look at objects and to be looked at, also encouraged the crowd to see itself as part of the spectacle, and therefore regulate its own behaviour as part of an ordered system of representation. This system of representation, Bennett suggests, determined that exhibitions and museums were organised to encourage popular identification with a particularly national spectacle; the pedagogic function of the Great Exhibition, for instance, was to identify Great Britain as a world leader in manufactures, and to represent Britain's imperial power through the display of goods produced by (or ransacked from) the colonies. Rivals to Britain's economic status, such as France, Germany or the USA, were provided relatively marginal sites within the exhibition, encouraging a popular self-identification of crowd with nation state, *civis* with *polis*.

In pinpointing the 'happy-clappy imperialism' of the Dome, Sinclair implicitly places it in the tradition of the 'exhibitionary complex'.[6] However, if all there is to celebrate in 'Mogadon Britain' is 'its beggars (native and imported), its hospitals converted into Wendy House estates, its care-in-the-community psychotics forced to discover that "community" had evaporated somewhere around 1953', then the Dome becomes a kind of simulacrum of the museum, a museum without objects, a ruined museum where there are no wares nor pedagogic impulse, only the disciplinary effects of spectacle and surveillance.[7] The date of 1953 (coronation year for Queen Elizabeth II) becomes a kind of zero-point of Britain's decline. In a Britain characterised by 'public clowns, holy fools, craven press, zombie culture, and state-sponsored know-nothings', the connection to the era of the Festival of Britain (pre-1953) or even the Great Exhibition seems curiously bound up with a kind of nostalgia, as all 'declinism' seems to be.[8]

Ronald Thomas has noted what seems to be an important difference between the Great Exhibition and the Dome. Whereas the Great Exhibition displayed the 'wares of the world', but also emphasised British mercantile and industrial power,

> The Millennium Dome (according to [Tony] Blair) would be designed to present an entertainment experience rather than a display of objects or industry. Accordingly, he describes the Dome *not* as a place but as a '*time* for the nation to come together to be excited, entertained, moved and uplifted.' The emphasis upon products and territory in the Great Exhibition, organized as it was as a virtual commodity map of the world with individual exhibits displayed nation by nation, has been replaced in the new millennium by the Dome's emphasis upon experience and time in a series of entertainment events and on redefining what it means to be a nation in a world defined by spectacle and simulation.[9]

Thomas suggests that the Dome was part of an ideological project to negotiate the seeming fracture of a unified British 'identity', which we encountered in Chapter 3, furthered by New Labour's commitment to a programme of partial political devolution, difference and community signified in Tony Blair's phrase 'time for the nation to come together' (which is to say, it is *not* 'together'). The Dome, with its spectacle of different 'zones', embodied this fracture within the illusion of a single space (the Dome itself). According to Bennett, however, even though the Dome relocates its exhibitionary complex away from space towards 'time', away from material objects and towards simulation, its disciplinary underpinnings are reflected in the terms of Thomas's analysis: an identification with centrality of the British nation-state, even more imperative in New Labour's (and Sinclair's) Britain.

Curiously, Sinclair visits the Dome before it opens, and not afterwards. The photographs in *Sorry Meniscus* show a building site, devoid of people, or the Dome silhouetted against grey skies from a distance. As I argued in the Introduction, Sinclair's excursions take place in an emptied urban landscape, where the psychogeographic signs can be decoded. Marc Atkins' photographs in *Lights Out for the Territory, Liquid City, Sorry Meniscus* and *London Orbital* tend to feature depopulated landscapes; the walk around the M25 itself takes place along verges, paths, country lanes. Although the Dome is identified with the exhibitionary complex, the disciplinary effects of spectacle and surveillance on the urban crowd, Sinclair recurrently represents evacuated space, often a symbol for alienation and a kind of 'spiritual' emptiness. In *London Orbital*, instead of partaking of the crowds and festivities in London on Millennium Eve, Sinclair and his wife make a deliberate decision to drive away from the city, to Waltham Abbey, where they eat a meal in a near-deserted Indian restaurant. Though couched as an escape from New Labour fakery, 'nothing much to see, a moving stream of fire that didn't, unremarkable fireworks', what characterises Sinclair's portrayal of the London festivities is a aversion to the crowd: 'trains not running or impossibly crowded. Young girls who fainted or were attacked and couldn't get to hospital, or were turned away from police stations. Epic traverses in unsuitable shoes, further and further east, to escape the crush, the craziness'.[10] The crowd here is unmistakeably the mob, the spectre that haunted London's governance before the disciplinary effects of the 'exhibitionary complex' and, sometimes, afterwards. In *London: The Biography*, Peter Ackroyd gives over a chapter to 'Mobocracy', where he catalogues the 'irritability and sudden changes of mood' of the crowd, and the anti-authority temper of many crowds in the eighteenth century.[11] He also charts a decline in the prevalence of rioting and civic disorder, but suggests, in the terms of his rather essentialist and universalising 'biographical' conception of the city, that the city 'is at once too large and too complex to react to local outbreaks of passionate feeling, and in the twentieth century the most marked characteristic of riots and demonstrations was their failure to make any real impression on the stony hearted and unyielding city'.[12] London's mobs, declares Ackroyd, 'have never yet dominated it'.[13] As we have seen above, it is probably not the case that 'London endures' because of its natural amelioration of the effects of crowd violence, but that historically, the mob was suppressed through the regulation of crowd behaviour and the promotion of other forms of civic involvement.

Where Ackroyd downplays the importance of the crowd or mob in London's history and social organisation, Sinclair's evacuation of the crowd from London's streets is even apparent when describing his return to London on a day when street demonstrations have disturbed the order of the city.

> The orderly processions of the morning, making its way up New Bridge Street towards Ludgate Hill, are now – thanks to armed response units, Samurai snatch squads – a small riot. Provocation and response, the dance at the end of the day. Battle honours, blood on the T-shirt, lightly worn . . . We sit in a bar in Smithfield, relishing the riptide of energy, the necessary civic argument in which we play no part. Let the city burn for the cameras. This is nothing. There is worse to come.[14]

This is another example of the disengagement or distancing effected by Sinclair in his position of 'documenter' that we saw in *Kodak Mantra Diaries* and *The Verbals* in the Introduction to this book. Sinclair depoliticises the violence by representing it as ritual, as a 'dance', fundamentally non-serious and a spectacle for the crowd and for the cameras. Sinclair clearly has little time for this kind of political activity, and never sees the violence; instead, he lies down 'in the middle of the road on Blackfriars Bridge to take a photograph of an arrowed sign saying: CITY'.[15] The act of taking the photograph, seemingly one of documentation, is in fact artfully composed to elucidate a fantasy of absence, 'London without cars'.[16] Rather than documenting the protest, Sinclair instead retreats to an artificial and fantasised image of London where the crowd, the mob, is absent, and cannot trouble the journey of the psychogeographer.

The crowd does appear in *Lights Out for the Territory*, where Sinclair and Marc Atkins follow the funeral procession route of 'The Colonel', Ronnie Kray, in East London. The crowd, a 'mob of voyeurs' is described in terms which once again underline Sinclair's distance from them: 'The jobless, the unwaged, the never haves, the ones who parrot the party line, and those who don't have the faintest idea of what is going on today or any other day. A restlessness is abroad. They all feel the buzz, the tremor'. Worse, the crowd become grotesque, hallucinated, a 'festival of the maimed in which we were no more than pretenders'.[17] Clearly, Sinclair does not identify with those who spectate (as he does), but deliberately marks off his 'investigation' from their blithe and unknowing consumption. Curiously, it is in this very section that Sinclair declares his rejection of the *flâneur* and instead validates 'stalking the city', terms that were investigated in the Introduction. This gesture, then, could be read as motivated by Sinclair's desire to distance himself from other forms of spectatorship and walking, directly produced out of his immersion in, and aversion to, the crowd. By the time Sinclair and Atkins reach the cemetery, at All Saints church on Chingford Mount (in the East London/Essex borderlands), there's 'no trace of ... tearful crowds', and 'with relief' they enter the 'peaceful avenues of the dead'.[18] In retracing the route of the funeral procession, Sinclair and Atkins have evacuated the streets and finally located a 'paradise garden': of the dead. Later in the section, Sinclair describes the crowd in terms of the disciplinary complex of the exhibition: spectators become part of the spectacle, the 'crowd taking its own portrait', the very model of the disciplinary regulation of public behaviour.[19]

The reason for this evacuation of the streets is unclear. Perhaps the aversion from the crowd is another indicator of the move away from the politics of the counter-culture I diagnosed in the Introduction. Just as Sinclair was a self-confessed 'observer' in the Grosvenor Square demonstrations in London against the Vietnam War, this distancing from the crowd perhaps represents a rejection of a populist politics that engage in demonstrations: the 'mob' always haunts the 'crowd'. Sinclair's independent trajectories then demonstrate an exhaustion of the communitarian imperatives that propelled counter-culture street demonstrations (in the May Events in Paris in 1968, in Prague, or on the streets of Chicago), and perhaps an anxiety about what the 'mob' may eventually provoke: violent reaction and suppression, the 'dance' between police 'snatch squads' and the rioting crowd. Another possible reason is to do with Sinclair's status as incomer to London (although he has now lived there for over thirty years): Sinclair's observing eye turns urban fabric into landscape, a possibility also suggested by *London Orbital*'s turn towards the 'paradise gardens' of London's green spaces (see below). Third, and perhaps most importantly, I would like to suggest a relationship between Sinclair and space which bears upon this, and which we investigated in Chapter 5: that Sinclair evacuates the streets of London in order to see their significance, because in his texts Sinclair necessarily reduces the complexity of London as it is lived into diagrammatic form, in order to investigate the relationship of forces that he diagnoses as investing its infrastructures.

The scenes described above, which attest to the disruptive potential energies of the urban crowd or mob, are minor but highly suggestive ones in Sinclair's work, and indicate the ideological work required by the Dome project to forge a unified representation of a fractured and disrupted Britain. As Ronald Thomas suggests, it is heavily ironic and somewhat significant that Greenwich was used to site the Dome (originally planned for Birmingham), as the introduction of a uniform British time (based upon the Mean Time calculated at the Greenwich meridian) 'gradually imposed a standardized experience of space (calculated station by station) as an increasingly frequent and precise schedule of operation regimented one's sense of time (according to departure and arrival timetables)'.[20] Greenwich Mean Time, whose position at the 'zero' point by which all other global times are measured (there were over a dozen prior to 1884), owes its position to political wrangling and to Britain's imperial and scientific eminence in the nineteenth century. Sinclair refers to this idea in *Downriver*, where Sinclair describes 'a women whose job it was to entrain daily for Greenwich to capture and fetch back the 'right time', so that the watchmakers of Clerkenwell could make a show of precision, repair their damaged stock with transfusions of the real'.[21] Uniform (or national) time, suggests Sinclair, was a 'privatised' time, dictated by the necessity for coherent railway timetables. 'Time could be a local affair [. . .] but now, by decree, anywhere and everywhere had to come over, check in, attach themselves to the machine (heart) locked within the dome on Greenwich Hill'.[22] As with the informing principles behind the exhibitionary complex of the Great Exhibition, the imperatives of the nation state are central to the imposition of uniform time, and we can perhaps sense nostalgia here for the loss of local variation. In *Sorry Meniscus*, Sinclair hints at the ideological significance of Greenwich and time.

> 'And the vision is?' I asked. 'Er, time,' Mr Gibbons replied. 'Time,' he repeated, after a significant pause, remembering to capitalise the abstraction. I understood: millennium, zero longitude, Greenwich. Prospects of future sports-fests. Berlin in the Thirties, without Leni Reifenstahl.[23]

The Dome inserts itself into the narrative (and ideological imperatives) of Britain's imperial past, its presumed centrality to global affairs, and to the affirmed condition of a 'unified' British culture and subjectivity. A political act, then, which emphasises its political or ideological significance: as David Harvey has argued, a standardised and compressed sense of space and time is a central component of the modern industrialised nation state, the necessity of which is reaffirmed in the Dome's homogenised space.[24] Not only that, but the reference to Berlin's 1936 Olympiad indicates a debased (totalitarian) utopianism at the heart of the Dome project, one also found in Speer's architectural monumentalism and Reifenstahl's films.

Both *Sorry Meniscus* and *London Orbital* explicitly connect the shape of the Dome to London's circular motorway. In *Sorry Meniscus*, Sinclair states:

> I had to admit that this shape, the dome, had its resonance. What if a dome could be stretched over the area circumscribed by the M25? A caul of translucent skin. A Blakean conceit, fierce, true, but held only in the mind [. . .] The Dome as a conceit, an emblem lifted into the consciousness of all who lived inside its limits [. . .] Imagine the Dome as it ought to be, rather than as it is: a poached egg designed by a committee of vegans.[25]

Compare a very similar passage contained in the very penultimate paragraph of *London Orbital*:

> Will Self, a fan of the M25, said that the mistake of the Dome was that it played safe. It was too modest. It should have spread itself to envelop the whole of London, right out to the motorway. An invisible membrane. A city of zones and freak shows separated from the rest of England. Ford Madox Ford's old fantasy [of vast concentric motorways spiralling to sixty miles out from London] finally activated.[26]

Sinclair displaces the vision of the supra-dome onto Will Self in the latter (and later) passage, a curious negation of his own 'conceit' in the earlier book, and a gesture familiar from *Rodinsky's Room*. The importance of the necessary impossibility of the Dome project places it squarely in the utopian tradition, a connection confirmed by the reference to Ford's imagination of a London which reaches out as far as Cambridge, Winchester and Oxford, served by motorways and 'moving platforms for pedestrians'.[27] This London, neither *rus in urbe* nor Garden City, but a super-metropolis so large that there is no difference between city and country, both prefigures the present but also paints it in utopian terms. Sinclair deploys it to indicate the roots of urban postmodernity, but also to signify the malign fulfilment *and* inversion of this vision that the current M25 and Dome represent. (Curiously, the Dome over London is a feature of Stephen Baxter's 1997 'sequel' to Wells's *The Time Machine*, *The Time Ships*. The Wells connection is strong in *London Orbital*.)

The imagination of a 'sixty miles out' London, and its vision of a Dome which encompasses centre and margins of the city, repeats the long history of London's 'development' from City to 'world city'. As Roy Porter's *London: A Social History* (2000) suggests, London's expansion to connect all its outlying villages and towns into one vast conurbation was a 'fungus-like growth', a history of private speculation, commerce and only latterly (in the Victorian-era Metropolitan Board of Works and after 1888, the London County Council) in governance and planning. London's network of communities, its history of borough and parish organisation, its very lack of a unified culture or government, meant that it resisted the regularity of Haussmann's Paris boulevards, or the utopianism of Ford, or the planning of a Le Corbusier – at least until the LCC's Architect's Department under Leslie Martin, builders of 'machines for living' in London's tower-block dominated post-war estates. The Dome and the M25, planned by a Conservative government whose abolition of the GLC was a destruction of a centralised opposing power in the capital, under the guise of returning London to the traditional governance of its boroughs, are perversely the very signs of 'utopian' planning made (very real) concrete and Teflon. Sinclair's identification with, and apparent validation of, Will Self and Ford's visions (to the extent that they both overlap with his own) indicates the undercurrent of utopianism that Sinclair inherits from the counter-culture, a utopianism that seems to run counter to his otherwise dystopian and/or apocalyptic imagination and the terms of his satirical critique of post-Thatcherite Britain.

In addition to Sinclair's circuit of the M25, there are two other, radial walks in *London Orbital*: the first begins in London and ends at Waltham Abbey, along the Lea Valley. This first walk, which takes place at the start of the book as a kind of prelude or prologue, sets out some of the key terms of Sinclair's critique of New Labour's Britain. Sinclair discovers a series of new-build estates on despoiled, polluted 'brownfield sites', such as the Gunpowder Mills at Enfield. The dominant term here is 'waste': the wasteland, toxic waste, the 'London Waste company'. In something like campaigning journalism, Sinclair uncovers the story of dioxin-infused ash that was used in road building, and houses built over badly decontaminated industrial areas. The Lea Valley is, for Sinclair, the prime site of New Labour's project: 'profit before people', gated communities, no-zones where 'memory is trashed'.[28] As a counterpoint to this walk, Sinclair later visits Samuel Palmer's 'Valley of Vision', a pastoral idyll in the Green Belt that surrounds London. No less than the urban planning that is a target for Sinclair's ire, the Green Belt was a construction of London County Council's planners in the first decades of the twentieth century, who tried to create a kind of 'lung' for Londoners, a 'parkway encircling London at a ten-mile radius from Charing Cross'.[29] In the section of *London Orbital* called 'Paradise Gardens', Sinclair opposes such plans to Thatcherite and New Labour valorisation of suburbia:

> Wilderness was abhorrent. Rough pasture must be rationalised into Best Value recreational zones, retirement homes for happy butterflies. Farm animals were smelly, dirty, unreconstructed: cull them. What was required was a vertical wedge through the landscape (the Lee [sic] Valley Regional Plan), a designated hierarchy (media, recreation, development). What was not required was an holistic vision, any talk of belts or girdles or circuits. What was lost was the old dream of paradise gardens.[30]

Sinclair deploys keys words in his lexicon (vision, circuit) in the service of a utopian conception of urban planning. The utopian impulse is clearly indicated in the phrase 'paradise gardens', and we can also detect a strong element of nostalgia here. Sinclair has often been described as a 'modernist', as noted with regard to his poetic practice in Chapter 2 of this book, and here we find a nostalgia for the urban restructurings of modernity (the Festival of Britain site on the South Bank, the Green Belt, the Garden City) and a rejection of the values of contemporary capital or 'postmodernity'. The Dome, then, is excoriated for the paucity of its utopianism, its failure of 'vision': to be a 'poached egg designed by a committee of vegans' rather than a supra-dome.

Margins and meridians

The Dome is what the French anthropologist Marc Augé has called a 'non-place' produced by the contemporary conditions of 'Super-modernity'. For Augé, 'place' is infused by the patterning and ritual that provides a relationship between people and their environment: 'place [. . .] can be defined as relational, historical and concerned with identity'.[31] Non-place, in opposition, involves a kind of dislocation in space, and is particularly located in 'airports and railway stations, hotel chains, leisure parks, large retail outlets'.[32] Augé writes:

What is seen by the spectator of modernity is the interweaving of old and new. Supermodernity, though, makes the old (history) into a specific spectacle, as it does with all exoticism and all local particularity. History and exoticism play the same role as 'quotations' in a written text: a status superbly expressed in travel agency catalogues. In the non-places of supermodernity, here is always a specific position (in the window, on a poster, to the right of the aircraft, on the left of the motorway) for 'curiosities' presented as such: pineapples from the Ivory Coast; Venice – city of the Doges; the Tangier Kasbah; the site of Alésia. But they play no part in any synthesis, they are not integrated with anything; they simply bear witness, during a journey, to the coexistence of distinct individualities, perceived as equivalent and unconnected.[33]

The 'spectator of modernity' is the *flâneur*, who is able to take in the city as a totality, a formulation which coheres with the subjectivity interpellated by the modern nation-state. The spectator of super-modernity, however, looks not at the city, but inside the Dome; not at the 'interweaving of old and new', but at a seemingly equivalent series of spectacles. As we have seen, Sinclair attempts to distance himself from both positions. The non-place, like the disciplinary spaces of the 'exhibitionary complex', asylum or clinic, interpellates a subjectivity which coheres with the imperatives of the nation-state in a time of globalised capital and the rhetoric of democratic liberalism.

Augé's non-places are signally the topography of the fiction of J. G. Ballard, the Shepperton-based author of *High-Rise* (1975), *Concrete Island* (1974), *Crash* (1973) and *Super-Cannes* (2000). Ballard is a vital presence in *London Orbital*, referred to many times and interviewed for the book (as Sinclair had done for his BFI Modern Classic on Cronenberg's *Crash*, and for the Sinclair–Petit film of *London Orbital*). Ballard's fiction is understood by Sinclair as prophetic: 'how does [Ballard] feel,' asks Sinclair, 'about predicting, and thereby confirming, the psychogeography of Heathrow's retail/recreation fallout?'.[34] Ballard's symbolic landscape – overlit highways, airport service roads, corporate campuses – is deployed in *London Orbital* as London's other, yet London's future. The Siebel building, which we looked at in the Introduction, is archetypically Ballardian, the real-world analogue of the Mediparcs and corporate campuses of *Super-Cannes*, a non-place that is the signature space of *London Orbital*. For Ballard, the margin represents a chink in a global system of psychic repression, where fantasy and desire can achieve perverse manifestation. Ballard, in Sinclair's *Crash*, says that

'I regard the city as a semi-extinct form . . . I think the suburbs are more interesting than people will let on. In the suburbs you find uncentred lives. The normal civic structures are not there. So people have more freedom to explore their own imaginations, their own obsessions'.[35] For Sinclair, the 'process of drift, from centre to margin' in *London Orbital* is largely a malign process. While 'this edge, this nowhere, is the place that will offer fresh narratives', these narratives do not signify escape from repression but dispossession, relocation, uprooting.[36] In Augé's terms, it is the move from 'place' to 'non-place', from a space marked by the impacted memories of real lives to a fabricated and repressive 'nowhere'.

Although Sinclair pays homage to Ballard by visiting him in Shepperton, his description of Ballard's 'project' indicates criticism rather than admiration:

> Ballard's poetic is anti-populist, anti-city. It's a demented meltdown of Thatcher and Aleister Crowley: do what you will is all of the law, repression is death. No interference from the state, no nannying. Canary Wharf triumphalism and the inalienable right to kill yourself on an orbital motorway as you fight your way to work. What is astonishing is the courage, the recklessness of Ballard's argument; the unashamed trust in his own psychopathology.[37]

In his book on Ballard's and Cronenberg's *Crash*, Sinclair enlists Ballard's vision into his demonology of Thatcherism. 'Had he [Ballard] activated a demonic psychopathology that could only be appeased by regular sacrifices?' asks Sinclair.[38] Ballard's world-view, suggests Sinclair, anticipates that of Thatcherite neo-liberalism. Not only does Ballard's work become 'prophetic', but in the magical thinking that Sinclair seems to derive from William Burroughs as well as from his reading of the literature of the occult, the act of writing brings about the malign future, the future of the suburb and post-Thatcherite New Labour. Thatcher is a key figure for Sinclair, as we saw in Chapter 3. In *The Verbals*, a book of interviews with Kevin Jackson, Sinclair suggests that '[Thatcher's] take, if you look at it, verges on the demonic. She wanted to physically remake London, the mob, all of those things, which finally through the Poll Tax brought her down. I can't look at it in any other way but as actual demonic possession'.[39] Note how Sinclair connects Thatcher with the disruptive force of the London mob, which she activates as part of a populist politics but which brings her rule to an end. To suggest that Ballard's poetic 'is a demented meltdown of Thatcher and Aleister Crowley' is therefore to attest to the malignity of Ballard's vision of London (and the future), not to celebrate it. If Ballard is the 'man who defined the psychic climate', who predicted the domination of suburban 'non-space', then in figures such as Vaughan in *Crash* or Wilder Penrose in *Super-Cannes* the 'cautionary tale' becomes much more attractive and therefore sinister.[40] If, as Sinclair suggests, Ballard 'isn't dealing in metaphors, he means it', then Ballard's work becomes a celebration, not a critique, of the psychopathology produced by suburbia and corporate capitalism, a symptom rather than a cure.[41]

Sinclair's move from centre to margins, from Whitechapel to M25, represents a change in symbolic topography: from the city to the suburb; from the specificities of the East End (Hawksmoor's churches, mythical alignments and triangulations of key buildings, urban myths and narratives) to the dehistoricised and anonymous corporate architecture of London's suburban ring; from the utopianism of modernity to the non-places of postmodernity. The 'drift from centre to margin' also repeats the movement of London's population from inner city to new town and overspill suburb in the post-war period. This movement finds its emblematic figure in David Rodinsky, the mystery of whose disappearance is finally 'solved' by Sinclair and Rachel Lichtenstein when Rodinsky's grave is discovered in Epsom, in Surrey. Longrove in Epsom was one of a 'ring' of asylums in London's Green Belt that also included Shenley and Colney Hatch, Victorian institutions which housed the 'mad' but also those who were the victims of social exclusion and repressive Victorian sexual morality.

Sinclair seems to adopt a Foucauldian reading of the asylum, which would understand the 'birth of the clinic' as part of a wider epistemological shift after the Enlightenment with regard to the maintenance of social order, from regimes of punishment to the establishment of disciplinary 'complexes' such as that identified by Bennett in the exhibition. Foucault identifies the prison and the asylum as emblematic spaces which signify the movement from spectacles of punishment as a form of control (public hangings, the pillory) towards scientific and medical discourses to 'explain' and control those that a society or culture deems as 'other', be they criminal or 'insane'. Roy Porter, in *Madness: A Brief History* (2002), suggests that the rise of the numbers in asylums can be explained by 'positivistic, bureaucratic, utilitarian, and professional mentalities [which] vested great faith in institutional solutions in general'.[42] Porter, though, does not entirely accept Foucault's positing of a 'great confinement', and suggests an interesting economic dimension: 'in urbanized Europe, and in North America, the rise of the asylum is better seen not as an act of state but as a side effect of commercial and professional society'.[43] Porter argues that private asylums promoted the curative or healthful effects of confinement, but perhaps one might suggest that the imperatives of trade and commerce in an increasingly globalised colonial economy also determined the necessity for disciplinary regimes and a re-ordering of the social structure. Peter Ackroyd, in *London: the Biography*, suggests that it was 'the restraints imposed by a mercantile culture, ruinous in its effects upon many who comprised the crowd, encouraged rapid volatility of rage and exhilaration'.[44] The disruptive effects produced by the need for social stability and order, to further Imperial commerce, themselves necessitated new regimes of order. The violence of the mob is coterminous with the disciplinary effects of the prison or asylum.

We saw in the Introduction how Sinclair adopts the discourse of the 'anti-psychiatrist' R. D. Laing in the late 1960s, and has since equated states of psychological 'otherness' ('vision', the 'mad' poet, the fugueur) with alienation and opposition to societal norms. David Rodinsky is incarcerated in Epsom not because he is 'mad', in these terms, but because his status as scholar *manqué* from a Jewish or Yiddish tradition makes his behaviour inexplicable, and therefore 'other', to health workers and social services operating in the East End. Rodinsky emblematises London's 'lost': those who were taken away from their communities and disconnected from cultural memory and history. Rodinsky symbolises not only those who were taken to asylums, but the 'diaspora' of London that settled in Essex, Hertfordshire, Kent and Surrey in the post-war years. In the course of his circuit around the M25, Sinclair discovers that many of the Victorian asylums have themselves been closed and 'erased' from history and memory, the archives lost (such as those from Epsom that might have detailed Rodinsky's time there). Sinclair 'logs' a process of transformation over time: 'We learn how the old estates were broken up and rebranded as asylums, retreats, drying out clinics, holding pens for troublesome inner-city aliens. Looking at my map, before the walk began, I logged: Shenley, Harperbury, Napsbury, Leavesden and, a little to the south . . . Friern Barnet'.[45] In the times of Thatcher and New Labour, these asylums are themselves broken up and 'rebranded' as 'gated communities', only the Italianate water towers of the original buildings betraying their history. In this regard there is an ambivalence at the heart of *London Orbital*'s project. On the one hand, the text memorialises these 'lost' communities and histories while, at the same time, it criticises the very principles which informed their construction and operation. Ironically, Roy Porter connects Laingian 'anti-psychiatry' with Thatcherite 'care in the community' policies that led to the closure of the asylums; Sinclair's own Laingian inheritance forces him to valorise the 'mad' outsider (the 'visionary') while lamenting the economic imperatives that drive the transformation of Shenley and Epsom from hospital to 'gated community' and push the vulnerable onto the street.

The Millennium Dome and the Asylum are crucial sites in *London Orbital*, signalling the erasure of history and community in contemporary Britain and its replacement with a series of spectacles and simulacra. Memory becomes central to Sinclair's project because it opposes these forces, and *London Orbital* and other texts are involved in a process of memorialisation. Several times in *Sorry Meniscus* and *London Orbital* Sinclair reminds us that the Dome was built upon what was once known as Bugsby's Marshes, 'toxic marshlands' on the Greenwich Peninsula, a name now suppressed. As read by Sinclair, the 'Teflon meteorite ... dropped in the mud' is an overwriting of history and place, of the spaces and usages of centuries of London life (good and bad).[46] In fact, Sinclair characterises it as a deliberate evacuation of space (place) and time (history) in order to replace it with a malign and artificial consumerist experience. The spatial memories of place are overlaid by a blank 'caul'; cultural memories and practices of everyday life are overwritten and countermanded by contemporary configurations of power, manifested in microcosmic form in the Dome.

Blood and oil

In the film *London Orbital* (co-directed with Chris Petit), Sinclair states explicitly of the M25 project: 'we were walking to exorcise the shame of the Millennium Dome'. Exorcism is a word Sinclair uses regularly to describe his own projects, a cloaking of critique in the terminology of the occult. In *London Orbital* Sinclair deploys Gothic tropes in his writing to critique the present, a critique which is itself

Gothicised and occulted (turned into 'psychogeography', 'shamanism' or other formulations). Not only does Sinclair seek to investigate (and bring forth) the repressed, suppressed and forgotten (in the manner of Gothic), he also seeks to turn the processes of occlusion, occulting and repression back upon the instruments of that repression: by occulting them. Psychogeography and the importance of walking (in a culture which ignores the pedestrian) already indicates the revisiting, recapturing and remembering of space found in Sinclair's other texts, a strategy to reveal and oppose its appropriation or erasure by the forces of contemporary capital.

Sinclair's project is to turn 'non-place' back into 'place', where life is practised on a daily basis, and where memory and history are *not* divorced from the spaces in which people live. This is why Sinclair's walk in *London Orbital* is anti-clockwise, and why Sinclair recurrently focuses on the Dome, located at the 'origin' of time in Greenwich. As he explicitly states: 'Our walk is a way of winding the clock back', to resist the subjectivity interpellated by the Dome and by Ballard's fiction.[47] In the *London Orbital* book, he writes: 'That's why our walk began at the most tainted spot on the map of London [the Lea Valley]. Exorcism, the only game worth the candle'.[48] *London Orbital* is not only an exorcism of the Dome, it is also an exorcism of Ballard's vision of the future, a vision Sinclair clearly believes is analogous to our own present. Curiously, the emphasis on exorcism is anticipated in a passage from *White Chappell, Scarlet Tracings*. The text suggests:

> Always erasure, not exorcism. Exorcism merely confers status on the exorcist: who claims, falsely, that he has the power to unmake. His tricks to stake the demonic, nail the black heart.
>
> Erasure acts over, is a discretion. Joblard's performance in the warehouse erased itself so that the voices were set free. They wound back the memory of the future.[49]

To wind back the memory of the future seems a distillation of Sinclair's project in *London Orbital*, to which we will return shortly, but he seems now to have compromised his own injunction. In the assessment of some critics, this has also brought his own judgement down upon his head: exorcism valorises the exorcist.

To exorcise the present, Sinclair returns not to the time of the Festival of Britain (1951), nor the Great Exhibition (1851), but somewhere in between, the Gothic texts of the *fin de siècle*, a literature not of suburbia but of the city. Although the first walk in *London*

Orbital is 'up the Lea valley', ending at Waltham Abbey, the true beginning and end of the M25 (if such a thing can be said to exist) is at the Thames crossing at Dartford, and this is in fact where the film of *London Orbital* begins and ends. Travelling anti-clockwise, on the north bank of the river, the first psychogeographic site is at Purfleet in Essex, the place of Carfax Abbey in Stoker's *Dracula*. This chapter (the penultimate, before 'Millennium Eve', the putative deadline for the completion of the circuit) makes explicit the centrality of Gothic to Sinclair's work and to *London Orbital*:

> Vampire scholars, such as Kim Newman, have always recognised that yesterday's Undead are today's asylum seekers, the Undispersed. The slow-detonating impact of Stoker's 1897 fiction came, not from its novelty, but from the sense of the book as an original rewrite, the recapitulation of a recurring fable. Beneath the breastbeating Shakespearean echoes (cod Irving), and the tent-show religiosity, is a considered and accurate geography.[50]

While the vampire signifies Sinclair's Gothicised, occulted critique of contemporary London, the deployment of Stoker's intertext is a doubled (Gothic) rhetorical move, also returning 'non-place' (the London/Essex fringes) to 'place', a palimpsest of history, narrative and power. The section in *London Orbital* called 'Blood and Oil', emphasises the conjunction of oil, real estate and south Essex's crime culture. Carfax Abbey is sited at Purfleet on the Essex fringes of London, where Exxon (which is, as Sinclair explains in the *London Orbital* film, the company of US President George W. Bush) has its storage tanks. The economic logic of vampirism as mapped onto contemporary capital. Although I have elsewhere suggested that Sinclair's mode of critique gestures towards the transcendent rather than being strictly materialist (or Marxian), the connection between Marx and vampirism occurs even in *Das Kapital*. Franco Moretti, in *Signs Taken for Wonders*, notes that vampirism is a 'metaphor for capital' in Stoker's *Dracula*. According to Marx, 'Capital is dead labour which, vampire-like, lives only by sucking living labour, and lives the more, the more labour it sucks'.[51] For Moretti, Sinclair's 'blood and oil' connection is already pre-encoded by *Dracula* itself, and Sinclair's rereading foreshadowed by Marx's own writings.

In Sinclair's *White Goods* (the title of which uncannily conflates colonialism or slavery with consumer durables), the kaleidoscopic prose piece called 'From the Thick End of a Purfleet Telescope' contains the Burroughsian invocation: 'IMMIGRATION. STORAGE. DISTRIBUTION'.[52] This signifies Dracula's invasion of London, his purchase of Carfax, and the spread of vampirism as a disease (Lucy Westenra turned into the 'Bloofer Lady'). If 'Stoker's themes are still active' (2002a: 409), then Dracula's vampirism becomes a metaphor for the oil industry in particular and for contemporary capital in general: 'Buy toxic. Buy cheap: madhouses, old chapels, decaying abbeys. Then make your play: storage and distribution'.[53] Dracula reread, rewritten, becomes a forerunner of the developers who turn the asylums into gated communities. The victims of this vampirism are Londoners. Their histories and memories are vampirised: they are displaced, distributed to asylums and the 'non-places' of London's margins. An 'original rewrite' (a term that echoes Sinclair's char-acterisation of Conan Doyle's mediumistic writing in *White Chappell, Scarlet Tracings*), *Dracula* is '[t]he Gothic imagination invading – and undoing – imperial certainties of trade, law, class. *Dracula* announces the coming age of the estate agent'.[54] Like *Crash*, *Dracula* is reread by Sinclair as an anticipation of the future. This re-reading becomes the source text; the original becomes rewritten. To rewrite the future (our present), the past (the progenitor of the present) must be rewritten. Extending the same symbolic structure, Sinclair writes: 'The Count's fetid breath warmed Thatcher's neck as she cut the ribbon' when opening the M25.[55] The M25 becomes an arterial system or four-chambered heart, the orbital motorway re-imagined as a somatic map, just as the London Underground system appeared as a network of veins on the cover of *Dark Lanthorns*. The connection of Dracula to Thatcher and the M25 suggest that not only does the (clogged) circulation of the orbital motorway attract the vampiric intentions of capital (from property developers to the Essex gangsters outlined in the film), but the heart must be staked. In the guise of staking London's heart, however, Sinclair is attempting to heal it. As the references to Magdi Yacoub and the Harefield hospital reveal, Sinclair is no longer the autopsist of *White Chappell, Scarlet Tracings*, but a surgeon attempting to restore failing life: 'we have to learn to walk the damage, repair the hurt'.[56]

Sinclair and Petit's film *London Orbital*, more a complementary text or companion-piece rather than filmic version of the book, stresses the theme of time through another late nineteenth-century intertext: H. G. Wells's *The Time Machine*. Over DV footage of daytime driving around the M25 (shot through the windscreen of Petit's car), Sinclair quotes from *The Time Machine* twice, once to suggest that 'there is no difference between Time and any of the three dimensions of Space except that our consciousness moves along it', and second in describing the nauseous effects of time travel itself: 'there is a feeling like that one has upon a switchback – of a helpless headlong motion!'[57] Driving the M25, then, is analogous to travelling in time, just as psychogeography and reading and writing enable the collision or conflation of two different historical eras, the connection illuminating both. As we saw above in Sinclair's conception of Ballard's *Crash*, the past text's anticipation of the future becomes the figuration of our own present, a present that can only be undone or challenged by rewriting the text, reappropriating memory and history. In the book *London Orbital*, it is *War of the Worlds* rather than *The Time Machine* that is the crucial Wells intertext, where it is used by Sinclair to indicate the invasion narratives of London that haunted the late nineteenth-century and which were usually set in the southern suburbs (Woking or Dorking). Wells, of course, was a son of the suburbs. In his *London: A Social History*, Roy Porter quotes Wells's vision of a future London:

> We are . . . in the early phase of a great development of centrifugal possibilities,' H. G. Wells argued at the dawn of a new century: 'the available area of a city which can offer a cheap suburban journey of thirty miles an hour is a circle with a radius of thirty miles. And is it too much . . . to expect the available area for even the common daily toilers of the great city of the year 2000, or earlier, will have a radius very much larger than that?[58]

Wells's prophetic vision of a London sub-region that extends thirty miles or more connects with the vision of the supra-Dome in *Sorry Meniscus*, and Ford Madox Ford's 'Sixty Miles Out' utopianism. The M25, however, is a dystopic inversion of these dreams, for there are no radial journeys on the M25: London is perpetually bypassed. The Ballardian suburbs are our suburbs, but *London Orbital* is haunted by the (lost) utopianism of Wells: what ought to be, rather than what is.

The *London Orbital* film makes effective use of found footage (CCTV, Sinclair's 8mm home movies from the early 1970s), digital video, and also techniques such as split screen. The split screen, modish in the 1960s, is thematically important to *London Orbital*. Both Sinclair and Petit narrate voice-over material on the film, usually alternating, and near the beginning of the film Sinclair acknowledges the 'split nature of our project' (between film and book, Sinclair and Petit, image and image). This resonates with the recurrence of the word 'split' in *White Chappell, Scarlet Tracings* and elsewhere in Sinclair's work, where it denotes a rupture in the body, the body politic, the space of the city, or the (in)ability to represent London as a whole. In the film, this rupture is accompanied by a sense of loss. If the book attempts to 'turn back time' as part of a political or critical project, the insertion of Sinclair's home movie footage of the early 1970s (particularly shots of Anna, Sinclair's wife, walking along crowded London streets) into the fabric of the film indicates a personalisation of that loss, and perhaps a sense of nostalgia for a time of 'wholeness'. Rosemary Jackson, in *Fantasy: the Literature of Subversion*, connects the split subjectivities of the Gothic to Freudian psychoanalytical symbolism, which illuminates Sinclair's use of 'split' across his texts:

> Many texts fantasize a return to a stage of undifferentiation, to a condition *preceding* [Lacan's concept of] the mirror stage and its creation of dualism. For prior to this construction, in a state of primary narcissism, the child is its own ideal, and experiences no discrepancy between self (as perceiving subject) and other (as perceived object). To get back, on to the far side of the mirror, becomes a powerful metaphor for returning to an original unity, a 'paradise' lost by the 'fall' into division with the construction of a subject.[59]

Sinclair's diagnosis of the 'split', a symptom of the conditions of contemporary social and cultural organisation, corresponds to the ideological work needed by the Dome to try to fuse a coherent (national) subject. The Dome, like the asylum and the 'paradise garden', are responses to stages in the development of capital, from the industrial revolution and modernity to the age of simulacra, spectacle and postmodernity/supermodernity. The 'paradise garden' then looks back to an originary state of wholeness; the project to 'turn back the clock' is an attempt to heal the 'split', a utopianism infused both with nostalgia and with traces of Christian myth.

In film (which is 'past', rather than tape, which is the future and 'disposable'), time can be 'turned back'; memories, the ghosts of the past, are materialised. The final sentences of the film are spoken by Petit, over blurred and slowed-down footage of the road, and then, vitally in terms of the desire for 'wholeness', a still photograph of Sinclair as a child:

Space, and not time . . . was the key to the M25, just as space, and the movement of the camera, is the real secret to cinema . . . We move through space *and* time, memory recedes, we become cosmonauts, we become lost.

We become lost; but as the film consistently stages, memories do not. Where, in Ballard's fiction, the future is collapsed upon the present, in Sinclair's texts it is the past (memory, history, the 'return of the reforgotten') that is immanent in the contemporary, which tries and fails to repress it. In *London Orbital*, Sinclair insists that London is certainly marked with histories of oppression, but it is also marked with histories of resistance, with traces of memory, which may still be read. They cannot be erased or simply 'Domed' over.

Notes

1   Iain Sinclair, *London Orbital* (London: Granta, 2002), p. 3.
2   Iain Sinclair, *Sorry Meniscus* (London: Profile, 1999), pp. 19 and 21.
3   Sinclair, *London Orbital*, p. 68.
4   Sinclair, *London Orbital*, pp. 29–30.
5   Tony Bennett, 'The Exhibitionary Complex', in D. Boswell and J. Evans (eds), *Representing the Nation: A Reader: Histories, Heritage and Museums* (London and New York: Routledge, 1994), pp. 332–61 (p. 333).
6   Sinclair, *Sorry Meniscus*, p. 19.
7   Sinclair, *Sorry Meniscus*, pp. 19–20.
8   Sinclair, *Sorry Meniscus*, p. 20.
9   Ronald R. Thomas, 'The Legacy of Victorian Spectacle: The Map of Time and the Architecture of Empty Space', in C. L. Krueger (ed.), *Functions of Victorian Culture at the Present Time* (Athens, OH: Ohio University Press, 2002), pp. 18–33 (p. 27).
10 Sinclair, *London Orbital*, p. 22.
11 Peter Ackroyd, *London: The Biography* (London: Chatto & Windus, 2000), p. 391.
12 Ackroyd, *London: The Biography*, p. 397.
13 Ackroyd, *London: The Biography*, p. 399.
14 Sinclair, *London Orbital*, p. 246.
15 Sinclair, *London Orbital*, p. 246.
16 Sinclair, *London Orbital*, p. 246.
17 Iain Sinclair, *Lights Out for the Territory: 9 Excursions in the Secret History of London* (London: Granta, 1998), pp. 72 and 78.
18 Sinclair, *Lights Out for the Territory*, pp. 83 and 84.
19 Sinclair, *Lights Out for the Territory*, p. 80.
20 Thomas, 'The Legacy of Victorian spectacle', p. 22.

21 Iain Sinclair, *Downriver* (1991) (London: Vintage, 1995), p. 170.
22 Sinclair, *Downriver*, p. 171.
23 Sinclair, *Sorry Meniscus*, p. 30.
24 David Harvey, *The Condition of Postmodernity: An Enquiry into the Origins of Cultural Change* (Cambridge, MA and Oxford: Blackwell, 1990).
25 Sinclair, *Sorry Meniscus*, p. 14.
26 Sinclair, *London Orbital*, p. 457.
27 Sinclair, *London Orbital*, p. 169.
28 Sinclair, *London Orbital*, p. 62.
29 Sinclair, *London Orbital*, p. 70.
30 Sinclair, *London Orbital*, p. 71.
31 Marc Augé, *Non-places: Introduction to an Anthropology of Supermodernity* (London: Verso, 1995), p. 77.
32 Augé, *Non-places*, p. 79.
33 Augé, *Non-places*, pp. 110–11.
34 Sinclair, *London Orbital*, p. 218.
35 Iain Sinclair, *Crash* (London: BFI, 1999), p. 84.
36 Sinclair, *London Orbital*, p. 14.
37 Sinclair, *Crash*, p. 110.
38 Sinclair, *Crash*, p. 117.
39 Iain Sinclair with Kevin Jackson, *The Verbals* (Tonbridge: Worple Press, 2003), p. 135.
40 Sinclair, *London Orbital*, p. 222.
41 Sinclair, *London Orbital*, p. 218.
42 Roy Porter, *Madness: A Brief History* (Oxford: Oxford University Press, 2002), p. 112.
43 Porter, *Madness: A Brief History*, p. 95.
44 Ackroyd, *London: The Biography*, p. 391.
45 Sinclair, *London Orbital*, p. 83.
46 Sinclair, *London Orbital*, p. 3.
47 Sinclair, *London Orbital*, p. 58.
48 Sinclair, *London Orbital*, p. 38.
49 Iain Sinclair, *White Chappell, Scarlet Tracings* (London: Paladin, 1988), p. 199.
50 Sinclair, *London Orbital*, p. 403.
51 Franco Moretti, *Signs Taken for Wonders: Essays in the Sociology of Literary Forms*, trans. S. Fischer, D. Forgacs and D. Miller (London: Verso, 1983), p. 91.
52 Iain Sinclair and Emma Matthews, *White Goods* (Uppingham: Goldmark, 2002), p. 43.
53 Sinclair, *London Orbital*, pp. 409 and 408.
54 Sinclair, *London Orbital*, p. 403.

55 Sinclair, *London Orbital*, p. 404.

56 Sinclair, *London Orbital*, p. 167.

57 Chris Petit and Iain Sinclair (dirs) *London Orbital* (2002).

58 Roy Porter, *London: A Social History* (London: Penguin, 2000), pp. 378–9.

59 Rosemary Jackson, *Fantasy: the Literature of Subversion* (London: Routledge, 1981), p. 89.

7

Borderlands

I like frontiers. (Iain Sinclair)[1]

In this final chapter, I will discuss Sinclair's three novels, *Radon Daughters* (1994), *Landor's Tower* (2001) and *Dining on Stones* (2004). All share structural similarities (as they do also with *White Chappell, Scarlet Tracings* and *Downriver*); there is a recurrence of motifs to do with journeys and roads; all place the significance of narration (and the narrator) centrally in the concerns of the text; and all manifest an increasingly conscious appreciation of issues of subjectivity and gender.

Radon Daughters

Radon Daughters is anomalous in Sinclair's novels in that it does not feature a first-person narrator, who is generally some kind of avatar of Sinclair himself: 'Sinclair', 'the Late Watson', 'Norton'. *Radon Daughters* concentrates upon Todd Sileen, who does not narrate his own story, though the free-indirect prose does offer his point of view. Sileen is a 'monopod', a one-legged denizen of London's book-running margins, who lives in squalor with a television 'weathergirl', Helen. The London of *Radon Daughters* is a grim, entropic place, the energies of Thatcherism exhausted and the long twilight of the John Major Conservative administration stumbling to its end. Todd Sileen is first presented as an inhabitant of the square mile around the London Hospital in Whitechapel, who for some reason is addicted to the fugue states that he achieves when being X-rayed by a rather dubious technician at the hospital. He is forced by his 'secret state' operator (and bibliophile), one Drage-Bell, to embark on a search to find the missing (and possibly mythical) manuscript copy of the sequel to William Hope Hodgson's *The House on the Borderland*. In the company of the 'eco-warrior' Rhab Adnam (a version of Renchi Bicknell, the artist who shares the walk around the M25 in *London Orbital*), Sileen performs a 'triangulation', on foot, between the traces of the church of St Mary Matfellon in Whitechapel, the Castle Mound in Oxford, and Cambridge. In Oxford, an eccentric academic named Hinton joins them (an allusion to C. Howard Hinton of *White Chappell, Scarlet Tracings*), and in Cambridge they encounter Simon Undark, the Prynne-like poet/academic who possesses the manuscript. As Undark performs a slide-show lecture to Hinton and Sileen (and as Sileen plots to grab the manuscript), Drage-Bell stages a raid on the room to expropriate the object of his and Sileen's quest. In a curious sub-narrative, Helen and another woman, Andi, fall in with the gangster Nicky Tarten and are persuaded to participate in a female boxing match, staged illegally in East London. Towards the end of the narrative, Sileen steals the manuscript from Drage-Bell and sets off with Helen to Ireland, to try to find the location of Hodgson's text. This is revealed as somewhat pointless, as Sileen learns that: 'he had been wrong from the start . . . There was no "House on the Borderland". A condition had been described, a pathology, *not* a specific location'.[2] This, then, is a self-negating quest, a journey to a place that only existed in a fiction, and a place that was only ever a state of mind or 'pathology'.

Radon Daughters is Sinclair's most 'plotted' and least episodic novel. It stands in contrast to the tripartite structure of *White Chappell, Scarlet Tracings*, and the 'twelve tales' that comprise *Downriver*. It is almost certainly no coincidence that it does not feature an avatar of Sinclair as a narrative focus ('the Late Watson' or 'Norton'): Sileen, cartoonish though he is – an X-ray addicted one-legged book-runner – is clearly an attempt at 'character' on Sinclair's part, and *Radon Daughters* itself endeavours to create the depth and coherence of a literary novel 'proper', rather than the deliberately fractured forms of Sinclair's other fiction and poetry. Curiously, it is also the densest of all Sinclair's novels, and, as Sinclair confesses in *The Verbals*, the most 'difficult'. One must make a distinction, however, between 'plotting' and narrative propulsion, as again, the linguistic (or perhaps poetic) properties of the writing tend to create a kind of 'drag'. As elsewhere, then, Sinclair uses the journey or walk to structure the text.

What the journeys do provide, however, are the narrative opportunities provided by what Mikhail Bakhtin, in 'Forms of Time and the Chronotope', calls 'the chronotope of the road'. A chronotope, he argues, is 'the primary means for materializing time in space', 'providing the ground essential for the showing forth, the representability of events'.[3] Several times Bakhtin uses the metaphor of the text 'taking flesh', becoming material, through the chronotope, but it is not simply a figure for analysing how space and/or time is represented in a text.[4] Rather, it is the means by which spacio-temporal relations are encoded in representation itself. As such, these relations are culturally and historically contingent, and change over time, as well as between different genres. Therefore, Bakhtin historicises his analysis, beginning with an investigation of 'adventure time' in the Greek romance, where he argues that the narrative events lie in series but not in what we would understand as chronology. Time is neither historical nor biological, it is 'undifferentiated'; characters do not develop, because their essence is unchanging. Space, similarly, is undifferentiated; it is abstract, lacking concreteness, and always alien to the hero. What determines narrative event on the journey or adventure through this space is, because of the undifferentiation of time and space, chance.

Bakhtin's 'chronotope of the road', by extension, is associated with the motif of 'encounter': 'the chronotope of the road is both a point of new departures and a place for events to find their denouement. Time, as it were, fuses together with space and flows in it (forming the road)'.[5] The road was central to the form of the picaresque novel, and the picaresque's episodic character and reliance on the fantastical and grotesque is reflected in the narrative journeys of Sinclair's fiction. The 'encounter' is crucial to the means by which Sinclair organises his narratives: Sileen meets Hinton, and they both encounter Undark in *Radon Daughters*; the narrator 'Norton' repeatedly meets the Ketamine Kreeps, Howard Marks, Joblard, and the central (mysterious) female character Prudence in *Landor's Tower*. While *Radon Daughters* has been seen as Sinclair's most 'plotted' novel, it is still organised around Sileen's London–Oxford–Cambridge triangulation, and the first section of *Dining on Stones* is even called 'Road', and is focused on the A13, the trunk road from London's East End out to Southend-on-Sea. The journey or 'chronotope of the road' is recurrently used by Sinclair in order to provide the linear narrative structure that his text, as spatial or 'open field' constructs, tend to de-emphasise. The element of chance in the encounter is, perhaps, also connected to the traces of situationist *dérive* (or drift) that Sinclair inherits in the position and practice of the walking subject: the subject is open to the chance encounters that reveal the occluded city, or in *Landor's Tower*, the nature of the borderland.

There are two types of time on Sinclair's road: that of the pedestrian, such as Todd Sileen, or Sinclair himself in the non-fiction; and that of the driver, such as Petit in the *London Orbital* film, or 'Norton' in *Landor's Tower*, who crosses and recrosses the border between Wales and England. As we have seen throughout this book, Sinclair obsessively returns to time and space throughout his texts, from the mythographic elements of *Lud Heat* and particularly *Suicide Bridge*, to the accreted historical locales of Whitechapel, to the suburban non-spaces of *London Orbital*. Bakhtin's 'chronotope of the road', with its emphasis on encounter and chance, is closer to the walking subject than that of the driver, who encounters nobody in her or his sealed experiential bubble. The space-time of the driver, hypnotically rendered in the *London Orbital* film, is a break from the historically situated time that Bakhtin analyses with regard to the historical novel, but more closely approximates the abstract, alien world of 'adventure time', where space and time are undifferentiated.

The borderland

In *Radon Daughters*, the journey is organised around the search for the sequel to William Hope Hodgson's *The House on the Borderland*. In *The Verbals*, Sinclair notes that 'it's completely impossible to write a sequel to *The House on the Borderland*, because it ends with the death of the cosmos, time, and everything else'.[6] This 'impossible' text becomes a kind of magical object, or even a map to be decoded; in the character Dr Hinton's words, 'the Borderland is a reality, a site, a map reference. It can (and *must*) be visited . . . There was, and is, a pivotal place. A gateway. A point of entry'.[7] As I noted above, this sense of the Borderland is countermanded later in the novel when Sileen realises that the borderland is a condition or pathology rather than a location: it is something you carry with you rather than something you find. The sequel, both Hinton and Sileen accept, somehow preceded *The House on the Borderland*, a reversal of normal causality that makes Hinton think the manuscript is a fake. This conception is a revisiting of the model of writing found elsewhere in Sinclair's texts, where writing at speed, automatically, or through 'dictation' from an occult elsewhere allows the writer to move ahead of events, and to write them. The problem is that for Hodgson, as it is for horror writers H. P. Lovecraft or M. R. James, that 'communication with the spirits' may prove to be a gateway to the diabolic. The borderland may be a threshold.

It is certainly connected with death. Sileen realises that the borderland is a 'pathology' soon before he meets his own death on the Burren, the limestone pavement in Ireland; and more poignantly, Sinclair suggests a connection between the borderland and Hodgson's own personal history. Hodgson volunteered to serve in the artillery in the First World War, with such fortitude that he recovered from a serious fall from a horse and re-enlisted, and ultimately he was killed on the Western Front. Sinclair quotes Hodgson's letter to his mother, wherein he describes '"that most atrocious Plain of Destruction. My God! Talk about a Lost World – talk about the END of the world . . . it is all here"'.[8] Taking the model of 'writing ahead of the present', Hodgson's fiction of the borderland becomes a prefiguring of the apocalyptic landscape of No Man's Land, a wasteland filled with despair and death. 'The borderland, the wire', considers a sobbing Sileen.[9] There is no transcendence here; in this 'space between', there is only the bleak history of warfare and destruction.

In *Landor's Tower*, however, the border between Wales and England becomes the zone of numerous crossings and recrossings by several characters. *Landor's Tower* is a less densely 'plotted' fiction than *Radon Daughters*, and assumes the episodic form of much of Sinclair's fictional texts. The protagonist is 'Norton', a name Sinclair previously used in *Slow Chocolate Autopsy*, and one that he uses again in *Dining on Stones*, for a character whose personal history approximates Sinclair's own. Norton travels up and down the M4 motorway, stopping at service stations (where he encounters the 'Ketamine Kreeps', one of whom offers rather brutal evaluations of Norton's/Sinclair's recent fiction), in haunted cottages (once occupied by Terry Waite), and conducts a kind of romance with 'Prudence', a female figure who is revealed not to have individual existence, but to be a form of *anima*: 'My soul was separate, a woman'.[10] Sinclair means more than 'soul-mate' here; Prudence is an occult object, a kind of 'fetch' or spectre, not unlike the female figures to be found in the Petit–Sinclair film *The Falconer*, or 'The Double Death of the

Falconer' in *Slow Chocolate Autopsy*. Norton's journeys are interweaved with the 'research' of Kaporal, who stumbles upon the dis-
graced Liberal Party leader Jeremy Thorpe in an idyllic garden; with
Dryfeld and Silverfish, bookdealers whose capers are somewhat comic;
and the arrival in Wales of Kwilt and Joblard (a cameo return for the
character based on Brian Catling, who was crucial to one of the
narrative threads in *White Chappell, Scarlet Tracings*, but who appears
here as a stuttering would-be assassin of a talking dog). In *Landor's
Tower*, then, Sinclair returns to the multi-stranded narrative that
characterises *White Chappell*, but the text is not so fractured in form.
Some of these narrative lines are self-consciously intertextual, pointing
the reader back to previous Sinclair fictions: this is a development
in Sinclair's fiction that becomes fully-fledged in *Dining on Stones*,
to which we will return later in the chapter. *Landor's Tower* is, in
parts, Sinclair's most comic novel, cartoonish without the savagery
of *Downriver*. There is even a small role for Howard Marks, the
Welsh, dope-smoking and dope-smuggling 'Mr Nice' (who Sinclair
also 'accidentally' encounters by the MI5 building in *Lights Out for
the Territory*) as a dealer in clothing remnants. Marks finally becomes
the unfortunate and mistaken target of a kidnap effort by Kaporal
and some Albanian migrants (they are really after the British singer
and entertainer Max Bygraves) in *Dining on Stones*.

For Norton, a crossing of the borderland between England and
Wales is a journey into personal history: as I noted at the very
beginning of this book, Sinclair spent his childhood in South Wales
(before being sent to boarding schools on both sides of the border).
Sinclair, alluding to the horror writer Arthur Machen (Welsh but
'exiled in London'), suggests a connection between 'the gothic horror
of the alleys and courtyards' of the capital, and the binary nature of
the Welsh border country. The borderlands are London's other, yet
London's double; the narrator finds the same occult forces breaking
through the surface of the countryside as were found in Sinclair's
'lines of force' in *Lud Heat* and elsewhere. Machen's grafting of one
significant space onto another is repeated by *Landor's Tower* itself.

Unlike *Rodinsky's Room*, however, *Landor's Tower* is no search
for origins. Norton does not find an authentic, unitary self in the
borderlands, but only fracture and mystery. Sinclair continuously
disavows any sense that the novel is in a recovery of personal history
or of his childhood, still less a sense of Welsh identity, by relentlessly
representing the Welsh through somewhat scurrilous caricature if

not with outright hostility. Some of this material, I would argue, is troubling, not least because of Sinclair's disavowal of Welshness as his own subject-position. As we have seen elsewhere in this study, Sinclair identifies with some ethnic or religious communities more than others: there is some problematic material with regard to the Bengali and Bangladeshi areas of Whitechapel in *Downriver*. It might be said of *Landor's Tower* that Sinclair identifies with the Welsh least of all ethnic or national communities. In spite of a scene where he is recognised by an old schoolfriend (turned nightclub owner and local crime boss), Norton goes to Wales not as a returning exile, but as a visitor, an outsider.

In *Landor's Tower*, the narrative re-imagines two quasi-utopian communities that were historically located in the Vale of Ewyas, that of one Father Ignatius, and also of the painter Eric Gill. The former is characterised as a kind of 'spiritual gulag' dominated by the domineering, charismatic priest.[11] The second, 'a prison colony, a pastoral hell', is created by Gill as a sexualised 'utopia' which reflected Gill's own sexual obsessions.[12] Robert Bond, in a short essay on the novel, considers the depiction of the two communities to convey a

> suspicion of ruralist, communitarian utopianism [which] is grounded precisely in Sinclair's identification of both the conversion of rural utopia to rural dystopia [. . .] and the degradation of spiritually-liberating space to a site of spiritual confinement.[13]

Bond goes on to suggest that it is the denial of the 'corruption of the flesh' attendant on urban experience, inside a 'sensual gulag', that marks the repression of these communitarians.[14] Gill's use of the women (and men) of the community for his own sexual ends is crucial, because it demonstrates Sinclair's increasing self-consciousness with regard to representations of gender in his texts. Gill's impetus towards his own sexual satisfaction, and his rendering of the women as sexual objects, is an index of his unpleasantness and the malignity of the 'utopia' he sets up. If Sinclair seems increasingly attracted, in his non-fiction, to alternatives to urban life (Samuel Palmer's 'Valley of Vision' in *London Orbital*, the investigation of the countryside in *Edge of the Orison*), in *Landor's Tower* Wales is certainly no retreat from, or contrast to, the deformations of life in the contemporary city. Power, domination and alienation (dis-location) are present in both.

If, in *Radon Daughters* and *Landor's Tower* the borderlands are a space in which the numinous emerges from the everyday 'real', then in *London Orbital* it is the exemplary site of contemporary capital. The M25 ring, the 'Thames Gateway', the communities of the Lea Valley, are all suburban or ex-urban non-places, where history has been evacuated or overwritten, and communities huddle in gated paranoia. In *London Orbital*, the M25 ring became bound up with the lost histories of the Victorian 'asylums' that encircled the city, to which the marginal and 'undesirable' (like David Rodinsky) of London were sent in a cruel analogue of the suburban dispersal of London's inner city communities after the Second World War. The Home Counties 'borderlands' are a malign place in *London Orbital*, because devoid of the markers of history and community that may still be traced on the streets of London, in spite of attempts to erase them. In *Edge of the Orison*, this rhetoric becomes more pointed still on the walk out from Essex to Northamptonshire: 'Disease, so often, seems to be a condition of residence of the edge-lands'.[15] We saw in Chapter 4 how Sinclair deploys the motif of 'exile' to denote the condition of alienation suffered by the 'shamans of intent' he celebrates in *Lights Out for the Territory*; in *London Orbital*, this 'exile' is no symbol, but the material relocation (and dislocation) of London's unwanted.

Self, double, third mind

The structural armature that is often visible on the surface of Sinclair's texts not only estranges the reader from an immersive consumption of it (thereby repeating Sinclair's critique of contemporary commodity capital at the level of reading), but also demonstrates the insistent spatiality and materiality of form that we have seen throughout Sinclair's work. The fragmentary nature of *Lud Heat*, for instance, with its collisions of found engravings, poetry, prose, journal entries and mythological speculation on place, indicates a kind of heteroglossia in Bakhtin's terms, what he calls *raznorečie*. Bakhtin asserts that:

> The novel asserts all its themes, the totality of the world of objects and ideas depicted and expressed in it, by means of the social diversity of speech types [*raznorečie*] and by the differing individual voices that flourish under such conditions. Authorial speech, the speeches of narrators, inserted genres, the speech of characters are merely those

fundamental compositional unities with whose help heteroglossia [*raznorečie*] can enter the novel; each of them permits a multiplicity of social voices and a wide variety of their links and relationships (always more or less dialogised).[16]

The phrase 'social diversity of speech types' indicates how the novel is a plural form, which imports a variety of different voices and discourses into it. It is inclusive and democratic, both reflecting the diversity of voices in the culture that produces it and resisting totalisation.

In Sinclair's fiction, however, all but one novel focalises its narration through an 'I' persona, variously named as 'Sinclair' or as 'Norton'. I would suggest that there is a tension between heteroglossia and the totalising 'I' of first-person narration in Sinclair's fiction that is borne of his originary (and ongoing) status as 'poet'. The 'I' persona of lyric poetry conflicts with the dialogism and heteroglossia that Bakhtin argues are central to novelistic form. Even though I have characterised them as 'open field' texts, Sinclair's novels do not produce true heteroglossia, even resist it, something that Sinclair himself seems to acknowledge. In the auto-critique offered in *Landor's Tower*, 'Bad News' (one of the Ketamine Kreeps) says: ' "Your women are a joke and you can't do working class. Or blacks or Jews or immigrants of any kind. As for kids – where are they?" '.[17] Sinclair's fictions are peopled with caricatures, grotesques, cartoons, such as Todd Sileen, Imar O'Hagan, S. L. Joblard; intentionally travestied historical personages, such as William Gull, Eric Gill or Walter Savage Landor; savagely satirised politicians such as Margaret Thatcher, 'The Widow'; or most revealingly, with avatars of himself. While this might suggest that the 'I' is totalising in Sinclair's fiction, it is possible to argue that Sinclair's main means by which to escape his damning auto-critique is to narrate through a problematic, often split, narrator, who has an indeterminate (or unreliable) connection with Iain Sinclair the author, thereby destabilising the 'I' persona.

In *White Chappell, Scarlet Tracings*, the tripartite narrative structure has two threads in which a version of the 'author' appears: once as 'Sinclair' in the narrative with Joblard centred on Truman's brewery; and again as 'the Late Watson', the third in the group of booksellers that also includes Nicholas Lane and Dryfeld. We assume a correlation between 'Sinclair', 'the Late Watson' and Sinclair himself, an assumption sustained by Sinclair's own recurrent suggestions that his novels are conflations of 'truth' and fiction. That the narrating subject seems to be 'split' (as we saw in Chapter 2 of this book, a crucial word in *White Chappell, Scarlet Tracings*) indicates the extent to which Sinclair attempts to destabilise the unitary, totalising 'I' from which the text appears to narrate. The same splitting occurs in *Landor's Tower*, in a scene in which the apparent Sinclair alter-ego 'Norton', accused of murder, is shown CCTV footage which seems to show him in a place he has not been, with a woman (the murder victim) who is not who the police say she is: 'Speed the tape. My car. A woman leaning against it. A woman in a ratty fur jacket. I am walking towards her. Very hip, Dogme-95 film-making; no close-ups, reverse angles ... I am chatting to Prudence'.[18] Although Norton, the 'I', rationalises the seeming double by suggesting camera trickery is involved, the 'split' is confirmed much later in the novel, where the narration abruptly switches from first person to third:

> I knew nothing about Landor's connection with the Vale of Ewyas when I made that first ascent – which I'm making again. In Hackney ...
>   The fiction of the tower dissolved as Norton plunged over the headland above Porlock ... The trajectory of Norton's non-life was over, spiked.[19]

In this moment of estrangement, the diegesis disintegrates and the ventriloquising voice of the 'author' (back in Hackney) is presented. The 'split' is revealed to be that between the (authentic, originary) 'author', the writing self, and the presented 'I'-narrator of Norton.

Radon Daughters's Todd Sileen is another split subject, but this is not revealed until near the end of his futile quest to Ireland, when, killed by his nemesis Taylor, it revealed that they are, in fact, one and the same person: 'Arms clasped, they drowned in air, both of them. Alone'.[20] In *Dining on Stones*, the 'split' subject is still more explicit. In this novel there are two versions of 'Andrew Norton', both authors: but of different texts. The first book, 'Estuarial Lives', is 'published' by 'Granita Books' and written by 'Andrew Norton'; the second, 'Allegories of Insomnia & Continuous Sky', is written by 'A. M. Norton' and published by Hamish Hamilton (as was, in fact, *Dining on Stones* itself); and the third, by 'Andrew Norton', is titled 'The Middle Ground' (subtitle of *Dining on Stones*) and is published by Albion Village Press. All the 'books' are presented in the text with a separate title page.

Dining on Stones is Sinclair's most formally disrupted novel, even more so than *White Chappell, Scarlet Tracings* and *Downriver*. In fact, it could even be said to adopt 'postmodernist' textual strategies in its foregrounding of formal structures and the actual printed page, its self-reflexivity, and its deliberate implication and play with our sense of the 'narrator(s)' Andrew and A. M. Norton and the 'author' Iain Sinclair. *Dining on Stones* is, one might conclude, a metafiction, a novel about the writing of novels, or perhaps more properly, like Federico Fellini's *8 1/2*, a fiction about the impossibility of writing fiction. In a fairly standard metafictional device, Sinclair even acknowledges his technique in the text:

> I rejected the alternate chapter technique, much abused by recent practitioners: historical pastiche interspersed with unconvincing passes at contemporary life. Those exhausted tropes: miraculously discovered journals, photos in shoeboxes, invented poems . . . The past as a website you can access for a small fee. Password: Metafiction.[21]

In the course of the novel, the two 'Norton' characters meet and come into conflict, and near a Travelodge on the A13 road out of East London: one runs to his death by decapitation, while the other lives on. The decapitated body, however, disappears: 'Of Norton, his head and his body, there was no trace. The man had vanished' (2004: 264). This symbolic sacrifice is a completion, of 'an unfinished triptych: *The M25 Slaughter*'.[22] Just as we saw at the end of *White Chappell, Scarlet Tracings* that 'the circuit [was] completed', here again we find an impulse towards closure: but it occurs just over half-way through the book, at the end of 'Estuarial Lives'.

In *Dining on Stones*, there are in fact three 'Nortons': 'Two Nortons were never going to be enough. Andy in room 234 with his files, his nostalgia. And his sterner, fiction composing doppelganger, A.M., sipping whiskey . . . Now Norton's third mind had broken cover, the writer, the watcher. The other two could never be reconciled'.[23] The notion of a 'third mind' or third presence is a recurrent one in Sinclair's fiction. As I noted in Chapter 2, as early as *White Chappell, Scarlet Tracings* reference is made to this idea: 'When two men meet a third is always present, a stranger to both'.[24] Much more direct allusion is made in *Landor's Tower*: 'It was a superstition: two men walking down a road will conjure the presence of a phantom third, the secret auditor'.[25] The 'third' is then associated with revelation, with a transcendental moment of insight. As I have argued before, we find here then cloaking of the material ('a true understanding of the relation of things' as the moment in which the distorting lens of ideology or false consciousness is removed) in the garments of the transcendental. One need not speculate on whether Sinclair himself actually believes in this 'doctrine of the three interconnected spheres' to understand that it is of a piece with the Gothicised, occulted mode of critique we found in Chapters 2 and 3 of this book.

The importance of the 'third' Norton is vital to what I believe to be a major departure for Sinclair's fiction. At the end of *Dining on Stones*, Norton reads the novel by his newly (re)discovered lover Marina Fountain/Ruth Alsop in her apartment, and discovers that it is so good that 'this book would make her name'.[26] He recognises not only a lover and partner, but an equal, an artist of value. He declines to return to his old life and space, a 'discontinued and discredited narrative', preferring instead to embrace the domestic and the complex relationships forged between himself, Marina, the researcher and leg-man Kaporal and the young woman Ollie (who he discovers is his daughter).[27] Curiously, considering his other novels, Sinclair chooses to resolve the narrative of *Dining on Stones* with a moment of happiness. While I do not find Marina Fountain much more convincing as a female character than Sofya Court in *Radon Daughters*, Edith Cadiz in *Downriver*, or Prudence in *Landor's Tower*, the happiness represented at the end of *Dining on Stones* is convincing, and one might even characterize it as romantic. *Dining on Stones* turns away from the voyeurism of the previous novels, from the mechanical self-pleasuring of Todd Sileen, the priapism of Eric Gill, or the masochistic and quasi-incestuous fantasies of Hinton in *White Chappell, Scarlet Tracings*. It turns to the domestic, and to something almost entirely absent from the sometimes brutal, and always strictly material, sex that is found elsewhere in Sinclair's fiction, but which is also present in the pages of *Edge of the Orison*: love.

Painting, photography, cinema

In *Dining on Stones* the concept of the 'third space' and borderland come together under the sign of the 'middle ground'. This, as noted above, is the subtitle of the novel itself, and is the title of the concluding 'book' of *Dining on Stones*. (It is also the title of a book written by another character in *Dining on Stones*, Marina Fountain.) 'The middle ground' is connected throughout the novel to the artwork of Keith Baynes, whose compositional style stresses foreground and background, but excludes the middle: 'There is a passage to be navigated into the "middle ground", a corridor he neither delineates, nor understands. A space where lives can be lost'.[28] The excluded middle is also explained, this time as a tool of poetic composition, by Basil Bunting, the British modernist poet and author of *Briggflatts*.

> 'Take the middle out of it', the moustached and bespectacled poet told me, eyes glinting, when I interviewed him for a radio programme (never broadcast). 'It's a different thing. The middle one is a nightmare or dream or whatever you fancy. But once you've got that, of course, the chronological structure is obvious.'[29]

Bunting's 'lifelong allegiance to shape' positions him as an antecedent to the 'open field' poetics that inform all of Sinclair's poetry and prose.[30] The middle, or middle ground, then becomes a missing element that provides the key to the entire structure. The middle ground, the third space, the supercelestial sphere, the borderland: all are spatial figures for the transcendent, though a transcendence that is fraught with possible dangers. It also represents the space of Sinclair's fiction, the space that the complex textual apparatus gestures towards continually: the space between actuality and fiction.

By way of contrast, in much of Sinclair's writing, photography is inextricably bound up with the very material act of voyeurism. Part of Sileen's sexual frisson in *Radon Daughters* is through watching and being watched (with the X-ray plates, he assumes a privileged insight into his own body). The text states explicitly: 'Sileen was a voyeur'.[31] In fact, these scenes in the first 'book' of *Radon Daughters* are interweaved with chapters which narrate Imar O'Hagan's voyeuristic photographic sessions with Sofya Court. Photography, sexual desire, watching others and oneself: all are intertwined.

Sinclair's representation of gender, and particularly of women, has come under some critical scrutiny. David Cunningham, in his *Literary Encyclopaedia* entry on *Downriver*, notes that 'each of the women appears in the novel, at one point or another, as the object of a voyeur'.[32] Perhaps the crucial scene of voyeurism in *Downriver* features Edith Cadiz, the emblematic dancer/victim/fantasy figure that haunts the narrative(s). Though a trained dancer (and self-defined artist), Edith's key dance is performed in a pub, as a 'stripper':

> She wears a costume of maps. There are rings sewn to districts that have previously been cut so they will tear away, at a touch. Heard from the street, the sound of the audience is elongated and alarming. They feel their tongues being slowly split with rusty shears.[33]

Edith is, then, presented as an object of the male gaze, a position
she accepts in order to perform. The implied gaze of the reader is
also voyeuristic; we are implicated in the description of the spectacle.
David Cunningham argues that one can read the voyeurism encoded
in *Downriver* and *Radon Daughters* as a kind of critique of a culture
where 'pornography (in its widest sense) becomes the most prevalent
of cultural forms', and a sense of complicity the reader feels in the
gaze would certainly open the text up to that reading.[34] Cunningham
suggests that *Radon Daughters* can be read as a deliberate attempt,
on Sinclair's part, to incorporate female subjectivity into his fiction,
which he judges not to be very successful. The textual self-consciousness and estrangement in Sinclair's novels often take the form of
split subject or characters as avatars of the narrator's/author's own
subjectivity; little wonder then, as Cunningham argues, that 'Sinclair
is probably at his weakest in his writing of the female characters'.[35]

Where, in his other novels, Sinclair uses the fractured narrator-
subject to distance the reader from the events of the narrative (such
as it is), in *Radon Daughters*, the very textual fabric of the novel is
disrupted by the estranging device of cinema. Terminology from film,
such as 'CU' (close-up), 'tracking', 'shock cut' are used to give a sense
of reality mediated, pre-edited on film. The narrative discourse
undergoes severe compression; the effect is highly visual and, indeed,
spatial. We have seen in Chapter 5 how Sinclair's texts are often self-
conscious in their deployment of visual material, and that Sinclair
has had an 'other' career as a filmmaker (from teaching film at
Walthamstow art college to his collaborations with Chris Petit). In
Radon Daughters, filmic techniques are used to defamiliarise (and
thereby make visible) the conventions of literary narrative itself.

Structures and forms

All of Sinclair's novels place the armature of narrative structure on
the very surface of the text. *White Chappell, Scarlet Tracings* and
Landor's Tower have three 'books', while *Radon Daughters* has four;
there are twelve 'tales' in *Downriver*, and *Dining on Stones* has three
'books' (presented as separate texts with separate authors) and three
sections (named 'Road', 'Coast' and 'Netherworld') that run concur-
rently, with two interpolated 'stories' by the female character Marina
Fountain. In addition, *Landor's Tower* has some final 'notes' and

biographical information, placed after the conclusion of the diegetic narrative, on the historical characters in the novel; *Radon Daughters* an 'Author's Note' which gives space to Brian Catling and Marc Atkins and their own responses to two crucial sites in the novel; and *Downriver* an 'Acknowledgements and Confessions'.

Sinclair himself puts a kind of mocking auto-critique into the mouth of a minor character in *Landor's Tower*.

> 'What's with this three-part structure? One: lowlifes running around, getting nowhere. Two: a baggy central section investigating "place", faking at poetry, genre tricks, and a spurious narrative which proves incapable of resolution. Three: *quelle surprise*. A walk in the wilderness. What a cop-out, man!'[36]

This characterises *Landor's Tower* very neatly indeed, even though it is delivered by 'Bad News', one of the double-act 'Ketamine Kreeps' the narrator encounters in a motorway service station, and therefore somewhat compromised in terms of authority. In a sense, this is a joking reference to (and defusing of) criticism of Sinclair's novels, and a pre-emptive gesture to ward off further critique, particularly from academia. Later on the same page in *Landor's Tower*, the narrator imagines being

> trapped in some off-piste New University in the Midlands, taking a kicking from a sixties harridan, a born-again slapper who had run through the catalogue of bad behaviour and was now taking revenge on white-world daddies who soaked up attention that rightly should be hers.[37]

A rejection of academic criticism may be understood in terms of Sinclair's turn away from officially sanctioned cultures and canon that we saw in Chapter 4, although the figure of Simon Undark (a version of J. H. Prynne), a poet/academic at Cambridge, has a major role in *Radon Daughters* and a cameo in *Landor's Tower* and is but lightly satirised. Towards the end of *Radon Daughters*, the protagonist Todd Sileen and his partner Helen embark upon a ship bound for Ireland, only to find it host to 'FLEXICON', a science-fiction convention peopled by 'deep-text colonists, pod people, copycat androids waiting in dormitory towns for the Venusian transfer . . . a strictly non-judgemental crowd, good sports'.[38] Unlike the lifelessness or malignity of the academic world, the fannish, para-critical space of FLEXICON is affectionately presented as a kind of carnival or party. It is not critical reading, then, which draws Sinclair's ire, but the official paraphernalia of academic criticism of which, it must be said, this book is a part.

Elsewhere in the novels, the narrator confesses to the texts' lack of narrative trajectory, even at one point quoting the words of John Clute, who argues in relation to *White Chappell, Scarlet Tracings* that 'Sinclair too frequently overloads a not remarkably powerful grasp of narrative syntax, and his quasi-Joycean rhythms consequently lose steam, become swayback, and stall'.[39] Clute himself straddles the worlds of fandom and academic criticism largely within science fiction, and was known to Sinclair during the latter's bookdealing days. I would concur with Clute's assessment with regard to Sinclair's narratives, but would suggest that Sinclair uses a set of compensatory devices to provide some kind of architecture for a novel-length prose fiction. One of these is the self-conscious presentation of the text's structure in the form of 'books' or sections that I noted above. What, in prose fiction, is generally the underlying narrative framework upon which the world of the fiction is built is, in Sinclair's novels, placed upon the surface, largely because there is very little narrative impetus. In fact, the representation of a world (post-consensus London or Britain in decline) is the dominant textual effect in Sinclair's writing. This is not 'at the expense' of narrative, as narrative event is secondary; just as we saw that in *Lud Heat* and *Suicide Bridge*, linearity is supplanted by models of the spatial, fragmentary and contingent.

In fact, Sinclair's novels, as Robert Bond has suggested, can, like his long poetry, be considered as 'open field' works, textual spaces into which a variety of discourses, formal devices and registers can be imported. David Cunningham, in a short essay on *Radon Daughters*, suggests that 'it is Sinclair the prose stylist who matters most', praising the 'sheer exuberance and richness of linguistic form displayed in his writing'. The novel itself 'revels in its own dazzling play with language, mixing the archaic with the colloquial, the poetic with the street wise'.[40] This linguistic 'exuberance', the deployment of different registers for a range of effects (often comic), is what, no doubt, causes John Lanchester to write: 'Sentence for sentence, there is no more interesting writer at work in English than Iain Sinclair'. (This is quoted on the back of the dust jacket for the hardback edition of *Edge of the Orison*.) Both Cunningham and Lanchester praise Sinclair for the sentence, for the dazzling linguistic surface, not for his narratives (or even the book as a whole). This is unsurprising; as I have noted elsewhere in this book, the brilliance of the sentence or line in Sinclair's work often creates a kind of 'semantic drag', a retardation of the narrative impetus. What I would argue here is that the novels force the attention of the reader to the level of the sentence, the brilliant phrase-making, and away from the narrative as a whole. The self-conscious performativity of the language (and, as I argued in Chapter 5, even of the material form of the texts themselves) means that Sinclair's novels do not offer the immersive pleasures of typical narrative fiction. Sinclair's novels deliberately estrange the reader, both in their linguistic play and in the self-conscious deployment of the structural armature of the narrative on the surface of the text.

In his Introduction to the collection of essays *Metafiction* (1995), Mark Currie makes an illuminating suggestion with regard to metafictions, or 'fictions about fictions', of which *Dining on Stones* could certainly be seen to be a part. Rejecting the paradigm of 'self-consciousness' with regard to this mode of writing, Currie instead proposes a 'definition of metafiction as a borderline discourse, as a kind of writing which places itself on the border between fiction and criticism, and which takes that border as its subject'.[41] The form of *Dining on Stones* is then particularly appropriate to Sinclair's ongoing preoccupations with borders, transitions, liminal states of subjectivity, and the fractured self. If Currie is correct, then metafiction is also a means by which Sinclair, as reader of other texts, as dealer in books, and as a writer, can forge a mode of writing which is at once critical and imaginative, neither prey to academic scholasticism nor the excesses of fannish enthusiasm. For metafiction is perhaps what truly characterises all of Sinclair's fictional texts: densely allusive or intertextual writing, with an author-figure (or semi-transparent alter-ego) implicated in the text, a recognisable cast of characters that seem to come straight out of Sinclair's own circle of friends and acquaintances, and an insistent return to (or less generously, recapitulation of) earlier fictions. In the Introduction to this book, I suggested that it is alienation that is crucial to Sinclair's world-view, the alienation of the 'visionary' poet or outsider, filtered through the politics and psychiatric discourses of the 1960s and the counter-culture. Sinclair's fiction, which refuses the pleasures of narrative immersion in its spatial organisation, linguistic dazzle, and metafictional devices, places readerly alienation at the heart of its practice. Like the poetry Sinclair celebrated and collected in *Conductors of Chaos*, Sinclair's texts are difficult, and make the reader work; therein lay their pleasures.

Notes

1 Iain Sinclair, *London Orbital* (London: Granta, 2002), p. 51.
2 Iain Sinclair, *Radon Daughters* (London: Jonathan Cape, 1994), p. 442.
3 M. M. Bakhtin, *The Dialogic Imagination: Four Essays*, M. Holquist (ed.), trans. Caryl Emerson and Michael Holquist (Austin: University of Texas Press, 1981), p. 250.
4 Bakhtin, *The Dialogic Imagination*, pp. 84 and 250.
5 Bakhtin, *The Dialogic Imagination*, pp. 243–4.
6 Iain Sinclair with Kevin Jackson, *The Verbals* (Tonbridge: Worple Press, 2003), p. 127.
7 Sinclair, *Radon Daughters*, p. 234.
8 Sinclair, *Radon Daughters*, p. 421.
9 Sinclair, *Radon Daughters*, p. 421.
10 Iain Sinclair, *Landor's Tower* (London: Granta, 2001), p. 234.
11 Sinclair, *Landor's Tower*, p. 180.
12 Sinclair, *Landor's Tower*, p. 215.
13 Robert Bond, ' "The Chapel at the End of the World": Lust and Spiritual Discipline in Iain Sinclair's *Landor's Tower*', *Literary London* 3:2 (2005) (accessed 1 December 2005). <www.literarylondon.org/london-journal/bond1.html>, par. 2.
14 Bond, ' "The Chapel at the End of the World" ', par. 3.
15 Iain Sinclair, *Edge of the Orison* (London: Hamish Hamilton, 2005), p. 146.
16 Bakhtin, *The Dialogic Imagination*, p. 263.
17 Sinclair, *Landor's Tower*, p. 285.
18 Sinclair, *Landor's Tower*, p. 162.
19 Sinclair, *Landor's Tower*, pp. 306–7.
20 Sinclair, *Radon Daughters*, p. 451.
21 Iain Sinclair, *Dining on Stones* (London: Hamish Hamilton, 2004), p. 282.
22 Sinclair, *Dining on Stones*, pp. 264 and 263.
23 Sinclair, *Dining on Stones*, p. 370.
24 Iain Sinclair, *White Chappell, Scarlet Tracings* (London: Paladin, 1988), p. 36.
25 Sinclair, *Landor's Tower*, p. 288.
26 Sinclair, *Dining on Stones*, p. 448.
27 Sinclair, *Dining on Stones*, p. 449.
28 Sinclair, *Dining on Stones*, p. 448.
29 Sinclair, *Dining on Stones*, p. 344.
30 Sinclair, *Dining on Stones*, p. 345.
31 Sinclair, *Radon Daughters*, p. 102.
32 David Cunningham, 'Downriver', *The Literary Encyclopaedia* (accessed 29 March 2004). <www.litencyc.com/php/sworks.php?rec=true&UID=5531>, par. 4.

33 Iain Sinclair, *Downriver* (1991) (London: Vintage, 1995), p. 63.
34 Cunningham, 'Downriver', par. 4.
35 Cunningham, 'Downriver', par. 4.
36 Sinclair, *Landor's Tower*, p. 285.
37 Sinclair, *Landor's Tower*, p. 285.
38 Sinclair, *Radon Daughters*, p. 414.
39 John Clute, *Look at the Evidence: Essays and Reviews* (Liverpool: Liverpool University Press, 1995), p. 62.
40 David Cunningham, 'Radon Daughters', *The Literary Encyclopaedia* (accessed 29 March 2004), <www.litencyc.com/php/sworks.php?rec= true&UID=2492>, par. 6.
41 Mark Currie, 'Introduction', in M. Currie (ed.), *Metafiction* (Harlow: Longman, 1995), p. 2.

References

Works by Iain Sinclair

Kodak Mantra Diaries (London: Albion Village Press, 1971).

Lud Heat (London: Albion Village Press, 1975).

Suicide Bridge (London: Albion Village Press, 1979).

White Chappell, Scarlet Tracings (Uppingham: Goldmark, 1987).

White Chappell, Scarlet Tracings (London: Paladin, 1988).

'An Aberrant Afterword: Blowing Dust on the House of Incest' to William Hope Hodgson, *The House on the Borderland* (1908) (London: Grafton: 1990), pp. 179–88.

Radon Daughters (London: Jonathan Cape, 1994).

Downriver (1991) (London: Vintage, 1995).

Lud Heat and Suicide Bridge (London: Granta, 1995).

'Introduction', *Conductors of Chaos: A Poetry Anthology*, I. Sinclair (ed.) (London: Picador, 1996), pp. xiii–xx.

with Dave McKean, *Slow Chocolate Autopsy* (London: Phoenix, 1997).

Lights Out for the Territory: 9 Excursions in the Secret History of London (London: Granta, 1998).

Crash (London: BFI, 1999).

Dark Lanthorns (Uppingham: Goldmark, 1999).

Liquid City (London: Reaktion, 1999).

and Rachel Lichtenstein, *Rodinsky's Room* (London: Granta, 1999).

Sorry Meniscus (London: Profile, 1999).

Landor's Tower (London: Granta, 2001).

'Introduction' to Sir Arthur Conan Doyle, *A Study in Scarlet* (London: Penguin, 2001), pp. vii–xxi.

'Introduction' to Alexander Baron, *The Lowlife* (London: Harvill/Panther, 2001), pp. v–xii.

London Orbital (London: Granta, 2002a).

and Emma Matthews, *White Goods* (Uppingham: Goldmark, 2002).

Saddling the Rabbit (Buckfastleigh: Etruscan Books, 2002b).

with Kevin Jackson, *The Verbals* (Tonbridge: Worple Press, 2003).
Dining on Stones (London: Hamish Hamilton, 2004).
'The Poet Steamed', *London Review of Books* 26:16, 19 August (2004), 27–9.
Edge of the Orison (London: Hamish Hamilton, 2005).

Films
Petit, Chris (director; Iain Sinclair, script), *The Cardinal and the Corpse* (1993).
Petit, Chris and Iain Sinclair (dir.), *The Falconer* (1998).
Petit, Chris and Iain Sinclair (dir.), *Asylum* (2000).
Petit, Chris and Iain Sinclair (dir.), *London Orbital* (2002).

Secondary works

Ackroyd, Peter, *Hawksmoor* (London: Hamish Hamilton, 1985).
Ackroyd, Peter, *London: The Biography* (London: Chatto & Windus, 2000).
Anderson, Perry, 'Dégringolade', *London Review of Books* 26:17, 2 September (2004), 3–9.
Anderson, Perry, 'Union Sucrée', *London Review of Books* 26:18, 23 September (2004), 10–16.
Augé, Marc, *Non-places: Introduction to an Anthropology of Supermodernity* (London: Verso, 1995).
Bakhtin, M. M., *The Dialogic Imagination: Four Essays*, M. Holquist (ed.), trans. Caryl Emerson and Michael Holquist (Austin: University of Texas Press, 1981).
Ballard, J. G., *Running Wild* (New York: Noonday Press, 1988).
Ballard, J. G., *Concrete Island* (1974) (London: Flamingo, 1992).
Ballard, J. G., *High-Rise* (1975) (London: Flamingo, 1993).
Ballard, J. G., *Crash* (1973) (London: Vintage, 1995).
Ballard, J. G., *Myths of the Near Future* (1982) (London: Vintage, 1999).
Ballard, J. G., *Super-Cannes* (London: Flamingo, 2000).
Ballard, J. G., *Millennium People* (London: Flamingo, 2003).
Barry, Peter, *Contemporary British Poetry and the City* (Manchester: Manchester University Press, 2000).
Barthes, Roland, 'The Photographic Message', *Selected Writings*, in S. Sontag (ed.) (London: Fontana, 1983), pp. 194–210.
Baxter, Stephen, *The Time Ships* (London: Voyager, 1997).
Benjamin, Walter, 'On Some Motifs of Baudelaire', in Hannah Arendt (ed.), trans. Harry Zohn *Illuminations* (London: Fontana, 1992), pp. 152–96.
Benjamin, Walter, 'The Work of Art in the Age of Mechanical Reproduction', in Hannah Arendt (ed.), trans. Harry Zohn, *Illuminations* (London: Fontana, 1992), pp. 211–44.
Benjamin, Walter, *The Arcades Project*, trans. Howard Eiland and Kevin McLaughlin (Cambridge, MA and London: Belknap Press, 1999).

Bennett, Tony, 'The Exhibitionary Complex', *Representing the Nation: A Reader: Histories, Heritage And Museums*, in D. Boswell and J. Evans (eds) (London and New York: Routledge, 1994), pp. 332–61.

Berger, John, 'The Moment of Cubism', in G. Dyer (ed.), *Selected Essays* (London: Bloomsbury, 2001), pp. 71–92.

Blake, William, 'Jerusalem', *Complete Writings*, G. Keynes (ed.) (Oxford and New York: Oxford, 1966).

Bond, Robert, 'Suicide Bridge', *The Literary Encyclopaedia* (accessed 29 March 2004a). <www.litencyc.com/php/sworks.php?rec=true&UID=10512>

Bond, Robert, e-mail, 17 November 2004b.

Bond, Robert, *Iain Sinclair* (Cambridge: Salt, 2005).

Bond, Robert, ' "The Chapel at the End of the World": Lust and Spiritual Discipline in Iain Sinclair's *Landor's Tower*', *Literary London* 3:2 (2005) (accessed 1 December 2005). <www.literarylondon.org/london-journal/bond1.html>

Brooker, Peter, *Modernity and Metropolis: Writing, Film and Urban Formations* (Basingstoke: Palgrave, 2002).

Bunyan, John, *The Pilgrim's Progress* (Harmondsworth: Penguin, 1986).

Burgin, Victor, *In/Different Spaces: Place and Memory in Visual Culture* (London, Berkeley and Los Angeles: University of California Press, 1996).

Burroughs, William S., 'Les Voleurs', *The Adding Machine: Collected Essays* (London: John Calder, 1985), pp. 19–21.

Bynum, W. F., *Science and the Practice of Medicine in the Nineteenth Century* (Cambridge and New York: Cambridge University Press, 1994).

Certeau, Michel de, *The Practice of Everyday Life* (Berkeley, CA and London: University of California Press, 1984).

Clarke, Bruce, 'A Scientific Romance: Thermodynamics and the Fourth Dimension in Charles Howard Hinton's "The Persian King" ', *Weber Studies: An Interdisciplinary Humanities Journal*, 14:1, winter (1997), supplement to ebr, Science Technology and the Arts (accessed 7 June 2004). <www.altx.com/ebr/w(ebr)/essays/Clarke.html>

Clute, John, *Look at the Evidence: Essays and Reviews* (Liverpool: Liverpool University Press, 1995).

Conrad, Joseph, *Heart of Darkness* (1901), Paul O'Prey (ed.) (London: Penguin, 1989).

Corcoran, Neil, *English Poetry since 1940* (London and New York: Longman, 1993).

Crang, Mike and Nigel Thrift (eds), 'Introduction', in M. Crang and N. Thrift (eds), *Thinking Space* (London: Routledge, 2000), pp. 1–30.

Cunningham, David, 'Downriver', *The Literary Encyclopaedia* (accessed 29 March 2004). <www.litencyc.com/php/sworks.php?rec=true&UID=5531>

Cunningham, David, 'Iain Sinclair', *The Literary Encyclopaedia* (accessed 29 March 2004). <www.litencyc.com/php/speople.php?rec=true&UID=4084>

Cunningham, David, 'Lud Heat', *The Literary Encyclopaedia* (accessed 29 March 2004). <www.litencyc.com/php/sworks.php?rec=true&UID=3810>

Cunningham, David, 'Radon Daughters', *The Literary Encyclopaedia* (accessed 29 March 2004). <www.litencyc.com/php/sworks.php?rec=true&UID=2492>

Currie, Mark, 'Introduction', *Metafiction*, ed. Mark Currie (Harlow: Longman, 1995).

Davis, Mike, *City of Quartz: Excavating the Future in Los Angeles* (1990) (London: Pimlico, 1998).

Debord, Guy, *The Society of the Spectacle* (Detroit: Black and Red, 1977).

DeKoven, Marianne, *Utopia Limited: The Sixties and the Emergence of the Postmodern* (Durham: Duke University Press, 2004).

Derrida, Jacques, *Of Grammatology*, trans. Gayatri Chakravorty Spivak (London and Baltimore: Johns Hopkins University Press, 1976).

Derrida, Jacques, 'from *Specters of Marx*', *The Derrida Reader: Writing Performances*, Julian Wolfreys (ed.) (Edinburgh: Edinburgh University Press, 1998), pp. 140–68.

Derrida, Jacques, and Bernard Stiegler, *Echographies of Television* (Cambridge: Polity, 2002).

Dun, Aidan, *Vale Royal* (Uppingham: Goldmark, 1995).

Eliot, T. S., *Collected Poems 1909–1962* (London: Faber, 1974).

Faraday, Michael, 'from *Experimental Researches in Electricity* (1839–55) (1852)', in L. Otis (ed.), *Literature and Science in the Nineteenth Century: An Anthology* (Oxford: Oxford University Press, 2002), pp. 55–9.

Fisher, Allen, *Place I–XXXVII* (London: Aloes Press, 1974).

Fischer, Susan Alice, 'A Room of Our Own: Rodinsky, Street Haunting and the Creative Mind', *Changing English: Studies in Reading and Culture*, 8:2, October (2001), 119–28.

Foucault, Michel, 'Body/Power', in *Power/Knowledge: Selected Interviews and Other Writings, 1972–1977*, ed. Colin Gordon, trans. Colin Gordon *et al.* (Brighton: Harvester, 1980), pp. 55–62.

Foucault, Michel, 'Of Other Spaces', *Diacritics* 16 (1986), spring, 22–7.

Foucault, Michel, *Discipline and Punish: The Birth of the Prison*, trans. Alan Sheridan (1975) (Harmondsworth: Penguin, 1991).

Green, Jonathon, *All Dressed Up: the Sixties and the Counterculture* (London: Pimlico, 1999).

Greenland, Colin, *Michael Moorcock: Death is No Obstacle* (Manchester: Savoy, 1992).

Gregory-Guider, Christopher C., 'Sinclair's *Rodinsky's Room* and the Art of Autobiography', *Literary London* 3:2 (2005) (accessed 1 December 2005). <www.literarylondon.org/london-journal/guider.html>

Harvey, David, *The Condition of Postmodernity: An Enquiry into the Origins of Cultural Change* (Cambridge, MA and Oxford: Blackwell, 1990).

Hawking, Stephen, *A Brief History of Time: From the Big Bang to Black Holes* (London and New York: Bantam, 1988).

Hewison, Robert, *Future Tense: A New Art for the Nineties* (London: Methuen, 1990).

Home, Stewart (ed.), *Mind Invaders: A Reader in Psychic Warfare, Cultural Sabotage and Semiotic Terrorism* (London: Serpent's Tail, 1997).

Horovitz, Michael, 'Afterwords', in M. Horovitz (ed.), *Children of Albion: Poetry of the 'Underground' in Britain* (Harmondsworth: Penguin, 1969), pp. 316–77.

Jackson, Rosemary, *Fantasy: the Literature of Subversion* (London: Routledge, 1981).

Jameson, Fredric, *Postmodernism, or, the Cultural Logic of Late Capitalism* (London: Verso, 1991).

Jameson, Fredric, 'Periodizing the Sixties', in Patricia Waugh (ed.), *Postmodernism: A Reader* (London: Edward Arnold, 1992), pp. 125–52.

Jarvis, Brian, *Postmodern Cartographies: The Geographical Imagination in Contemporary American Culture* (London: Pluto, 1998).

Jenks, Chris, 'Watching Your Step: the History and Practice of the *flâneur*', in C. Jenks (ed.), *Visual Culture* (London and New York: Routledge, 1995), pp. 142–60.

Laing, R. D., *The Divided Self* (Harmondsworth: Penguin, 1965).

Lefebvre, Henri, *The Production of Space*, trans. Donald Nicholson-Smith (1974) (Oxford: Blackwell, 1991).

London Psychogeographical Association, 'Why Psychogeography?', in S. Home (ed.), *Mind Invaders: A Reader in Psychic Warfare, Cultural Sabotage and Semiotic Terrorism* (London: Serpent's Tail, 1997).

Loomba, Ania, *Colonialism/Postcolonialism* (London: Routledge, 1998).

Luckhurst, Roger, 'The Contemporary London Gothic and the Limits of the "Spectral Turn"', *Textual Practice*, 16:3, December (2002), 527–46.

Luckhurst, Roger, *Science Fiction* (Cambridge: Polity, 2005).

McKenzie, A. E. E., *The Major Achievements of Science* (New York: Simon & Schuster, 1973).

Mengham, Rod, 'The Elegiac Imperative' [Review of *Lights Out for the Territory* and *Liquid City*], *Kenyon Review*, 23:1, winter (2001), 173–7.

Merrifield, Andy, 'Henri Lefebvre: a socialist in space', in M. Crang and N. Thrift (eds), *Thinking Space* (London: Routledge, 2000), pp. 167–82.

Moorcock, Michael, *Mother London* (1988) (London: Scribner's, 2000).

Moore, Alan and Eddie Campbell, *From Hell* (Paddington, Queensland, Australia: Eddie Campbell Comics, 1999).

Moretti, Franco, *Signs Taken for Wonders: Essays in the Sociology of Literary Forms*, trans. S. Fischer, D. Forgacs and D. Miller (London: Verso, 1983).

Moretti, Franco, *Atlas of the European Novel 1800–1900* (London: Verso, 1998).

Moretti, Franco, 'Graphs, Maps, Trees: Abstract Models for Literary History – 2', *New Left Review* 26, March–April (2004), 79–103.

Moretti, Franco *Graphs, Maps, Trees: Abstract Models for a Literary History* (London: Verso, 2005).

Murray, Alex, 'Exorcising the Demons of Thatcherism: Iain Sinclair and the Critical Efficacy of a London Fiction', *Literary London* 3:2 (2004) (accessed 1 December 2005). <www.literarylondon.org/london-journal/murray.html>

Nairn, Tom, 'The Crisis in the British State', *New Left Review* I/130, Novemeber–December (1981), 37–44.

Olson, Charles, 'Projective Verse', in Paul Hoover (ed.), *Postmodern American Poetry: A Norton Anthology* (New York and London: Norton, 1994), pp. 613–20.

Onega, Susana and John A. Stotesbury (eds), *London in Literature – Visionary Mappings of the Metropolis* (Heidelberg: Universitätsverlag C. Winter, 2002).

Parsons, Deborah L., *Streetwalking the Metropolis: Women, the City and Modernity* (Oxford: Oxford University Press, 2000).

Perril, Simon, 'A Cartography of Absence: The Work of Iain Sinclair', *Comparative Criticism: An Annual Journal*, 19 (1997), 309–39.

Phillips, Tom, *A Humument: A treated Victorian Novel* (London: Thames & Hudson, 1997).

Philo, Chris, 'Foucault's Geography', 'Henri Lefebvre: A Socialist in Space', in M. Crang and N. Thrift (eds), *Thinking Space* (London: Routledge, 2000), pp. 205–38.

Pile, Steve, 'Memory and the City', in J. Campbell and J. Harbord (eds), *Temporalities, Autobiography and Everyday Life* (Manchester: Manchester University Press, 2002), pp. 111–27.

Pinder, David, 'Ghostly Footsteps', *Ecumene* 8:1 (2001), 1–9.

Poe, Edgar Allan, 'The Man of the Crowd', *Selected Tales* (Oxford: Oxford Classics, 1980), pp. 97–104.

Porter, Roy, *The Greatest Benefit to Mankind: A Medical History of Humanity from Antiquity to the Present* (London: Fontana, 1999).

Porter, Roy, *London: A Social History* (London: Penguin, 2000).

Porter, Roy, *Madness: A Brief History* (Oxford: Oxford University Press, 2002).

Potter, Rachel, 'Culture Vulture: The testimony of Iain Sinclair's *Downriver*', *Parataxis* 5 (1992–3), 40–8.

Prynne, J. H., *Poems* (Newcastle: Bloodaxe, 1999).

Rawlinson, Mark, 'Physical Graffiti: The Making of the Representation of Zones One and Two', in S. Onega and J. A. Stotesbury (eds), *London in Literature – Visionary Mappings of the Metropolis* (Heidelberg: Universitätsverlag C. Winter, 2002), pp. 233–53.

Re/Search, *J. G. Ballard*, 8/9 (San Francisco: Re/Search Publications, 1984).

Rushdie, Salman, *The Satanic Verses* (London: Viking, 1989).

Samuel, Raphael, 'Unravelling Britain', in A. Light with S. Alexander and G. S. Jones (eds), *Island Stories: Unravelling Britain, Theatres of Memory volume II* (London and New York: Verso, 1998), pp. 41–73.

Sawday, Jonathan, *The Body Emblazoned: Dissection and the Human Body in Renaissance Culture* (London and New York: Routledge, 1995).

Sheppard, Rob, 'Disobedient Versions 2002' [Review of *Saddling the Rabbit*, Etruscan Books 2002] (accessed 22 June 2004). <www.terriblework.co.uk/disobedientversions2002.htm>

Sheppard, Robert, 'Elsewhere and Everywhere: Other New (British) Poetries', *Critical Survey*. 10:1 (1998), 17–32. Online version (accessed 22 June 2004), <www.dgdclynx.plus.com/lynx/lynx1310.html>

Shields, Rob, 'Fancy Footwork: Walter Benjamin's Notes on *flânerie*' in *The Flâneur* (London: Routledge, 1994), pp. 61–80.

Sinfield, Alan, *Literature, Politics and Culture in Postwar Britain* (Berkeley and Los Angeles: University of California Press, 1989).

Soja, Edward W., *Postmodern Geographies: The Reassertion of Space in Social Theory* (London: Verso, 1989).

Spivak, Gayatri Chakravorty, 'Translator's Preface', in J. Derrida, *Of Grammatology*, trans. Gayatri Chakravorty Spivak (London and Baltimore: Johns Hopkins University Press, 1976), pp. ix–lxxxvii.

Stevenson, Randall, *The Last of England? The Oxford English Literary History*, v. 12, 1960–2000 (Oxford: Oxford University Press, 2004).

Stoker, Bram, *Dracula* (1897) (Kerry, Eire: Brandon, 1992).

Tester, Keith, 'Introduction' in *The Flâneur* (London: Routledge, 1994), pp. 1–21.

Thomas, Ronald R., 'The Legacy of Victorian Spectacle: The Map of Time and the Architecture of Empty Space', in C. L. Krueger (ed.), *Functions of Victorian Culture at the Present Time* (Athens, OH: Ohio University Press, 2002), pp. 18–33.

Walkowitz, Judith, *City of Dreadful Delight: Narratives of Sexual Danger in Late-Victorian London* (London: Virago, 1992).

Ward, Geoffrey, 'Nothing but Mortality: Prynne and Celan', in A. Easthope and J. O. Thompson (eds), *Contemporary Poetry meets Modern theory* (New York and London: Harvester Wheatsheaf, 1991), pp. 139–52.

Watson, Ben, 'Iain Sinclair: Revolutionary Novelist or Revolting Nihilist?', *Critical Literalism* (accessed 21 June 2004). <www.militantesthetix.co.uk/critlit/SINCLAIR.htm>

Watson, Ben, 'Iain Sinclair: The Right Kind of Schizophrenia (a Note on *Downriver*)', *Literary London* 3:2 (2005) (accessed 1 December 2005). <www.literarylondon.org/london-journal/Watson.html>

Wells, H. G., *The Time Machine* (London: Heinemann, 1911).

White, Glyn, *Reading the Graphic Surface: The Presence of the Book in Prose Fiction* (Manchester and New York: Manchester University Press, 2005).

Williams, Raymond, *Resources of Hope*, Robin Gable (ed.) (London and New York: Verso, 1989).

Wise, M. Norton, 'Electromagnetic Theory in the Nineteenth Century', in R. C. Olby, G. N. Cantor, J. R. R. Christie and M. J. S. Hidge (eds), *Companion to the History of Modern Science* (London and New York: Routledge, 1990), pp. 342–56.

Wolfreys, Julian, *Deconstruction: Derrida* (New York: St Martin's Press; Basingstoke: Macmillan, 1998).

Wolfreys, Julian, *Victorian Hauntings: Spectrality, Gothic, the Uncanny and Literature* (Basingstoke: Palgrave, 2002).

Wolfreys, Julian, 'Londonography; Iain Sinclair's Urban Graphic', *Literary London* 3:2 (2005) (accessed 1 December 2005). <www.literarylondon.org/london-journal/julian.html>

Woods, Tim, 'Allen Fisher's *Place* Project and the "Spatial Turn"', *Parataxis* 8 (1996), 39–46.

Woolf, Virginia, 'Street Haunting: A London Adventure', *Collected Essays* Vol. 4 (London: Hogarth Press, 1967), pp. 155–66.

Wright, Patrick, *On Living in an Old Country: The National Past in Contemporary Britain* (London and New York: Verso, 1985).

Wright, Patrick, *A Journey through Ruins: A Keyhole Portrait of British Postwar Life and Culture* (London: HarperCollins, 1993).

Žižek, Slavoj, 'The spectre of Ideology', in Elizabeth Wright and Edmond Wright (eds), *The Žižek Reader* (Oxford: Blackwell, 1999), pp. 53–86.

Films

Frears, Stephen (dir.; Hanif Kureishi, screenplay), *Sammy and Rosie Get Laid* (1987).

Jarman, Derek (dir.), *The Last of England* (1987).

Keiller, Patrick (dir.), *London* (1992).

Index